WITHDRAWN

THE AGONY
AND THE
TRIUMPH

Papers on the Use and Abuse of Myth

By

HERBERT WEISINGER

MICHIGAN STATE UNIVERSITY
PRESS

★
★ ★
★
★

Manufactured in the United States of America

To my wife

Contents

Acknowledgments

I want to express my most sincere thanks to my friends whose invitations to address meetings of scholarly groups at their institutions and societies were the occasion of many of these papers; to the editors of *Proceedings of the Conference in the Study of Twentieth-Century Literature, First Session* at East Lansing, *Bucknell Review, Bulletin of the New York Public Library, The Centennial Review, Daedalus* and the American Academy of Arts and Sciences, *The History of Ideas Newsletter, Journal of American Folklore, Journal of General Education, Literature and Psychology, Midwest Folklore, The Monthly Review, Proceedings of the International Comparative Literature Association Congress* in Chapel Hill, *Shakespeare Quarterly* ("The Study of Shakespearean Tragedy since Bradley," Vol. VI, No. 4, Autumn 1955, pp. 387-96), and *Studies in the Renaissance* for their permission to reprint the papers which first appeared in their journals; to Dr. Lyle Blair, the Director of the Michigan State University Press for suggesting that I gather the papers into book form; and to the Michigan State University Research Fund for assistance in the preparation of the manuscript. My deepest debt is recorded in the dedication.

East Lansing, Michigan
November, 1963

Introduction

I suppose it must be transparently obvious to any one who happens to read these papers but it was not until I had brought them together and had read them one after the other that I realized how irritatingly ambivalent they are toward myth, their ostensible unifying theme. They are not only ambivalent toward myth; they are equally ambiguous with regard to their corollary theme, science, as well, and, in retrospect, I can see now that this double ambiguity is the necessary consequence of my original equivocation. In some of these papers, I find myself genuinely believing in myth as a still viable and fecund form of thought, and indeed, in one paper, I go so far as to argue that all thought processes are ultimately reducible to the mind's figuring forth of itself in the form and in the scenario of the myth and ritual pattern. In other papers, however, I discover that I take altogether the opposite point of view, that myth represents but an early stage in the intellectual development of man which served its purpose as well as it could when it did but is now no longer capable of competing for the solution to modern problems with the more historically recent methods of reason and science. Pandora's box is myth; opening it is science.

Similarly, I sometimes hold the position that only the methods of science can give us control over the processes of nature and that the more we can gain such control, the better off all of us will be. On the other hand, I just as often think of science as nothing more than another kind of magic, deceiving magician and spectator alike into imagining that it can indeed yield fruit, as Bacon and his enthusiastic virtuosi had so fondly hoped, only for us to be shocked into our awakening from our dream of learning by the acrid taste of the apple of forbidden knowledge. In short, I veer from one point of view to its opposite, depending on what I am working on, on the papers and periodicals I persist in provoking myself with, and on the lows and the lower lows in the glass of my personal barometer of native pessimism, and, when I advance one view, I feel obliged, emotionally and logically, to disparage the other.

If I could find any trend in these papers toward one or the other of these attitudes, I would simply attribute their ambivalence to the fact that they were written over a period of ten years and that they therefore constitute the record of a changing mind, lamentable perhaps from the point of view of a consistent and identifiable critical position, but at least humanly understandable. I cannot claim even such a feeble excuse; the last two papers are as much opposed to each other as the first two (I am speaking of their chronological composition and not their ordering in the text). Furthermore, the high-water mark of my belief in myth does not occur in these papers; that took place in *Tragedy and the Paradox of the Fortunate Fall,* published in 1953. Neither does the low-water mark apear here; that came in a piece published in *Myth and Mythmaking,* edited by Henry A. Murray, in 1960, which was originally done when I was asked to criticize a prevailing mode of Shakespeare criticism for a Modern Language Association meeting and proceeded, Cronos-like, to devour my own child, a previous paper providing a myth and ritual analysis of Shakespearean tragedy. Between the flood of faith and the drought of denial, then, the ardor of belief in these papers rises and falls as I keep circling around and around the idea of myth, this time passionately dedicated to it, that time unalterably hardened against it, certain only that I am hardly likely ever to arrive at a definite destination.

To make matters worse, I simply have no means of reconciling these differences. I am not even able to make up my mind whether the ambivalence is due to the innate irreconcilability of the mythic and scientific modes of thought, or, of far less concern, to the limitations of my own mind and knowledge. I realize of course that this is certainly not a unique experience for these times, but this is merely a comfort of sorts and scarcely a contribution. I am afraid I am too much of a contemporary American to give up the convenience and ease of my power-steering, my hi-fi set, my electric blanket, my automatic dishwasher, and my electric toothbrush for the dubious—at least in these days—pleasures of prophecy. And yet I am also too much of a humanist to be able to live in a world devoid of the works of the mind and of the spirit, the makings of the unique and endlessly-varied creativity of the myth-makers; Gulley Jimson may very well be a pain in the neck to have around the house all day long but I know of no scientist who can make you look into the horse's mouth —and, after all, both poet and scientist are conducting substantially the same tour but by different routes—in quite the same way that he does. Scientists seem to me to bow to three sets of gods—authorities (their senior professors), statistics, and foundations—but Gulley bows to no one. An experiment can be, is expected to be, and is reproduced if it is to gain acceptance; a work of art is *sui generis* and confirms itself.

The great debate between the two cultures of which we hear so much these days boils down, not so much to a matter of knowing either the second law of thermodynamics or Shakespeare, as Snow and Leavis seem to contend, but rather to two opposing views of the nature of human nature and to the two opposing views which stem from them. The humanist sees human nature as a mixture of good and evil in which the evil may be expected to dominate at least no less, and probably even more than, the good; it is therefore a tragic view in which the nature of the future is irrelevant for the reason that external change cannot affect the intrinsic condition of man. The scientist is more cheerful; change external circumstances, he argues, and you do change human nature; moreover, it is entirely probable that changes in external circumstances will make those affected by them better and happier than they were without them; and, in any event, you will be accomplishing something, and that is a good in itself for action is life. To deny this is to lay oneself open to the charge of reactionary selfishness, and, given the direction of affairs, the charge is, I fear, convincing to most men. It would be brutally heartless and lacking in all compassion and understanding to say to those who have nothing now that they will not necessarily be better or happier once they acquire the things they so envy us for having, nor, by the same token, would I wish to perpetuate suffering as the price of art. I must add that I am as sick and tired of being patronized for my Western lack of spirituality as I trust my Eastern friends are of being criticized for inadequate plumbing. Historically, art has been produced by and for a minority in the main indifferent to the needs of the many; today the division is not so much along class lines within a nation as it is between nations. A favored few nations in the West can have both autos and art; for the rest, poverty, illiteracy, discrimination, and disease are more real, more pressing, and surely, at this moment of history for them, more immediate than the dilemma of tragedy. Perhaps a world freed of its ills and with material prosperity for all will be a terribly dull place in which to live but I have noticed that the pleasures of the tragic *frisson* are better appreciated on a contented stomach.

But this formulation of the dichotomy between the humanities and the sciences is really quite askew. I am more and more convinced that the conflict between the two cultures is not so much a conflict which arises out of the assumed discordance between the different disciplines involved as it does out of the much more fundamental differences in the men who practice them. Anyone who has spent any time at all in academic life must be very blind indeed if he does not quickly see that the meaningful distinction is not between disciplines as such but between men; not between what they do and how they do it, but between each man's ability to understand the significance of what he does beyond the immediate limit of professional practice. It is not the arts and sciences which are in contention with each other; it is the humanists and scientists; and it is not all humanists against all scientists; it is men of understanding and vision from both sides joined against those, again from both sides, who are incapable of raising their eyes from their test-tubes and text-books. Though they may ostensibly belong to opposing parties, pedantic humanists and pedestrian scientists bear a relationship to each other very like that of the Southern Democrats and right-wing Republicans: at the first sign of threat to the academic *status quo* they perpetuate, they immediately and invariably cross party lines. But I see I am being unfair to the pedantic and the pedestrian; the one at least knows a subject, boring or trivial as it may be; the other performs useful work at a certain level. What I am really aiming at is the academic nullities, the men who believe little, profess less, and know nothing except the date of their retirement: the men who, precisely because they neither propose nor oppose, dispose. Such men are found in both camps where, fearing equally the radical values of the humanities and the radical values of the sciences—and by radical here I mean that effect of both the humanites and the sciences which forces one to transform one's self and one's environment—they stifle the fervor and the ferment of the humanities and the sciences alike. They are the faceless and fearful enemies of the inquiring mind, whatever direction it happens to take; and if education is ultimately permanently revolutionary, they are permanently reactionary.

What all this comes to in the end is the rather obvious and trite conclusion that the differences with which I have been concerned here are not the result of differences inherent in the different disciplines but are the result of differences between men as such. Neither art nor science is a way of life but a way of making a living, and there is nothing about either which gives one or the other the force of a more than human fiat; art is what men who are artists do and science is what men who are scientists do, and since artists and scientists are men first, as men they are fallible, subject to the same passions and prejudices as other men, and therefore accountable as men. The values and ideals which motivate and inform men away from bench and book are derived from an area of experience greater and far more complex than that of art or science alone, and if the humanities do not necessarily humanize, it does not follow that science must therefore necessarily objectify. The choice of values and ideals, the stance and style of a man, are his own responsibility. Science and art, politics and economics, philosophy, faith, myth, brute experience, accident, and other men, each in its own way, may help (or hinder) him; but, for good or for ill, the decision is his, for in the end he bears the consequences of his choice, not because he is an artist or a scientist, but because he is a man. I should add that the time he spends away from book or bench is in a certain sense of more significance than the time he spends at his work; in any case, however, he cannot be two different kinds of person.

And here we hop right back on the merry-go-round of the closed circle of change. If we are to improve education, we have to educate the society which supports it; if we are to educate the society which supports education, we have to improve the education of our students who become the alumni whose voice determines in large measure the character of the very society we ought to be educating against; if we are to improve the education of our students who become the alumni who determine the character of society, we have to change the temper of mind of our faculties; if we are to change the temper of mind of our faculties, we have to change the education of those who become teachers; if we have to change the education of those who become teachers, we have to change the minds of those who are already teaching; but, since those who are already teaching are by and large those who, having been taught by teachers with nothing to profess to begin with, themselves profess nothing to the children of alumni who have been taught by teachers with nothing to profess, who therefore profess nothing themselves, and who constitute a society, which, professing nothing, will support only the kind of school system which turns out students who profess nothing, who in their turn—where and by whom are the lever and fulcrum of change to be placed? The answer, of course, is: "Physician, heal thyself," but to that I can only say that, after some thirty years in the academic profession as a student and as a teacher, I have come to the most distressing conclusion that the gravest danger to education lies, not outside the academic walls, but directly and deeply within them, and this is the third of the ambiguities to which I can only confess but which I cannot resolve. About the best I can do at this point is to repeat the admonition of my teacher, Erwin Panofsky, that if the ivory tower is a place of refuge, it is also a place from which warnings may be sounded, and, I add faintly hopefully, heard as well. After all, it is something to know that even an emperor looks funny with no clothes on, especially if he is out of condition because he does not exercise his responsibilities.

I have many regrets about this collection of papers, but, with one exception, I shall not name them since they will all too readily reveal themselves. There are, sad to say, abilities which one simply does not have, but saddest to say, one comes finally to an age when one does not so much moan their lack as savor the nostalgia of their absence; lest I be accused of sentimentality, let me say that I am far from weeping the harsh tears of Ford Madox Ford's hero at all that I have not done and all that I will never do; I do not take myself all that seriously. The exception is my regret at not being able to deal with contemporary literature with any sort of competence. Here I speak only as an amateur of contemporary literature, but I speak at least as an amateur in both senses of the word.

As an amateur, then, I read contemporary literature and contemporary criticism with that particular and choice pleasure which one gets when he reads under no constraint to be an expert. And from my confessedly unsystematic reading in more quarterlies than I know are good for me, I cannot help noticing that the study of contemporary literature appears to suffer from the same social ambivalence of the able but poor boy from the wrong side of the tracks trying to cross over and rise in the world, that is, undecided whether he should crash or wheedle. For myself, I do not see why it is so important to be admitted into the country club atmosphere of traditional literary study which at the present moment seems rather bored with its own company and which, in addition, shows no little guilt feelings about its restrictive practices; I think that the burden of rejection is far heavier than the desire for admittance.

The charges I find leveled against the study of contemporary literature as a serious scholarly discipline seem to me to go to the heart of the profession, for if they can be sustained, they would, I fear, ultimately emasculate the study not only of contemporary literature but of all literature. In essence, explicit and concealed, these criticisms reduce themselves to an irreconcilable schism between scholarship and criticism since they predicate the absolute necessity of their separation. It is my conviction that if this cut is allowed to open beyond the point of healing then we will find ourselves in precisely the same position to which classical studies have sunk and for precisely the same reasons. Scholars and critics exist for literature, not literature for them.

The first objection I find is: how do you know when contemporary literature begins? As an historian of the ideas of the Renaissance, this question strikes me with a certain wryness; I do not know when any period begins, least of all the Renaissance, but so far as contemporary literature is concerned, the question can be answered much more satisfactorily, at least so far as I myself am concerned. Naturally and obviously, contemporary literature begins in the year of my birth; when else? I shall not try to impress with a freshly worked up erudition of names and dates, but surely literary lightning struck in and around that year, not only in England and the United States, but on the continent as well; and not only in literature but in the arts as well, as *The Rites of Spring* and the Armory Show in New York will recall; and in those sciences upon which literature has drawn so fruitfully; *Totem and Taboo* appeared in 1913. The very fact that the lights were going out in politics seems to have meant that they were to be rekindled in the arts, and I believe that the experience of World War I gave contemporary literature a seriousness and relevance unmatched in previous periods of literature.

Another criticism of contemporary literature is that you must wait at least a half century before you can determine what is worth studying. But the very pleasure of contemporary literature is precisely in its contemporaneity. After all, the aim of scholarship is to reconstruct by every means at its command the contemporaneity of the past, that is to say, to put the modern reader in the same position *vis à vis* a work of literature which he would have had had he been contemporary with it. What other justification is there, after all, for our texts, our introductions, our annotations, our footnotes, our source studies, our audience studies, our social environment studies, our histories of ideas, our whole scholarly panoply in fact, if not to make the modern reader a contemporary reader? For us, this must be a matter of elaborate and painful effort which by its very nature cannot ever exactly hit the mark; one is always conscious of missing a note, of overlooking a sign. But in reading our own literature, we bring to it an apparatus naturally acquired merely by virtue of our having lived through the same era, the same experiences, the same turmoil; we do not have to reconstruct, we have only to recall; and we therefore bring to the reading of contemporary literature a density and depth, a special feel for it, so to speak, which no amount of scholarship can really hope to reproduce. Simply stated, it is the difference between a live and a recorded performance, no matter how hi the fi; scholarship alone cannot produce the overtones which the contemporary hears.

A third criticism of contemporary literature is that it neglects the individual character of national literatures. Precisely so. But literature is no longer nationally isolated so that no longer is it necessary to pursue such dreary quests as the character of the national character, or what is the great American novel, or what is the English element in T. S. Eliot, and so on. The internationalization of travel, communications, and education has forced us to become citizens of the world, whether we like it or not; I get my *TLS* and *New Statesman* book reviews on the same day my English colleagues do; a few weeks ago Olivier appeared in a French play in Detroit; a few weeks from now I expect to see a Lorca play here in Lansing; and the local movie house has in successive weeks shown French, German, Italian, Swedish, and Japanese films. Writers seem to flit from country to country, and, thanks to Fulbrights and the like, academics are not far behind. We must face up to the fact that the groves of academe now include the flora and fauna of the most remote and exotic places. In view, then, of the international dispersement of literature, our methods of studying it must correspondingly expand. If up to now we have pictured literature in a series of parallel columns separated by vertical national lines, we must now redraw the graph: the vertical lines need to be erased and we must show instead how the same phenomena appear virtually simultaneously around the globe within particular periods; the dividing lines, if such devices are to be at all useful, must be horizontal. I am not arguing here for the acceptance of comparative literature as such for the simple reason that there is no such thing as comparative literature as such; it is simply in the nature of our studies, contemporary or otherwise, that we disregard national boundaries.

Introduction

It is argued that contemporary literature has not historical roots. On the contrary, it is *par excellence* a learned literature. One reason for this is the obvious fact that more writers have gone to college than ever before and something of what we have tried to teach them has surprisingly rubbed off. You may recall Arthur Miller's discussion of tragedy in the preface to his collected plays; that derives directly from Professor Norman Nelson's lectures in criticism at Ann Arbor; I know because I sat near Miller when he was taking his notes. Malcolm Friar's and John Brinnin's poetry are well known; I heard them read their poetry in a coffee joint across the street from Angell Hall. And John Ciardi learned his art and his criticism in Ann Arbor as well. It does not take long to draw up a list of examples, even from one's own limited experience. I do not know of another body of literature which demands more learning, more understanding of the literary traditions from which it stems and from which it deviates, than that of contemporary literature. Not even the King Canutes of the new criticism can stem the tides of learning which flood through contemporary literature, and, as to criticism, why, Frazer, Marx, Darwin, Freud, Jung, Lovejoy, Whitehead, Tillich, and Buber are only the starting texts for beginning critics.

Indeed, the very fact that we bring to bear on the study of contemporary literature such a wide range of relevance has forced the re-reading and the re-evaluation of the classics of the past. Were it not for this pressure, we would be content, I am sure, with a Madame Tussaud's of judgment; fixed, permanent, and dead. But just as classical studies were revived at virtually the last moment by the anthropological school, so is the literature of the past being refreshed by the impact of the new methods brought into action by the necessity of dealing with the expansive forces of contemporary literature. The heightened awareness which contemporary literature demands is easily transferred to the literature of the past, and we now read it with a sensitivity, a passion, and a concern which scholarship in isolation cannot generate. In brief, we read literature as literature, that is to say, as intense response to the intense problems of man's condition; we read literature where it was made, in the arena, not the library.

To deny the significance of contemporary literature is to deny the significance of one's own life. The problems, the doubts, the fears, the hopes of contemporary literature are, after all, my problems, doubts, fears and hopes. It therefore speaks to me in a special way which no other literature, whatever its qualities, possibly can. I am not of course denying the greatness of the literature of the past; I am simply assessing the unique quality of contemporary literature to me. And I suspect that the literature of the past which we call great has been able to speak across the centuries to us precisely because it spoke as directly to its contemporaries. When Milton spoke of fame I am sure he did not mean embalmment in our journals; he meant that we should be as passionately concerned with the human predicament as he was.

Finally, it seems to me that the study of contemporary literature imposes on us a responsibility which, if we avoid, vitiates our claims, scholarly, pedagogical, and critical, on literature altogether. That is the necessity for judgment of literature as it comes. It takes no great critical acumen to decide that Shakespeare was a great writer of plays. But it takes the courage of one's critical convictions to evaluate that literature which has not yet been enshrined by generations of consensus. One can play it safe, and be dull; or one can gamble, but lose or win, one is at least alive. If we are really seriously concerned with literature, we are always examining and re-examining it, and re-estimating its worth, and the fortuitous fact that a book came out today does not give us the right to postpone our judgment of it for fifty years from now, that is, for someone else to take the responsibility. If our scholarship has not provided us with the tools of criticism and the scales of judgment, I frankly do not see our justification. The verdict of history is here and now.

On the History of Ideas

I T IS NOW over fifty years since Arthur O. Lovejoy's first essay on the history of ideas, "Some Eighteenth Century Evolutionists," appeared in *Popular Science Monthly*. In that time, the method of the history of ideas has achieved no small status in literary history; indeed, the work of Lovejoy and his followers is now an indispensable tool for scholars in nearly every branch of the study of literature. For this very reason, it seems to me that it would be a useful thing to re-assess the defects and merits of the method, for it is only by continuous scrutiny that we can keep it fresh and vital.

What are the larger values to be gained from the study of the history of ideas, the profits beyond those obvious ones secured by the careful and subtle analysis of ideas alone? To repeat Lovejoy's main contentions, the first is the achievement of proper historical perspective, the ability of the historian to select, not what seems important to him, but what seemed important to other men. Seen from this point of view, the truth or falsity, goodness or badness, of ideas take on a different aspect, for, while in any complex of beliefs, some may be true, some false, some good, and some bad, the really important question of value about any complex is, what specific *parts* of it are logically sound, or ethically right, or have had benign or injurious effects upon the individuals or the cultures they have influenced? This does not mean that judgment must be eternally suspended or that no judgments are possible, but it does mean that historical judgment is less parochial, less dogmatic, more informed, more tempered, and, in the long run, more useful than others arrived at by different methods. Speaking of Romanticism, for example, Lovejoy has urged that it is the duty of the historian of ideas to render such a complex psychologically intelligible by tracing how such manifold and discrepant phenomena have all come to receive the same name. Such an analysis would, he is convinced, show us a large mass of purely verbal confusions operative as actual factors in the movement of thought in the past century and a quarter, and it would—this is the important point—by making these confusions explicit, make it easier to avoid them.

Furthermore, it is Lovejoy's conviction that the history of ideas ". . . enables the reader to recapture, in writings of earlier times, aesthetic values which had been lost because the frame of reference, the preconceptions, the mood which gave them such value for their contemporaries were no longer current." The history of ideas, then, serves a humanistic function; it illuminates the nature of human nature; it shares with the other humanistic disciplines the task of confronting man with his own past that he may learn from it, and it differs from them mainly in precision of its methods.

I should like to consider now some of the inadequacies and limitations which I find in the method. I start with the definition of ideas. My difficulty here is not with the objects of study in themselves, but with the criteria, or, as it seems to me, the lack of criteria, for the choice of ideas to be studied. There is not, I think, any way of differentiating between them as to their worth. It is clear enough that such concepts as 'the great chain of being' or 'nature' satisfy the demands of range, seriousness, and consequence, but these criteria are not inherent in the method itself. Lovejoy would no doubt argue that only after analysis, only after we have chosen what was considered important to the past, will that importance be in the end revealed to us in the present. But he has already severely restricted the range of choice by his theorem that in the history of ideas the number of significant ideas is small, so that what is left is the search not so much for new ideas as for the ways in which the old ones are combined and recombined. If this is so, and I rather think it is, what is to prevent the future student of the history of ideas from dissipating his energies on the trivial? One of Lovejoy's chief arguments in favor of his method is that it has saved the study of literature from running into the shoals of pedantic and narrow scholarship, as indeed it has, but I strongly suspect that without satisfactory criteria of values, the history of ideas may simply bring us to the same shoals by another road.

Next, I think Lovejoy's theory of the oscillatory character of the movement of ideas is surely a frail reed upon which to depend. Teggart has subjected the cyclical theory of history to sharp criticism, and I need not repeat his arguments here. Professor Lovejoy tends to see ideas as moving of their own accord in a heaven of their own, fundamentally unaffected by forces outside their own tracks. But men and the ideas they hold cannot be separated so simply and so drastically. It is men who make ideas, and men who break them, and to account for the reasons that some are taken up and others neglected, we have to look beyond ideas to the men who manipulate them. One explanation for this failure lies in Lovejoy's own stringent scepticism; his revolt against large terms and general concepts has made him suspicious of philosophies of history which account for changes in men's thoughts by antecedent or concomitant changes in men's actions.

Third, there is implied in the method the claim that it follows more stringent scientific procedures than do competing methods. But if the assertion to be scientific is to be taken seriously, then literary theory must be expected to meet the minimum requirements of scientific procedure, namely, consistency, verifiability, reliability, predictability, progress, and an exact descriptive language. If it is to be accepted as true in the scientific sense of the term it must, first, demonstrate a high degree of consistency within itself, both logically and methodologically; second, it must be able to demonstrate an equally high degree of correlation between its theoretical constructs and the objective, observable phenomena outside of itself (the reality of their subject matters is assumed by all the sciences, at least for practical purposes) with which it is particularly concerned; and it must be able to present its findings in language altogether drained of ambiguities and overtones. Merely to state these requirements is to argue their inapplicability to literature and the study of literature. The nature of literature, the purposes for which it is studied, the means by which it is studied, and the manner of expression of the results of that study are of such a kind and character that scientific purposes and procedures are simply irrelevant to them and can serve, if their application is insisted upon, only to confuse rather than to clarify problems of literary theory and method. We have the lesson of the failure of traditional historical scholarship (the result of a faulty and misleading version of evolutionary determinism) to support the rejection of the claim—and the need—of literary theory to be scientific.

But it can be argued, and with much more sophistication, that these are criteria derived from the experimental and applied sciences and are therefore not germane to literary theory, but that the proper model for it to follow is mathematics. And that is what Northrop Frye in the conclusion to *The Anatomy of Criticism* does propose; asserting that the subject matter of mathematics is itself ". . . a disinterested conception of numerical relationships, concerned more and more with its inner integrity, and less and less with its reference to external criteria," he draws the analogy that just as mathematics is an autonomous language, so is literature. Indeed, he even goes so far as to suggest that the irrational numbers of mathematics may be compared to prepositions in verbal language; that both proceed from postulates, not facts; that the metaphor and the equation, the units of literature and of mathematics alike, are similar in form; and that "pure literature, like pure mathematics, contains its own meaning." Overlooking the shaky parallelism—is it literature is to mathematics what literary theory is to science or is it literary theory is to mathematics what literature is to science, surely a difference of no mean significance—we should not forget that the fascination which numerological speculation has held for the man of letters is an affair of long standing; it was already an old story by the time of the Plato of the *Timaeus;* but, as is often the case with such infatuations, it has been sadly one-sided. Speaking with all the authority of one who has systematically failed mathematics from his elementary school days onwards, I must repeat what my mathematical friends have patiently drummed into me, that careful distinctions must be drawn and maintained between mathematics as an instrument of expression of the behavior of phenomena, as an intellectual discipline with its own purposes and procedures, and as a source of religious and/or philosophical vision; romanticizing the second and believing the third of these approaches are not, to put it mildly, regarded either as mathematics or science.

It is therefore not surprising that the only physical scientist to whom Frye refers should be Sir James Jeans whose *The Mysterious Universe* culminates in a vision of a universe stripped down to pure mathematics. Nature may very well love the number seven, or any other number for that matter, but this charming news comes to us from men, not nature, which, so far as I know, neither likes nor dislikes anything, one way or the other. For we must remember that mathematics is, like any other language, an invention of man, first silently fobbed off on nature as it were by a conspiracy of methodological assumption, and then jubilantly proclaimed as a law of nature, unexpected and therefore true. But surely the discomfiture of physicists, when they were informed that the law of parity was invalid, would have been much less if they had recalled that it had never been passed in the first place, at least not by nature. For a mathematician—or a critic—to share Jeans' vision of a mathematically pure universe is a matter of personal conviction based on non-mathematical (though none the less moving) compulsions, but it is not a deduction from mathematics, let alone from astronomy or paleontology or astrology. There is something annoying, yet touching, in the attempt to convert God the Father into God the mathematician but the danger in this transformation is that while a poor parent may be a good mathematician and a good mathematician may be a poor parent, what if the result should be a poor parent and a poor mathematician both?

It is time to get down to cases; how do we apply a scientific approach to the problem of *the* meaning of *Othello*. If we categorize the various approaches which have been taken toward the play, we get a list something like this: the neo-classic theory of decorum as represented by Rymer; the introspective transference of Coleridge; the romantic adulation of Hazlitt; character analysis as practiced by Bradley; the "modern" anti-heroic view of Eliot; the application of the traditional humors psychology as done by L. B. Campbell; the pure stage convention view of E. E. Stoll; the Marxist approach of Smirnov; the social convention through professional type study of J. W. Draper; the imagery analysis of Robert P. Heilman; the neo-Christian approach of Paul N. Siegel; the persistence of medieval form and type of Bernard Spivack; the persistence of the medieval world-view into the Renaissance of Willard Farnham; the psychoanalytic approach of Kenneth Burke; and the myth and ritual approach of G. Wilson Knight. Confronted with this formidable list of the best which has been thought and said about *Othello*, we are immediately struck by their diversity, variety, and contradictions, both within and *vis-à-vis* each other. How are we to determine which of these is better than another? And in what sense better? How do we disassociate our own understanding of the play from the play itself, let alone our understanding of the

critics' understanding of the play? If we wish to combine
the individual virtues of the various approaches, on what
grounds do we reject one and accept the other, or portions
thereof? Do we read the play first and formulate our theory
of our understanding of it after, which is, incidentally, what a
prominent school of criticism suggests that we do, or ought to
do (but how? how do you repeatedly recover lost innocence?),
or do we read by and through assumptions, some derived
from our previous study of literature, some from our previous
study of criticism, and some, perhaps the most important of
all, derived from a range of experience far removed from
either literature or criticism? These are the kinds of questions
which literary theory has to answer; the problem is, how can
scientific method help us solve them?

If we take as our guide the procedures of the physical sciences, we begin with the immediate assumption of the objective reality of the phenomenon under observation, that is,
Othello. Even if such considerations as the accuracy of the text
are dismissed as trivial, what, actually, is *Othello?* The one
thing that it is not is its physical presence: the words on the
printed pages sewn into the form of a book. Despite its tangi-
bility, the book as such is meaningless, except to bibliog-
raphers, collectors, and booksellers; its only function, so far as
we as readers are concerned, is to embody a set of marks which
serve to establish a relationship between us and the author
who put them down; its reality resides only in perpetuating
that relationship. If we must use scientific terms, then the
book, *Othello,* is a spectroscope in which the single white light
of the author's mind is gathered up, translated into the colors
of language, and refracted into the reader's mind; and, in the
case of the play, *Othello,* there is the double refraction of
the book and of the performance both. To continue with the
analogy: the more complex the phenomenon to be observed
and measured, the greater is the margin of error in the instrument of observation and measurement, in the bias of the observer, in the observation and measurement, and therefore in

the statement of what has been observed. Consequently, in the case of so complex a phenomenon as *Othello,* the margin of error, that is to say, the attempt to arrive at *the* meaning of the play, must be so great that no single instrument, observer, measurement, or statement about it can encompass its totality.

For though the best computer so far built, weight for efficiency, the brain, swiftly brings to the reading of a work of literature a range of experience so wide and so deep that the reader does re-experience the experience of *Othello* in lesser or greater part, no computer and no brain has built into it the total range of experience which enables its possessor to re-experience the total experience of *Othello.* For each time we read the play, we are ourselves different, even if the text remains the same: we know more about Shakespeare, his plays, the Elizabethan period, the Renaissance, history, men, women; we have seen more, read more, done more, more things have happened to us; we are older: we are not the same person who read the play before, even if it was only yesterday. And this is precisely the meaning of the critics whose differences of understanding seem so upsetting; they stand for different ways of seeing, different angles of vision, different ages—in both senses—of men. It is therefore not a matter of their rightness or wrongness—and I include even Rymer, whose assumptions, once we grant them, are logically carried out—but of their breadth and depth. The scientist looks ever upward; the truth is just beyond the next peak; for the humanist the truth is around him, at eye level.

If we now take as our guide the procedures of mathematics, we begin, as before, with an immediate assumption, this time the inner self-containedness of our theoretical construct, not *Othello,* but what we think about *Othello.* What we think about *Othello* is a function of what we think about literature, and what we think about literature is the product of the analysis of the formal properties of individual pieces of literature, generalized, systematized, and expressed in non-emotional and non-evaluative language. This approach sets two goals for itself, though these are not always consciously realized by its practitioners: one is mathematical, that all the elements in the criticism of a piece of literature should be consistent within their own terms; the other is biological, that the piece of literature should exhibit the characteristics proper to its phylum, class, order, family, genus, species, and variety. Passing over as unimportant the odd Alexandrianism latent in this approach, I think it is best viewed as an attempt to introduce the model theory of mathematics into criticism, that is, as a theoretical construct whose value is in proportion to the tightness of its own inner logic. As I understand it, the model in mathematical theory is the model itself; its frame of reference is itself, in its own inner development and in the resolutions of its own inner tensions, so that the more it turns in on itself, so to speak, the more beautiful the demonstration of its closed consistency; and its chance utilization elsewhere, as in physics, has nothing at all to do with it as such.

It might be argued at this point that since I have already rejected the reality of *Othello,* that all we know about *it* is what *we* know about it, I should have no objection to the extension of model theory to criticism. But this is not what I said: what I did say was that the set of stimuli known as *Othello* remains constant; what varies is the degree of response to those stimuli, dependent on what we bring to bear on them. There are, in art, no adequate substitutes for the work of art; the ideal theoretical model of *Othello* is *Othello* itself. No matter how faithful and ingenious the translation of *Othello* or Opus 133 or *Guernica* of the Kaufman house into the language of criticism, however consistent within itself, the work of art retains its stubborn independence. But in this sense only, for, as an artifact, it is indeed *sui generis,* but it is an artifact whose significance is altogether dependent on the total experience of the man who made it and of the men who study it; it is a social phenomenon as well. It is this simultaneous double character which gives art its unique quality and distinction and forces criticism into the status of applied science, that is to say, a field of inquiry which cannot live off its own assumptions.

It is therefore not surprising that the exponents of model

theory do in the end take one step more in translation, a step which mathematics does not take, and that is the transformation of neutral model theory into some kind of ethico-aesthetic statement. Thus Frye says: "While we read, we are aware of a sequence of metaphorical identifications; when we have finished, we are aware of an organizing structural pattern of conceptualized myth." The leap from metaphor to myth is the confession of a leap from the description of behavior to belief, from the cold of process to the heat of judgment. For myth is far from being a neutral term; it implies a nexus of belief, even faith, with a correspondent hierarchy of values, more often extra-literary in character than not; and it poses more ethico-aesthetic problems than it solves. Thus model theory is forced to acknowledge, in spite of its theoretical fastidiousness, the rough edges and the harsh textures of the living work of art. Or to illustrate with a triple somersault from formal through mythical to Christian, this passage from J. A. Bryant, Jr.'s *Hippolyta's View:* "Shakespeare's plays are fundamentally developments of the great archetypal myths of the human race, whereby his dramatic fables, whether drawn from English history, Roman history, Italian novella, or English fabliau, are revealed as participating in an action which, from the poet's point of view, is Christian, divine, and eternal." Not even G. Wilson Knight will go that far, though it is a nice question whether English delicacy is to be preferred to American bluntness.

In short, the search for the identity of Othello, Iago, and Desdemona cannot by the very nature of the object being sought attain its end; there is, in art, no one source of the Nile. Each new critic of *Othello* reads the play in the light of his experience as a critic and as a man, and since he is different from both, let us say, Marvin Rosenberg—who tends to see the sexual side of *Othello*—and from me—who does not, he gives it a different reading; he is neither more right nor more wrong, boners apart; he is different. His knowledge of the past cannot be the same as mine, nor yet his experience of the present; as humanists, as readers of English literature, and as students of Shakespeare, we do share some assumptions in common and we do meet at *Othello*, intensely perhaps, but only briefly. That makes for a fine moment, but the sheer weight of numbers of men and of ideas has walled us apart, nor is there any way of turning back to a society founded on mutually evolved and accepted agreements on matters of taste, thought, and belief, if in fact there ever was one, so that though we would dwell within a della Francesca frame, we must exist in a Di Chirico landscape. Much as we would, we cannot relate in unity; we can relate only in synthesis, picking and choosing as we go, interpretations of *Othello* included. Barring atomic incineration, there will be more, and one would hope that as a consequence one will be able to see more and more deeply, though there is just as good a chance that one will be bewildered even more, like a motorist lost in a multi-level cloverleaf intended to help him on his way.

Finally, the ideas method tends to regard literature as a kind of backwash of philosophical ideas in dilution; questions concerning artistic values have been relegated to a place of secondary importance by the passion for the collection and analysis of ideas, nor have greatness and importance in art been sufficiently discriminated from the secondary and the commonplace. Theoretically, the method, by placing an author in his intellectual milieu, by examining the ideas which go into his work, and by contrasting the ways in which he has used ideas, ought to be able to distinguish the original from the commonplace, the skillful from the awkward. Unfortunately, in practice, far too little critical judgment has been shown in the treatment of literature not as the vehicle for ideas but as an art. The method enables us to make more detailed and precise comparisons between similar works of art, but the standards of judgment which we employ in making those comparisons are not contained in the method as it is at present constituted. When we survey the bulk of the work done by means of it, we notice that most of the scholarship has been concentrated on the literature of the seventeenth and eighteenth centuries, less on the literature of the Middle Ages and of the Renaissance, less again on nineteenth-century literature, and virtually none at all on contemporary literature. The reason for this diminuendo of interest is not hard to find: the literature of the eighteenth century is *par excellence* one whose ideas are clearly visible on the surface of the texts, but as we get away from these literatures in either direction, ideas are seen to play a less prominent role. I do not mean to say that ideas play a less significant role in them, but they are harder to detect, and they are imbedded in literature in such a way that our first impulse is to think of them critically rather than historically. We know that there is scarcely an "original" thought in Shakespeare, and we know that Milton is full of theological commonplaces, but what are we to make of this knowledge? The answer here lies outside the realm of the history of ideas, and judgments of value, far from being ancillary to the history of ideas, are what ought to be in the fore.

For when all is said and done, the main—I am almost tempted to say the sole—justification for scholarship concerned with the arts is the light it can throw on them, and, in the last analysis, this light has to be a critical light. We are, after all, in our capacities as scholars, as critics, and as men, concerned with rightness and wrongness. By avoiding these problems, by putting them on a plane where judgment is considered either irrelevant or automatic, the history of ideas tends to encourage us to abdicate our proper functions. To be sure, our standards come out of history, and it is the merit of the history of ideas that it shows us where we can anchor ourselves to the good traditions of the past, but history alone cannot compel us to make the right choices, nor having made them, give us the courage and the will to accept the consequences of those choices in scholarship, in criticism, and in our other activities as men. When it comes face to face with the problems of standards, standards of artistic value and the promotion of humanities, the history of ideas turns disappointingly vague and imprecise. I do not think that scholarship is its own excuse for being, but I do think that its values can be stated with more exactness, with more conviction, and I dare say, with more passion than the history of ideas has been able to do.

(1955, 1962)

The Study of Shakespearean Tragedy Since Bradley

UNTIL RECENTLY, Bradley's analysis of the nature of Shakespearean tragedy has been substantially accepted as fundamental to our understanding of the tragic pattern in the plays. Something of the excited approval with which Bradley was first accepted has been described by one of his severest latter-day critics; in her article, "Bradley Revisited: Forty Years After," Lily Bess Campbell has recalled the enthusiasm with which critics and teachers alike greeted the appearance of Bradley's study. And it was no wonder that he should have been given so hearty a reception, for if we glance at the state of Shakespearean study in the twenty years or so preceding the publication of his book we can see how great an advance he made in the analysis of Shakespeare's tragedies and to what a high level he lifted Shakespearean criticism.

However, just as Bradley's learning and critical depth put an end to nineteenth-century didactic, impressionistic, and romantic interpretations of Shakespeare's tragedies, so now a number of developments in modern criticism and scholarship have tended in turn to undermine his labors. These are, first, the emphasis on text instead of idea, characteristic of the new criticism; second, the effect of studies of imagery; third, the reading of Shakespeare's characters in the light of Elizabethan psychology; fourth, the emphasis on native medieval elements in Elizabethan drama; fifth, the semantic revolt against generic terms; and sixth, the assertion of the impossibility of the creation of tragedy at all. The cumulative direct force of the first five of these approaches, plus the indirect influence of the sixth, has brought about a general disparagement of Bradley's point of view and a corresponding devaluation of the idea of tragedy and its applications.

The most formidable of these approaches is the application of the methods of the new criticism to Shakespeare's plays. By asserting the unique integrity of a work of art, ". . . a pattern of resolutions and balances and harmonizations, developed through a temporal scheme," as Cleanth Brooks puts it in *The Well-Wrought Urn,* the new criticism effectively cuts off from the consideration of a piece of literature all matters which are not immediately intrinsic to it. More important, however, is the denial of the element of judgment in the new criticism. It is significant, I think, that for all his talk about tradition, Eliot has been very uneasy about making any statement of criteria of values, and even his principle of tradition is hardly vital enough for more general use, as Alick West has sharply shown in his remarks on Eliot as a critic in *Crisis and Criticism.* Moreover, I. A. Richards' notion of the therapeutic value of poetry, phrased as it is in technical psychological terms, is either too specific for use on any scale, or, if it says what I suspect it to mean, places him in the very camp which he is at some pains to oppose. And the best that Brooks can do is, by amplifying a suggestion of Richards, to suggest:

. . . a kind of scale for determining the value of poetry. Low in the scale one would find a rather simple poetry in which the associations of the various elements that go to make up the poem are similar in tone and therefore can be unified under one rather simple attitude —poems of simple affection, positive, 'external' satires, etc. Higher in the scale one would find poems in which the variety and clash among the elements to be comprehended under a total attitude are sharper. In tragedy, where the clash is at its sharpest—where the tension between attraction and repulsion is most powerful—one would probably find the highest point in the scale.

The effect of such a procedure is to utilize criteria ". . . in terms of the organizations of the poems themselves—not by having to appeal to some outside scale of values." But such a statement is either too narrow and personal to be of any widely applicable significance or says in a rather specialized and tortured way what most ethical critics—Arnold, for example—would normally accept.

At bottom, despite its sophistication, the new criticism rests on a postulate in theory which it must violate in action. This is the notion that the best reader of a poem is he who comes to it with a *tabula rasa* which prevents him from reading into the poem what is presumably not there. Unfortunately, his first reading must of necessity be his last since by that very act he has acquired too much knowledge. Ironically, it is amusing to note that two of the most important lyrics of our times, Eliot's *Waste Land* and Auden's *Christmas Eve Letter,* have been published with notes and explanations by the authors themselves, a clear violation of the doctrine of aesthetic self-containedness. Actually, one of the most stimulating things about the new criticism is the brilliant use it has made of insights outside the works themselves, that is, the implications of Frazer, Freud, and the recent students of language, such as Urban and Langer. The truth seems to be that when the new method is strictly applied to a work of the magnitude of the *Divine Comedy* or *Macbeth* it is simply wanting in the requisite range of applicability. Nor, as he himself admits, does Brooks' analysis of the clothed daggers and naked babe images in *Macbeth* tell us by any means the whole of the meaning of *Macbeth.* Finally, for all the strictures he heaped on Bradley's discussion of *Macbeth,* L. C. Knights finally manages to say pretty much the same thing about the play that Bradley does, and in words not very different from Bradley's.

If the new criticism suffers from a kind of aesthetic primitivism, studies of imagery suffer from a kind of tautology. Miss Spurgeon and the others who have followed her have gone to great and useful pains to catalogue the images Shakespeare used in his plays as evidence of his intent and have discovered that, in every case, the images used have matched that intent. That this method has resulted in many fresh insights into Shakespeare's methods of composition there is no doubt, particularly in the very subtle and revealing analyses by Edward A. Armstrong, who has applied recent discoveries in the study of the processes of word association to recreate what must be very close to Shakespeare's "subconscious and subliminal" methods of imagery making. Armstrong has an illuminating description of the probable method of imagery formation in Shakespeare; but when the imagery method gets out of hand, when, for example, Miss Spurgeon writes in *Shakespeare's Imagery:*

In the case of a poet, I suggest it is chiefly through his images that he, to some extent unconsciously, 'gives himself away,' . . . the poet unwittingly lays bare his own innermost likes and dislikes, observations and interests, associations of thought, attitudes of mind and beliefs, in and through the images . . .

and then proceeds to make him out verily a Victorian poet in mind and body: ". . . Healthy in body as in mind, clean and fastidious," or when Armstrong suggests that he disliked both painted women and dogs, then the legitimate boundaries of investigation have indeed been crossed.

But studies of imagery can tell us only how Shakespeare's mind worked; they have not been able to tell us the significance of the results of that working, that is, the patterns of action and meaning which the combinations of images ultimately constitute. There is, for example, nothing in the previous pages of Brooks' analysis of the imagery of *Macbeth* which prepares us for such a statement as:

. . . Macbeth is thus caught between the irrational and the rational. . . . Macbeth in his general concern for the future is typical

—is Every Man. He becomes the typical tragic protagonist when he yields to pride and *hybris*.

These are statements plainly derived from a study of the play which far transcends analysis of imagery and must be judged in terms of a larger concept of tragedy than the imagery method affords. Nor is Armstrong's notion that in Shakespeare's:

> . . . imagination the ideas Life and Death were supreme. . . . There are certain other important contrasting images of almost equal relevance to Life and Death intimately connected with them and constantly like them, set in opposition, such as Love and Hate, Light and Darkness.

particularly more helpful since these antitheses are at once too narrow and too large to be of much guidance in the interpretation of the tragic pattern in Shakespeare. But it is after all no wonder that the images match the intent for the simple reason that the play is conveyed to us through poetry, that is to say, though the succession of images proper to the experiences being conveyed. Thus it would be rather difficult, I imagine, to convey the atmosphere of murder in *Macbeth* without the imagery of murder, and it is as though to say that *Twelfth Night* is not *Macbeth* because it does not contain the imagery of despair and death. As a matter of fact, Bradley was not at all unaware of the use of imagery analysis, as witness his treatment of the animal imagery in *Lear*. But he recognized that imagery study is not an end in itself; his concern was properly with the patterns of motifs and ideas created by the use of the imagery pertinent to the patterns.

More determined, however, is the attack on Bradley's scholarship by Campbell. If in her book the criticism of Bradley was implicit, in her article she has quite openly stated that Bradley's ignorance of Elizabethan psychology and philosophy vitiated his entire treatment of the tragedies. However, a number of unexamined assumptions have gone into her criticism, and it might be well to examine them here, since they underlie other scholarly repudiations of Bradley as well. In the first place, Campbell seems to assume a kind of well-integrated and consistent Elizabethan psychology and philosophy which was known to all writers of the Renaissance, and which, in the second place, Shakespeare naturally used. But as Louise C. Turner Forest has so well shown, Elizabethan psychology is in reality a creation of recent scholarship which has given a false unity to what was actually a number of contradictory and fragmentary psychologies and pseudo-psychologies. Moreover, the assumption that Shakespeare did in fact use them is impossible of proof; the most that Campbell can show is that some Elizabethan psychologists said some things about some kinds of people which are something like what Shakespeare said of stage characters something like them.

Furthermore, there is in Campbell's method another assumption, one which is made by other Elizabethan scholars too, which postulates that the extrapolation of an intellectual background is indeed that background which the particular writer being studied did in fact use. But out of the totality of experience which is possible to a man within his lifetime, only those aspects which seem significant to him and which fit his particular needs are the ones which he does use. To say that Bradley was ignorant of Elizabethan philosophy is to assume the existence of such a philosophy and, further, that Shakespeare employed it. But if there is one safe generalization about the Renaissance, it is that the number of philosophies it propounded was legion; the real question is which, if any, did Shakespeare actually use, or granting the existence of such use, is the problem rather not one of asking how Shakespeare used those ideas, what modifications did he make in them—that is, what is distinctively Shakespearean, the unique quality which differentiates him from others, rather than of reducing him to the level of his contemporaries? Thus the effect of such studies as those of John W. Draper is to make Shakespeare into a compendium of Elizabethan social and psychological common-places in which the characters of the plays merely serve as the final illustration in a long series of equivalent Renaissance types.

But there are further implications in Campbell's method which lead us to the problem of the evaluation of the native medieval elements in Elizabethan tragedy. As a result of the reaction against Burckhardt's formulation of the Renaissance as *sui generis*, the gradual fusion of the Renaissance with the Middle Ages, a process expanded by the eighteenth-century historians on the basis of numerous Renaissance hints, has resulted in the virtual disappearance of the Renaissance as a distinctive era, and parallel with this development, has come the repudiation of the role of the revival of classical culture in the Renaissance and the substitution of a medieval world-view in its place. The onslaught against the Renaissance has been especially strong in the history of science under the leadership of Lynn Thorndike, but it is no less widespread in the present study of Elizabethan literature, particularly the drama. The medieval world picture, as described by Professors Campbell, Farnham, and Tillyard—to name only a few—has been so completely merged with the Renaissance that both it and its classical heritage have been all but covered over. And so far as the idea of tragedy in particular is concerned, the trend culminates in the reading of Shakespeare as a kind of superior writer of medieval exempla. As Farnham puts it in *The Medieval Heritage of Elizabethan Tragedy:*

The story of a fall from felicity into misfortune cast in the form which Boccaccio devised bore the name of tragedy down through the Middle Ages and even later. In Elizabethan England it bore the name without apology along with the newly born dramatic tragedy, and there is small evidence of anybody's critical concern that it should not do so.

Thus, the medieval fall of princes theme has been studied in detail by recent scholars with the purpose of showing that

Shakespearean tragedy is a natural outgrowth of native forces which have their origins deep in the Middle Ages (in fact, in late Roman culture, according to Farnham) and which culminate in Elizabethan drama which in turn differs from its medieval forebears only in degree but not in kind. Bradley had already recognized this relationship; in stating the more obvious characteristics of Shakespearean tragedy he had pointed out that it dealt with the exceptional suffering and calamity of a conspicuous person, which made the whole scene a scene of woe. These ideas, he said, ". . . would more than suffice to describe the whole tragic fact as it presented itself to the medieval mind," and he adduces Dante, Chaucer, and Boccaccio: "A total reverse of fortune, coming unawares upon a man who 'stood in high degree,' happy and apparently secure,—such was the tragic fact to the mediaeval mind." But he adds: "Shakespeare's idea of the tragic fact is larger than this idea and goes beyond it; but it includes it." That Shakespearean tragedy includes the medieval theme of the fall of princes is without doubt true but that it goes beyond it is equally true, and much more significant.

Theodore Spencer has suggested that for the Elizabethans tragedy was not "the imitation of an action . . . through pity and fear effecting the proper purgation of these emotions"; it was "merely a story that ended in death":

> And tragical, my noble lord, it is;
> For Pyramus therein doth kill himself.

Thus he rejects both the Aristotelian view of tragedy and also the medieval fall of princes theme and insists rather on a conception of tragedy which is the outcome of the conflict between two views of man in which the pathos of the omnipresence of death, inevitably covering all, strikes the proper tragic tone. Tragedy, then, is the sad flowering of the contempt of the world theme, inherited from the Middle Ages, and given more anguished and more passionate utterance, and its effect is ultimately one of despair, the individual briefly lighting the world with the flash of his ego, only to be buried in the darkness which encompasses us all.

Now, just as the so-called optimism of the Renaissance has had to be toned down by reference to its equally widespread pessimism, it is necessary to insist again that the Renaissance cannot be characterized exclusively by medieval or modern; it is much too complex for such oversimplified contraries. Again, the assertion of the nobility of man in the face of the overwhelming annihilation of both personality and ideals implicit in the expansion of the contempt of the world theme is made groundless by the very terms of the theme itself; Farnham sums up his conclusions by telling us that: "All that Shakespeare alone will permit us to say is that the yoke of life is hard but supremely worth the bearing in the interest of the general good." Thus stated, the assertion signally fails to do justice to the range of Shakespeare's thought and is self-contradictory as well. What seems to be happening here is that those who hold to the primary influence of the medieval fall of princes theme on Shakespearean tragedy are reading it in the light of Stoicism, even though one of the major aims of their work is to repudiate the influence of Seneca on Elizabethan drama.

Though Eliot expresses the hope that his essay will prevent the appearance of a Stoical or Senecan Shakespeare, nevertheless his prestige is such that the Stoical Shakespeare has been accepted by many critics and, for all the disclaimers, by Eliot himself. For in his account of "the penetration of Senecan sensibility," to use his phrase, he insists that ". . . the attitude of self-dramatization assumed by some of Shakespeare's heroes at moments of tragic intensity," an attitude characteristic of the Elizabethan dramatists as a whole, with the exception of Marlowe, is a terrible exposure of human weakness, the result of a philosophy which is ". . . the refuge for the individual in an indifferent or hostile world too big for him." But the best authority on the influence of Senecanism on the Renaissance drama, H. B. Charlton, in his lectures on *Shakespearean Tragedy,* expressly delimits the role of the Roman conception of fate in its effect on tragedy, particularly as it had been modified by the sixteenth-century mind. In his previous study of the growth of the Senecan tradition in Renaissance tragedy, Professor Charlton had already surveyed the dramatic qualities of Seneca's tragedies, established the nature of their appeal to the Renaissance, demonstrated the greater importance of Latin tragedy over Greek tragedy in the Renaissance, and examined in detail the development of the Senecan tradition in Italy, France, and England.

But is the Senecan influence an adequate explanation of Shakespearean tragedy? Is it, in fact, sufficient for Elizabethan tragedy as a whole? So far as the form of Elizabethan tragedy is concerned, we know that many of the formal elements attributed to the influence of Seneca are as much medieval in their origin as they are Roman. The five-act division of the play; the use of the chorus; the violation of the unities and of stage decencies; the employment of the messenger and of ghosts; the utilization of the revenge motive, the taste for rant, sensationalism, and sententious precepts, all these have their native medieval analogues and traditions. But it is in the realm of ideas where the difference between Elizabethan, and particularly Shakespearean, tragedy and Senecan tragedy is at once most sharp and most significant. For Senecan tragedy is based on postulates which by their very nature cannot possibly result in the kind of tragedy which we find in Shakespeare. That Christianity absorbed much of Stoicism is more than obvious, especially in the case of Paul and Augustine, and in the development of political theory. But if Christianity enveloped Stoicism, it also changed it, and this change is indeed radical, and all the more so when it is considered in context with the Renaissance insistence on freedom within limitation of the moral agent.

Stoicism is a philosophy of withdrawal, a rejection of the society of man, and a repudiation of the responsibility of man for man. Under such intellectual circumstances, the social basis of tragedy, tragedy as ritual, as a means of placing man in rapport with God and nature through the free struggle of man to attain understanding in his own way, through suffering passing from ignorance to knowledge by confronting evil directly and by actively overcoming it—in such circumstances tragedy must inevitably wither.

For if the Elizabethans worked more closely within a medieval framework than perhaps Burckhardt was prepared to admit, it still remains true that classical attitudes and ideas were at least as familiar, if not more so, to them than were the medieval attitudes and ideas which are now being rediscovered. And if they took their medieval ways for granted, they consciously and deliberately interpreted them in the light of the revival of classical culture. The result of the combination was not the mere addition of two elements, but rather the creation of a new synthesis on a level higher than either taken by itself. That behind Shakespeare there is indeed a medieval heritage of tragedy there is no doubt, but the measure of his artistry is not that he was absorbed and lost in that heritage but rather that he converted it to his own uses; he emphatically did not write yet another variation on *The Mirror for Magistrates*. For tragedy transcends mere exemplum; it is on a different and higher esthetic and ethical level.

The current revolt against generic terms such as "Renaissance," "Romanticism," and "Classicism" has left us so fearful of them that it is not surprising that the suspicion of generalizations should be extended to the concept of tragedy as well. The result has been that while the critic has been permitted to speak of particular tragedies, he cannot any longer speak of tragedy in general; the parallel situation in regard to Romanticism comes of course immediately to mind. Yet it does not seem unreasonable to ask whether, if Romanticism is in fact a series of romanticisms, a series of romanticisms cannot be Romanticism, and the same is true of the concept of tragedy as well. It must be obvious, I think, that to accept the denial of the universality of tragedy is to leave criticism virtually impotent, for if only particular definitions of tragedy applicable only to particular ages or even more narrowly to particular plays are valid, then generalization as to the nature of art is made impossible, and criticism, which has traditionally proceeded by the method of comparison and contrast over the widest range of relevance, is rendered impotent. However, the most serious consequence of the reaction against generic terms is the undermining of the element of judgment in criticism. The effect of semanticism run wild is to shatter the integrity of the individual artist; and to separate his work into disparate and often contradictory ideas often yields as false a picture of his work as the equally extreme manufacture of a system out of his ideas when there is none; certainly, the extreme of the one is not the corrective to the extreme of the other. Likewise, the tracing of ideas as though they had an independent life of their own and obeyed the special laws of their own being which only accidentally happened to place them within the work of a writer results in a loss of a focal place from which to exercise judgment, especially since it is in the less important writers that the most typical expression of an idea will ordinarily be found; again, there is the danger of so completely merging the great writer in the flood of parallel expressions that his uniqueness is drowned out. Judgment is thus lost in history which should be instead the highest kind of judgment.

It remains finally to assess the effect on the idea of tragedy of the theory that it is impossible, for sociological and ideological reasons, to write tragedy at this time. This theory rests on the valid principle that tragedy is ultimately optimistic in intent and needs an ethical view of the world on which to rest, but draws the false conclusion that no tragedy can be written because these conditions do not, and more important, cannot hold today. The effect of such ideas is to relegate the discussion of the idea of tragedy to an academic backwater, without the vital influence of the possibility of actual attainment to give the discussion point and purpose.

Yet the frame of mind which Joseph Wood Krutch has so well caught in his *The Modern Temper* is so widespread as to make the study of tragedy look almost exclusively to the past, when its purposes should be to establish a theoretical basis on which new tragedies can be written.

Krutch's argument stems from his insistence on the fundamental split between art and philosophy on the one hand and science on the other. If, he writes:

... the world of poetry, mythology, and religion represents the world as a man would like to have it, while science represents the world as he gradually comes to discover it, we need only compare the two to realize how irreconcilable they appear. For the cozy bowl of the sky arched in a protecting curve above him he must exchange the cold immensities of space, and, for the spiritual order which he has designed, the chaos of nature. God he had loved *because* God was anthropomorphic, because He was made in man's own image, with the purposes and desires which were human and hence understandable. But nature's purpose, if purpose she can be said to have, is no purpose of his and is not understandable in his terms. Her desire merely to live and to propagate in innumerable forms, her ruthless indifference to his values, and the blindness of her irresistible will strike terror to his soul, and he comes in the fullness of his experience to realize that the ends which he proposes to himself—happiness and order and reason—are ends which he must achieve, if he achieve them at all, in her despite. Formerly he had believed in even his darkest moments that the universe was rational if he could only grasp its rationality, but gradually he comes to suspect that rationality is an attribute of himself alone and that there is no reason to suppose that his own life has any more meaning than the life of the humblest insect that crawls from one annihilation to another.

But since tragedy can only arise when ". . . a people fully aware of the calamities of life is nevertheless serenely confident of the greatness of man" and is ". . . the triumph over despair and of confidence in the value of human life," ". . . a profession of faith, and a sort of religion; a way of looking at life by virtue of which it is robbed of pain," the effect of science has been to rob man of his dignity by ripping his faith in God and nature to shreds. The consequence is that it is only by the most painful effort of reconstruction that we can partially recreate the conditions which make the reading of tragedy somewhat possible, and as for the creation of tragedy itself, that is altogether impossible. But it seems to me that Krutch's position is based on a misreading of the philosophical implications of science. In the first place, it is not at all certain to me that the picture of the universe which Krutch attributes to science is correct. There is implied in his statement the notion that the new science of the Renaissance reduced man's stature in the universe and cut him irrevocably loose from his moorings in the orderly universe of the Middle Ages. But as Lovejoy has shown in *The Great Chain of Being,* the place of man in the new picture of the universe as drawn by Renaissance science was on the contrary much higher and nobler than the Middle Ages had accorded him; as Lovejoy writes: ". . . to remove man from the centre of things was to raise him from his low estate." In the second place, this reading of the history of science fails to recognize that so far as the early scientists themselves were concerned, the oppressive effects of science on man's place in the universe which Professor Krutch postulates were not regarded so pessimistically; and while they were recognized, as for example by the Cambridge Platonists, they were felt to be capable of being overcome by the other implications of science which promised man's control over nature and his emancipation from his bondage to scarcity. Finally, I am not at all sure but that the so-called crisis in science is not so much a crisis in science itself as a crisis in the society in which science now happens to find itself. That is, it seems to me that the picture of the universe which science has drawn and the place to which it has assigned man is not so pessimistic or so fraught with terror as Krutch would have one believe. But the crisis is rather the result of the clash between the bounty of science and a social structure which seeks to contain and stratify it; it is not a crisis in science itself, then, but in the control over the methods of making the results of science available. I do not therefore see that Krutch's position is tenable on the terms in which he has stated it, and it is possible to draw quite opposite conclusions concerning the impact of science.

Despite the trends which I have briefly characterized here, the kind of approach which Bradley represents still seems to me the most fruitful for the understanding of tragedy. However, I do not at all mean to suggest that we must forthwith return to him in his entirety for there is, after all, a lack in his work which must be supplied, a necessary correction which must be made, before his criticism can be employed in its proper perspective. I must indeed confess that Bradley often seems to proceed as though Shakespeare wrote with Aristotle by his side, and it is of course true that the Aristotle of the Renaissance is certainly not the Aristotle we have, and more important, it is scarcely conceivable that Shakespeare deliberately set himself to write within the Aristotelian framework. But it still remains true that, tautological as it sounds, Shakespeare did write tragedies and that, as a consequence of the nature of tragedy in general, both Aristotelian theory and Greek practice are indeed germane to the consideration of what Shakespeare wrote, even assuming that he knew nothing at all of them. What is missing is a bridge, valid on esthetic, historical, and ideological grounds, which can link Athenian and Elizabethan tragedy together in such a way as to close the gap in Bradley's treatment. Such a link would have to fit the pattern of Athenian tragedy, retain its vitality in the Middle Ages, and appear again as central to Shakespearean tragedy. Moreover, it would have to include within itself the possibility of a valid parallel between the Greek idea of *hybris* and the Christian doctrine of sin; it would have to be able to create a pattern of tragic action applicable both to Sophocles and to Shakespeare; and it would have to be able to take into account the parallel dialectical transformation of Greek myth into Greek tragedy and of Christian exemplum into Elizabethan tragedy.

(1955)

40

The Attack on the Renaissance in Theology Today

E VER SINCE THE Renaissance first invented itself some six
hundred years ago, there has been no agreement as to
what it is. Its definitions have been as many and varied as the
legions of scholars who have dealt with it, and the more that
is learned about the Renaissance, the less certainty there is
as to its extent, nature, purposes, and results. I need not re-
hearse the labyrinthine story of the idea of the Renaissance;
the study of studies of the Renaissance has become a scholarly
field in itself; and Wallace K. Ferguson has written the history of the idea of the Renaissance with just the proper mixture of authority, wonderment, and exasperation which it
deserves. I should like to call attention to a single recent episode in the history of the idea of the Renaissance, first,
because it is concerned with an area of discussion of the Renaissance problem a little off the beaten track of conventional Renaissance scholarship; second, because it illustrates a peculiar
power of the Renaissance itself, that is, its inevitable and in-
variable ability to provoke heat and passion; and third, because it opens a kind of Beaumont's window into the motivations of history writing which affords us that perspective in

depth so essential to its understanding but so difficult to obtain. I refer to the attack on the Renaissance which is a strong and surprising feature of the theology being written today.

What is unexpected about the attack on the Renaissance from this quarter is the almost unanimous agreement on this point of the theologians of all the major western faiths, Catholic, Hebrew, Greek Orthodox, and Protestant, and, among the Protestants, virtually all the denominations. The sharply critical theological treatment of the Renaissance, which often takes on an asperity a little at odds with Christian charity, is in turn related to the contemporary crisis of faith with which the theologians are primarily and naturally concerned. It is their view that the crisis of faith today is directly attributable to the Renaissance, that those ideas which have brought about the contemporary spiritual crisis originated in and were developed by the Renaissance, and that the crisis is in fact the infection of the Renaissance come to a head today. Failure of nerve, crisis of spirit, loss of faith in traditional values, doubt, depression, frustration, suffocation of spirit, nihilism, defeatism, indifference, totalitarianism of mind and body, compromise with principle, moral obfuscation, fatalism, materialism: these words and phrases, and others like them, mark the symptoms of the crisis of spirit of our times and appear over and over again in one form or the other in contemporary theology.

The deep spiritual malaise of which we are accused today stems from the Renaissance, which passed its fatal heritage on to us through a succession of ideological movements which intensified and deepened it. There appears to be common agreement among the theologians that despite the wide variety of philosophies since the Renaissance, they are at bottom essentially all alike in bearing the Renaissance taint. T. E. Hulme, in *Speculations*, declared without qualification: ". . . all philosophy since the Renaissance is . . . the *same* philosophy. The family resemblance is much greater than is generally supposed. The obvious diversity is only that of the various species of the same genus." And in *The Degrees of Knowledge,* Maritain goes so far as to accuse all modern philosophy of exhibiting the same error: "Whether they be neo-Kantians or neo-positivists, idealists, Bergsonians, logistics, pragmatists or neo-Spinozists, or neo-mysticists, one ancient sin works in the roots of all modern philosophies—the old error of *nominalism.*" The fatal descent goes from seventeenth-century science to the Age of Enlightenment, through romanticism, Hegelianism, Darwinism, Marxism, and on to existentialism; as Berdyaev writes in *Towards a New Epoch:*

Renaissance humanism affirmed the autonomy of man, and his freedom in the spheres of cultural creation, science and art. Herein lay its truth, for it was essential that the creative force of humanity should surmount the obstacles and prohibitions that medieval Christianity had put in its way. Unfortunately, however, the Renaissance also began to affirm man's self-sufficiency, and to make a rift between him and the eternal truths of Christianity. In this lay its error. Here we have the fountain-head of the tragedy of modern history, the tragic dialectic of humanism in which man's self-sufficiency becomes a denial of man and thus leads to anti-humanism. A divorce is effected between religious and anti-religious humanism. In opposition to the divine-humanity of Christ—that is the simultaneous activity of the two natures—the divine principle began to work against the human, and the human against the divine. God became the enemy of man and man the enemy of God.

In the view of the theologians, then, the major ideological movements produced by western civilization since the Renaissance have been, because of their corrupt origin in the Renaissance, false roads leading us on to the dead end of spiritual crisis. As the influential German Catholic theologian Karl Adam puts it in *The Spirit of Catholicism:*

The individualism of the Renaissance, the dismemberment of man and his relations in the Age of Enlightenment, and finally the subjective idealism of Kant, whereby our minds were taught to relinquish the objective thing, the trans-subjective reality, and to indulge in boundless subjectivism: these influences tore us from the moorings of our being, and especially from our true and essential basis, that humanity which produces, supports, and enfolds us. We became imprisoned within the walls of our own selves, unable any more to attain to humanity, to the full, whole man. The category 'humanity' became foreign to our thought, and we thought and lived only in the category of self.

What were the steps by which the Renaissance has inexorably and treacherously lured us to our present spiritual and intellectual dilemma? First of all, it shifted the emphasis from a theocentric to an anthropomorphic view of the world. As Etienne Gilson has put it: "The difference between the Renaissance and the Middle Ages was not a difference by addition but by subtraction. The Renaissance, as it has been described to us, was not the Middle Ages plus man, but the Middle Ages minus God, and the tragedy is that in losing God the Renaissance was losing man himself." The same idea is repeated by Berdyaev, who is quoted with approval by John Baillie, the Scots theologian; Berdyaev writes in *The End of Our Time:* "The Renaissance began with the affirmation of man's creative individuality; it ended with its denial." Agreement on this point comes as well from the Protestant Hopper who sums up the argument of the theologians in this way, in *The Crisis of Faith:*

Medievalism had reached a point of *stasis,* which brought about in the thirteenth to the sixteenth centuries a crisis of affirmation, in which the pristine principles of Christian and classical vitality broke through the formalism—intellectual and ecclesiastical—which sought to encircle it. The succeeding centuries confused the essence of this new vitality, and so the period suffered by degrees that fatal amputation of the spirit which left the period doubly vitiated from within by (1) a rejection of the faith and (2) an appeal to self-sufficiency. The Renaissance-modern mind, therefore, proposed to itself a two-fold experiment—an experiment in thought and an experiment in culture—the one an attempt to find meaning by way of reason alone, the other an attempt to ground the self creatively upon its own limitless powers. The failure of these experiments brings us to the true crux of all human choosing and instructs us in our fundamental poverty apart from God.

The Renaissance raised this *hybris* of civilization, as both Dawson and Niebuhr call it, to a new and absurd height, and we are now suffering from the dizziness of our belated realization that we have been left dangling on an unsupported perch.

The transfer from the medieval to the Renaissance point of view brought about far-reaching consequences of which the Renaissance in its naive enthusiasm for novelty was unaware but from which its descendants now suffer. Hopper lists the shifts as follows: the substitution of personality for the doctrine of original sin; the substitution of perfectibility and progress for hierarchy and order; the substitution of history, or a teleological, for an ontological world view; and the substitution of "a sceptical suspension of decision on ultimate questions" for religious faith, all opening the way for rationalism, scepticism, empiricism, the self-sufficiency of reason, the subjectivity of knowledge, and the deification of science. As Berdyaev dramatically declares in *The Fate of Man in the Western World:* "In making himself God, man has unmanned himself." Niebuhr is more sober but no less uncompromising in his rejection of the Renaissance: "The Renaissance is the real cradle of that very unchristian concept and reality: the autonomous individual." Answering his own question, what is the chief cause of this crisis, Berdyaev replies in *The Realm of Spirit and the Realm of Caesar:*

Since he moved out of the Middle Ages, man has followed a path marked by the autonomy of different spheres of creative activity. In the period of modern history, which has already ceased to be modern and has become very old, all spheres of culture and of social life began to live and develop by their own laws, independent of any spiritual centre. Hence some of the creative powers held captive in the Middle Ages could develop—politics, economics, science, technics, nationality, etc.—none of these will recognize any moral law, any spiritual element higher than themselves. Machiavellism in politics, capitalism in economics, scientism in science, nationalism in the life of peoples, the integral power of technics over man—all of these are the results of those autonomies. The basic and fatal contradiction in the fate of European man was that the autonomy of various spheres of his activities was not the autonomy of man himself, as an integral being. Man became more and more the slave of these autonomous spheres of activity, which were not under subjection to the human spirit.

It is worth noticing how, once the logic of this argument is accepted, even the staunchest Protestant is forced to elevate the Middle Ages at the expense of the Renaissance, and, worse yet, to suspect the Reformation itself because of its inextricable connections with Renaissance humanism. "The Reformation, like the Renaissance," declares the professor of systematic theology of St. Andrew's College, Saskatoon, Canada, Dr. Randolph C. Chalmers, "must assume a certain amount of responsibility for the disunity of European life following the close of the Middle Ages." And it is the Protestant Reinhold Niebuhr who submits the Reformation to the most searching criticism, especially those aspects of it which he describes under the heading of sectarian Protestantism, that is, ". . . the impulse towards the perfection of individual life expressed in the pietistic sects and . . . the impulse towards the fulfillment of history expressed particularly in the Anabaptist and socially radical sects." Similarly does he subject the Lutheran and Calvinistic Reformation to the most stringent scrutiny and he concludes that despite the Reformation ". . . polemic against the premature transcendence over history in Catholicism, it is as frequently tempted to commit the same error as Catholicism (though with the use of different instruments of pretension) as it is to commit the opposite error." The Protestant Hopper makes what seems to me a rather half-hearted defense of

Luther against Maritain's scornful "Spoilt Saint"; "the truth is," says Hopper, "that Luther and the Reformation are still an issue." And Berdyaev goes so far as to regard the Reformation as part of the disintegration of the Renaissance.

A major aspect of the Renaissance with which the theologians today find fault is what they term its excessive rationalism. The Renaissance discovery of the autonomy of reason led to the "real tragedy of the Renaissance," as Hopper calls it, and he continues:

For these two principles—that of the primacy of faith and that of the free criticism—were severed. The insights of Luther were accommodated to a dogmatic authoritarianism not less stringent than that against which Luther had protested; and the free criticism of experience became the notion of free inquiry operating in the interests of empirical investigation. Thus the spirit of man, which had experienced the momentary release into a life of faith and wisdom, was hurriedly closed off from both by the interception of a new dogmatism on the one hand and an empirical reduction of the criticism of experience upon the other. This left the self both naked and exposed, desperately introverted, and subject to a dialectic of gradual disillusionment and frustration. Secularity displaced the faith; freedom was debased into 'emancipation'; humanistic good sense shrivelled into 'enlightenment'; the individual lost his newly found dignity in the humiliating 'discoveries' of a naturalistic science. Meanwhile faith, uncriticised by life and experience, congealed into a Protestant scholasticism, or eddied into pietism and the several sects or cults of religious experience (feeling); and free inquiry followed the path of rationalism, empiricism, utilitarianism, evolutionism, experimentalism, down to this present hour.

Hopper reaches the unhappy conclusion that ". . . the man who discovers himself in the beginning of the Renaissance loses himself at the end of the Renaissance." From the disparagement of the claims of Renaissance rationalism, the path of theological criticism leads through the condemnation of Montaigne's scepticism and on to the inevitable full-scale onslaught against science in general and Descartes in particular. Perhaps on no other point are the theologians of all faiths in such concerted agreement as on their attack on Renaissance science. The Protestants Alexander, Brunner, Hopper, Tillich, and Zehrer; the Greek Orthodox Berdyaev; the Hebrew Buber; and the Catholics Gilson, Maritain, and Sheen fire their heaviest salvos at Renaissance science and Descartes. As one Protestant theologian has stated the case for the prosecution:

Beginning with the new dispensation (the new covenant) of the Copernican revolution, setting free the 'moribund' intelligences of medieval minds (to speak from within the revolution), and conferring on the 'modern' man a sense of liberation and emancipation from Church authorities and dogmas, it ushered in the 'age of reason and of man.' In the eighteenth century this science took on a role more hallowed still: it became Revealer, and the age was called the age of Enlightenment. Thence came the 'century of hope,' the century in which science as 'the new Messiah' offered men a new salvation—the salvation of indefinite progress, the bliss of material achievement, with comfort, goods, and conveniences for all. The twentieth century acknowledged this new Kingdom, projected its utopias, complied with all pragmatics, and sought to usher in the Kingdom for the masses. Accepting Marx as its latter-day prophet, it sought the rationalization of all mankind (as Lenin said, the 'electrification' of Europe).

Probably the most sustained attack on Renaissance science and its subsequent pernicious effects on modern science, philosophy, and religion has been made by Msgr. Sheen. His book, *Philosophy of Religion,* written by the scholar and philosopher and not the TV entertainer, takes up in careful detail the impact of scientific concepts on physical theory, comparative religion, and historical methodology. The effect of this influence was to create two different metaphysics of man, one the Natural or Liberal Man, the other the Frustrated Man, neither of which is capable of sustaining itself in the face of the spiritual crisis. In sum, science, "metaphysically presumptuous and religiously naive," is accused of dehumanizing and depersonalizing man by cutting him loose from his spiritual connections.

"The defect of Descartes' *Discourse on Method*," Unamuno has stated in *The Tragic Sense of Life:*

. . . lies not in the antecedent methodological doubt; not in his beginning by resolving to doubt everything, a merely intellectual device; but in his resolution to begin by emptying himself of himself, of Descartes, of the real man, the man of flesh and bone, the man who does not want to die, in order that he might be a mere thinker—that is, an abstraction.

But it is Maritain who returns to the attack on his "dear enemy," Descartes, as he calls him, time and again. In his essay, "Religion and Culture," Maritain simultaneously praises and indicts Descartes as the ". . . one genius at all events among the many responsible for the evils which afflict us." Descartes' dualistic knife, cutting in every direction, irrevocably and tragically split free spirit from geometrical extension, and through the gap poured those evil ideas of science, materialism, and rationalism which have inevitably led us to our moral and spiritual impasse. Maritain amplified this criticism in his 1934 lectures at the University of Santander where, in the section titled "The Dialectic of Anthropocentric Humanism—The Tragedy of Man," he declared:

In the case of man it is observable that in the beginnings of the modern age, first with Descartes, then with Rousseau and Kant, rationalism had set up a proud and splendid image of the *personality* of man, inviolable, jealous of his immanence and his autonomy, and finally, good in essence. It is in the name of the rights and autonomy of this personality that the polemic of rationalism had condemned any intervention from outside in this perfect and sacred universe, —whether such intervention comes from revelation and grace or from the tradition of human wisdom, the authority of a law of

49

which man is not the author, or of a sovereign good which solicits his will, or finally, of an objective reality which would measure and regulate his intelligence.

Yet in little more than a century, this proud anthropocentric personality has perished, and been involved in rapid ruin through the dispersion of its material elements.

In the wake of Descartes came Darwinism, which struck a mortal blow at the rationalist conception of human personality, and Freudianism, which administered the *coup de grâce* by making man a "monster, dear to himself." The ultimate disintegration of the personality thus leaves the way clear for the collective man of Communism. Maritain continued the attack on Descartes in his *Philosophy of Nature,* where, under the similar heading, "A Tragic Misunderstanding," he wrote:

> You can see how Descartes' rigorously mechanistic philosophy of nature was,—and this indeed is what condemns it as a philosophy, —a marvellously servile adaptation of philosophy to the dynamic state of the sciences and of scientific research during his time. He transferred into the philosophic order the very outlook that science needed from its methodological point of view and in the physico-mathematical order.

But it is in *Three Reformers* and *The Dream of Descartes,* particularly the latter, that Maritain most fully analyzes the defects of Cartesian thought. In *Three Reformers* Maritain accuses Descartes of importing ". . . into the sphere of the human the prerogative of the angel: intuitive knowledge, innate in origin and independent of the world of things." And in *The Dream of Descartes,* Maritain charges Descartes with distorting the concept of science; of destroying ". . . the foremost and most immaterial of human hierarchies, the order of intellectual disciplines"; and, finally, of disjointing man into independent and opposite substances. Maritain sums up his indictment in one incisive sentence: "On the balance-sheet we should inscribe: rupture of the impulse which was directing all the labour of human science towards the eternal, toward conversation with the three divine Persons—upsetting to the plan of knowledge."

Once Renaissance science and Descartes are convicted of such widespread and thorough-going epistemological deception, which betrayed man into the false paths of pride, solipsism, individualism, and vanity, the attack on the character of the Renaissance spreads in all directions. Berdyaev accuses the Renaissance of putting up man without God and against God; Peter Wust condemns it for substituting a secular culture for the life of faith; "From the Renaissance onwards," he states in his essay, "Crisis in the West," "the Christian concept of God recedes steadily into the background." And it is Niebuhr who write the theological epitaph on the Renaissance in *The Nature and Destiny of Man:* "The mistake of the Renaissance was to overestimate the freedom and power of man in history."

I may also mention four important but less frequently expressed criticisms of the Renaissance made by the theologians today. The first is by Bishop Anders Nygren in his stimulating *Agape and Eros* where he sharply distinguishes the Renaissance from the Reformation by declaring: "The Renaissance takes up the Eros motif, the Reformation the Agape motif." And he goes on to say that in Ficino's thought, for example, ". . . empirical man is made, in a way such as never before, the centre of the universe. In a word, it is a quest of the human god." A second theological criticism of the Renaissance is that it gave rise to the idea of nationalism, to the independent state, and to the consequent conflicts which followed in the train of nationalism. Baron von Hugel puts the case this way:

Then there came the Renaissance and the birth of the strictly modern Nations, with their supposed utter mutual independence of each other, and their supposed omnipotent Governments—two wild and poisonous suppositions. Here the entire self-sufficingness, pure selfishness, and boundless competitiveness of the several Nations and States becomes the fashionable doctrine. With Hobbes, we find a conception of the State in full parallel with that of the individual man, and of both as purely predatory. The single man is a wolf to his fellow-individuals—a single wolf amongst and against the other single wolves, until the omnipotent state undertakes to do, for these single wolves, the prowling and preying upon the other packs of wolves with a perfection of force and cunning utterly beyond all private competition.

His remarks would find a particularly strong echo in Berdyaev, who goes so far as to say that concurrently with nationalism the Renaissance produced as a new way of life the form of social organization known as capitalism, a way of life prodigiously destructive to the spirit of man. And Maritain is as critical of what he calls bourgeois humanism as he is of socialism; indeed, in many of the theologians who criticize the Renaissance, the idea of the rejection of the world as it is, including its dominant nationalistic and capitalistic institutions, is certainly implicit, if not often explicit. However, Niebuhr at least grants to the Renaissance a greater liberalism with regard to toleration and the state than either the Catholics or Protestants showed in practice. "The chief source of toleration in modern history," he writes, "has been in the various forces of the Renaissance movement, both sectarian and secular." And he concedes that the Renaissance "recognized the perils of conflict in the dynamic elements of social existence."

Another argument against the Renaissance is that it fell prey to historicism. According to Msgr. Sheen, both the Reformation and the Renaissance opposed the transcendent divine principle in history, for they ". . . wiped out the past and gave us discontinuous history." A most subtle and sustained attack on secular views of history is to be found in Niebuhr's *Faith and History;* he begins his critique by pointing out that the Renaissance returned to the classical cyclical interpretation of history but ". . . historical cycles became spirals of advance in Renaissance historiography. Its passion for a return to old disciplines was submerged by its enthusiasm for man's new and growing powers." The effect of this transformation was to destroy the concept of endlessly returning cycles with their implied despair; time lost its mystery; and history was ". . . no longer an enigma. It became the assurance of man's redemption from his every ill." From this root, the concept that history is rationally intelligible, grew the subsequent modern views of history, views which Niebuhr condemns as too simple morally, for he holds that ". . . man's life and history can be made intelligible only within the framework of a larger realm of mystery and meaning discerned by faith." It is this view informing the second volume of Niebuhr's Gifford lectures which leads him to conclude that, from the standpoint of the Christian faith, ". . . history is not meaningless because it cannot complete itself; though it cannot be denied that it is tragic because men always seek prematurely to complete it."

The final criticism of the Renaissance made by the theologians today is directed against its art. I do not refer to adverse judgments of the art of the Renaissance on technical or esthetic grounds but criticism which stems directly from theological presuppositions. In his Mellon lectures, Maritain summarizes the course of western art since the birth of Christ as passing ". . . from a sense of the human Self first grasped as object, and in the sacred exemplar of Christ's divine Self, to a sense of the human Self finally grasped as subject, or in the creative subjectivity of man himself, man the artist or the poet." In Byzantine, early Christian, and Romanesque art, the mystery of the Person emerges as object; in Gothic architecture, and in the work of Duccio, Giotto, Angelico, and Grunewald, this mystery discloses its more human depths; and in the art of the Renaissance ". . . the sense of the human Self and of human subjectivity enters a process of spiritualization, and passes from the *object* depicted to the *mode* with which the artist performs his work." The results of this shift were a *prise de conscience* of the intellectual energy of art, a *prise de conscience* of the working ego, and, above all, ". . . the unconscious pressure of the artist's individuality upon the very object he was concerned with in Nature came to exercise and manifest itself freely in his work." This criticism is made by Peter Wust in another way when he speaks of the Renaissance artist's absorption in classical and secular culture as ends in themselves which ". . . inevitably effected a cleavage within his soul between his Christian belief in the supernatural" and profane culture. This he names the "modern malady" and he warns that ". . . the time will soon come when the artist will no longer find his way back to the foot of the Cross when he has laid down his brush." But the most consistent and detailed application of the theological criticism of Renaissance art has been made by E. I. Watkin, a Catholic writer much influenced by Christopher Dawson, whose historical studies are based on his Catholic point of view. Watkin's book, *Catholic Art and Culture,* contains six sections whose headings tell in brief the history of Western art as he sees it: classical autumn; Christian spring; summer: medieval Christendom; late summer: the disintegration of the medieval order, the Renaissance; autumn: the age of Baroque; and winter: the modern world. Watkin derives his critique of Renaissance art from his idealization of the medieval synthesis in theory, realized in practice in the Summa, the *Divina Commedia,* and in the cathedral where ". . . medieval religion-culture achieved a harmony of the vertical and the horizontal movements of the human spirit, reconciled detachment with appreciation, built and ordered the earthly city with a vision directed to the heavenly." But the tension between the religious and vertical and the secular and horizontal movements was too delicately poised, and Renaissance art is the record of the disturbance of that tension. Watkin likens the Renaissance to an adolescent too eager and undisciplined in his enthusiasms: "Scholarship had opened to him the world of the past, exploration was opening up the entire world of the present, science offered the alluring prospect of a brave new world in the future." The result was that the ". . . Renaissance tensions were thus largely due to the imperfect assimilation of the new matter, not yet digested." The logic of Watkin's position thus forces him to praise baroque art, the art of the counter-Reformation which he defines as ". . . an effort to re-establish in every sphere the Catholic culture of the Middle Ages in forms and by methods suited to the novel conditions," so that baroque art may in turn be defined as ". . . the employment of classical forms by Gothic feeling." He says of baroque art: "I love it. . . . it was the ripe fruit of the Catholic religion-culture. . . . It will teach us how to be free without being lawless, to be humanist without being secular, to rise high yet range far, to live a life hid with Christ in God yet regard no human interest as alien."

In essence, then, these are the criticisms which constitute the theological attack on the Renaissance today. For the most part, they are none of them unfamiliar to anyone who has studied the history of the idea of the Renaissance. They have appeared singly or in combination in the work of critics of the Renaissance whose methodological presuppositions have been quite free of theological conditioning and they will be found in their appropriate places in Ferguson. I do not want to get involved in the reasons for the extent and virulence of this attack except to say that, once you commit yourself to a denunciation of the salient features of the world as it is, you are inevitably led to the condemnation of the Renaissance, and the process works both ways. Many of the most persistent critics of the Renaissance have insisted that not only did it never exist but it was also a very bad thing, but here you cannot have it both ways: for if it was a bad thing, it must have existed, and if it did not exist, it certainly cannot be blamed for what then could only have happened in the Middle Ages, obviously from the theological point of view, the wrong time for bad things to have happened.

What attitude ought one to take toward this theological

attack on the Renaissance? Religious considerations apart, there seem to me three possible approaches. The first impulse of the defender of the Renaissance is naturally to expose the errors in fact, and there are not a few, in the attack, and it is to this task that Coulton has exuberantly devoted himself. But it is not so much the facts which are at stake as the interpretation of the facts, nor can one question the accuracy of facts when it is the impetus behind a point of view which forces the accumulation of new information. Much more sophisticated is the approach which turns the tables by arguing that at its best the Renaissance exhibits those Christian virtues which it is accused of denying. "The classical humanism of the Renaissance was fundamentally medieval and fundamentally Christian," Douglas Bush has said, and he has back of him a reputable body of scholarship to sustain his point of view. But while this approach does in part redress the balance, it cannot nor does it intend to encompass the variety and complexity of the Renaissance as a whole. Finally, I would suggest that one can approach the Renaissance without bias or rancor, to accept it as an historical phenomenon which, whether we like it or not, did take place as it did. Perhaps if we had been given the opportunity and the power to rearrange the history of man, we would have seen to it that it would not be as messy as it has turned out to be. But there it is, not as we would like it to be, but as it is, for good or for ill, and I cannot see that anything is to be gained by taking issue today with events which occurred six hundred years ago, especially since we have other, and I think, more significant and more immediate problems to solve if we expect to have a future in which to continue to debate the Renaissance problem. If the world is as bad today as the theologians tell us it is, the blame rests not with Michelangelo or Shakespeare or Bacon but with us, and the remedies lie not in their hands but ours. But do not think that I am going to plead for the exclusion of bias and passion from scholarship. On the contrary, only conviction and zeal create the drive which uncovers new materials and yields fresh points of view. When the idea of the Renaissance was tied to the ideas of science and progress in the seventeenth century, it was alive and meaningful; when it became the exclusive property of the antiquarians, it languished and lost contact with living issues. History is a mirror in which we look into the past to see how we ought to appear in the future and I would keep no one from pursuing this oblique utopianism. And since we know that it is not the mirror which lies but the beholder, we need constantly around us scholars who can tell the emperor whether his suit fits or not, or indeed if it is on at all.

Reassuring indeed; but then, scholars are themselves hardly the glass of fashion and the mould of form. Who, when they appear in print with their doublets unbraced, no hats upon their heads, their stockings fouled, ungartered, and down-gyved, who is to dress *them* down?

> O, woe is me,
> T' have seen what I have seen, see what I see!

(1955)

Theatrum Mundi: Illusion
as Reality

I T WOULD BE a rather amusing task to make a little list of all
the sixteenth- and seventeenth-century works whose title
begins with the word *theatrum* or *teatro:* the world becomes
a grandiose spectacle, filled with floating images and a constantly changing scenery, rather than a structure clearly organized and intellectually penetrable." So Panofsky once wrote
me, throwing off in his characteristic way a suggestion at once
challenging and consuming, a mere lifetime labor. This was
some time ago when I was younger and stronger and still
under the impression that the way to academic fame was
through scholarship, and I dutifully began to compile my
little list. The list grew longer, the amusement duller, and
when at last I realized that I never would be missed, I gave up
the list. I will spare you the details; let it suffice to say that the
image of *theatrum mundi*, though not quite so prevalent as I
had anticipated, is still found frequently enough in Renaissance thought so as to constitute a genuine intellectual commonplace in it. While it is true that the concept has been
intensively studied within the past year or two by Bernheimer,
Rossi, Secret, and Yates, their interest in it has been limited:

they are concerned primarily with the Renaissance art of memory in which the image of *theatrum mundi* serves as a unifying mnemonic device; the *Theatrum Mundi* of Giulio Camillo is probably the outstanding example of this particular genre; at least, it is the one which has been most intensively studied. To be sure, both Curtius and Battenhouse have looked at the metaphor within a larger philosophical context than that of the art of memory alone, but, so far as I know, its main ideological implications are still untreated, and are likely to remain so even at the conclusion of this paper. Nevertheless, I should like, taking its existence and dispersal in Renaissance thought for granted, to suggest some tentative answers to a few significant questions about the image of *theatrum mundi,* that is, its role on the stage of Renaissance thought, the nature of its character and motivation, and its subsequent stage history.

Theatrum mundi is, as you realize, an extended metaphor; the world is symbolized as a theatre, and all its events, or plot, and all its inhabitants, or *dramatis personae,* are depicted as taking place and acting within its confines and within its particular terms as a medium of representation. Now, while the external form of the metaphor remains constant, that is, the world as a stage, its inner content changes, and changes drastically. So far as I can see, there are three separate and distinct types of expression of the *theatrum mundi* concept, each deriving from different ideological presuppositions and therefore with different, and indeed contradictory, intellectual consequences. And these differences, it seems to me, are the consequence of two drastic and sharp shifts within the metaphor itself, the first the shift in the location of the spectator within the image, the other the shift in attitude toward the meaning of the action being performed on the stage of the theatre of life.

In the first type, the spectator is placed in the center of the theatre and looks toward and up to the stage; he is in effect the audience, the witness to the proceedings on the stage of life; and he is put there for the sole purpose of admiring the skill and accomplishment of the author and/or producer and/or director of the drama of creation. "Every man should seriously apply himself to a consideration of the works of God," writes Calvin in *The Institutes,* "being placed in this very splendid theater to be a spectator of them," and in Vives' *Fable about Man,* Jupiter, at Juno's request and since he is all-powerful, improvises an amphitheatre, and:

. . . at a command of almighty Jupiter, by whom alone all things are done, this whole world appeared, so large, so elaborate, so diversified, and beautiful in places, just as you see it. . . . The great Jupiter was director of the play, and when he saw that all were there, he gave the signal. Since he was the maker, he ordered everything and explained it to all that they might understand. Lest something be done differently from what he himself liked, he prescribed to the company of actors the entire arrangement and sequence of the plays, from which not even by the breadth of a finger, as they say, should they depart.

The scene which this use of the *theatrum mundi* image evokes is, at least to me, essentially closer to that of a spectacle rather than that of a drama; it is not so much a performance which is being put on as a demonstration which is taking place. The most vivid pictorial representation of this sense of the metaphor which I can recall is Raphael's "Disputa del Sacramento" in the Stanza della Segnatura in the Vatican (I realize that I am doing violence to Raphael's position in the history of styles), with its carefully ordered levels of celestial and earthly hierarchies all neatly circumscribed within a solid, classical arch, the proscenium arch of the theatre of the universe inside of which the drama of all creation takes place. This arch imposes on the scene the comforting feeling of order and limit and visualizes for the beholder a real deity in a real universe whose components are logically arranged in the correct descending order; it is, in effect, the Christian concept in a classical setting; for, as Lovejoy has reminded us, the cosmical scene of the Middle Ages, and I would add of Christian orthodoxy at any time, has ". . . the essential qualities of a work of classical art." In this form of the metaphor, then, *theatrum mundi* may well have been designed by Alberti, the set by Piero della Francesca, the costumes by Dürer, the program notes by Cinthio, and the play itself by Dante, and, naturally enough, it is a comedy.

The second type of *theatrum mundi* metaphor wrests the spectator from out of his comfortable and safe seat in the audience and thrusts him over the footlights into the turmoil on the stage of life itself. This I would regard as the typical classical expression of the image; Curtius traces it back to Plato's poignant question: "May we not regard every living being as a puppet of the gods, which may be their plaything only, or may be created with a purpose?" Not unexpectedly, this use of the metaphor is revived in the Renaissance, but makes a rather late entrance in, for example, the work of Ronsard, Calderon, and Campanella; in England, the earliest reference to it which I could find is that by Udall in 1548. Though Spenser and Donne seem in their poetry to overlook the larger philosophical implications of the image, More and Raleigh do make serious use of it, but of course the best known expression is by Jacques in *As You Like It,* who amplifies Antonio's brief allusion in *The Merchant of Venice.* The Duke speaks:

> Thou seest we are not all alone unhappy.
> This wide and universal theatre
> Presents more woeful pageants than the scene
> Wherein we play in.

And Jacques replies:

> All the world's a stage,
> And all the men and women merely players.
> They have their exits and their entrances,
> And one man in his time plays many parts,
> His acts being seven ages. . . . Last scene of all,
> That ends this strange eventful history,

Is second childishness and mere oblivion,
Sans teeth, sans eyes, sans taste, sans everything.

Shakespeare thus links the *theatrum mundi* metaphor to the powerful, brooding Renaissance theme of time, and if, in the first use of the image, time is static and therefore timeless, in the second use time is turned into the destroyer, the enemy of man, and the drama of life becomes a conflict in which, though the final resolution is certain, the time for the last curtain to be rung down is unknown. I have described the first use of the metaphor in terms of High Renaissance style; I must therefore describe the second use in terms of Mannerist style. To the regulated ranks of hierarchy in the Raphael painting we must oppose the writhing, interpenetrating forms of Vasari's "Immaculate Conception," a difference in style which Vasari himself discriminated in the Preface to the third part of the *Lives*. Our theatre now is designed by Bernini, the set by Parmigianino, the costumes by Salviati, the program notes by Michelangelo, and the play itself by Tasso; again, it is a comedy, but a comedy with a difference, the difference, say, between *Twelfth Night* and *Measure for Measure*. Our spectator is now an actor who is playing from a script still being written in the wings by an harassed author as the play inexorably moves on just ahead of his flying pen.

The third form of the *theatrum mundi* metaphor carries the combined theatre-time concept to its ultimate conclusion: the very *mythos* of the play of life is itself a falsehood:

Life's but a walking shadow; a poor player,
That struts and frets his hour upon the stage,
And then is heard no more: it is a tale
Told by an idiot, full of sound and fury,
Signifying nothing.

A play heaped together by an idiot, a play saying nothing and meaning nothing, is no longer a play, nor, by the same token, can there be a theatre in which it can be housed; the fabric of intelligible form has been irreparably shredded. I therefore cannot assign a style to this form of the metaphor; it is below and beyond history.

These, then, are the three variations of the *theatrum mundi* image as I have found them expressed in Renaissance thought, and, as I have tried to show, while all three employ the same theatrical vocabulary, they do so for different purposes and different effects, the first envisioning the metaphor in terms of an amphitheatre or colosseum in which the glory of creation is endlessly proclaimed, the second conceiving the image in terms of a stage upon which the struggle for existence is fiercely performed, and the third simply destroying both meta- phor and meaning together. Of the three, the first is the most respectably orthodox, having behind it the authority of a divinely ordered and therefore morally acceptable hierarchical arrangement of existence; the second is the one most favored by the humanist tradition of half-scepticism and half-faith; while the third is unique for its time, yet for us perhaps the most influential of all. The metaphor itself has an instructive history beyond its Renaissance occurrence. It appears to be a product of late classical thought; I have found no uses of it in the myths of the ancient Near East nor in Greek thought be- fore Plato, nor have I found it in Latin literature until the satirists. It receives Christian expression only where a strong classical influence may be shown, as in Paul, Augustine, and particularly John of Salisbury; on the other hand, it is not sur- prising that the medieval systematizers should have avoided it, not merely because the absence of actual theatres would not have brought the metaphor to mind, but for more fundamental reasons, as I shall try to show. The metaphor was revived again in Renaissance thought, and again, significantly, in later rather than in earlier Renaissance humanism. In short, I should characterize its appearance as a symptom of sophisticated disil- lusionment, and we should therefore not be surprised to find it appearing again as a theme in modern literature, as it does in such widely differing versions as *Six Characters* and *The Connection*.

I should like now to consider some of the implications which each of these conceptions suggests. In the first form, God retains his divine attributes and powers but he has at the same time been imperceptibly turned into a cosmic impresario, a Belasco or Reinhardt or Stanislavsky operating on the grandest possible scale, and thus begins his progressive professionalization from God the father to God the divine architect, mathematician, sculptor—this is Miss Nicolson's nomination—watchmaker, referee, and partner in industry. The line of descent runs straight downward from the Renaissance commentaries on Genesis, through Hakewill, Burnet, the Cambridge Platonists, the Restoration scientists, Shaftesbury, Addison, all those pre-Romantic dispossessed second-son versifiers so tenderly treated by Professor Fairchild, Wordsworth, Tennyson, converted atomic physicists, the Sunday supplement, and the Sunday sermon. Where, in Hebrew prophecy and Christian mysticism, God works directly in and through his creation to manifest his power and mercy, in the first form of the *theatrum mundi* metaphor he puts on a show, colossal, dazzling, gorgeous, a cast of millions, the biggest sets, the most scenes, earthquakes, fires, floods, pigeons, rainbows, and, of course, lots of sex. As spectators, we are naturally overwhelmed; it is a stupendous show. But it is only a show; the point of the plot meanders and finally gets lost in the spectacle, the effects become tiresome, the impresario runs out of novelties; in the end the demonstration defeats itself. The simple realization that things really are not that way is of course the starting point of contemporary crisis theology. In the age of the overkill, the exhibition of the divine providence and wisdom is a little hard to take, and anyhow, you cannot see out of a fallout shelter.

In the second form of the *theatrum mundi* metaphor, the divine author-impresario gets the show started all right but is not quite sure how to manage the ending, leaving the actors to fend for themselves, knowing only that there will be a final curtain. The situation is oddly analogous to the way in which a film is made; individual scenes are photographed but not in the order in which they will appear, nor is this order necessarily known to the cast or even to the writer at the time of filming; the final order may be the decision of the director, the producer, the Eastern bank's Hollywood representative, or a public opinion poll. It is the awareness of this uncertainty implicit in the *theatrum mundi* metaphor which elicits Sancho's sceptical response to Don Quixote's eloquent exposition, and which makes Shakespeare abandon faith for astrology in Sonnet 15:

> When I consider everything that grows
> Holds in perfection but a little moment,
> That this huge stage presenteth nought but shows
> Whereon the stars in secret influence comment; . . .

In this form of the metaphor, then, man crawls, stumbles, and crawls again through his predestined seven ages: the infant pukes, the schoolboy whines, the lover sighs, the soldier postures, the justice mouths, the old man pipes:

> I have liv'd long enough: my way of life
> Is fall'n into the sere, the yellow leaf;
> And that which should accompany old age,
> As honour, love, obedience, troops of friends,
> I must not look to have; but in their stead,
> Curses, not loud, but deep, mouth-honour, breath,
> Which the poor heart would fain deny, but dare not.

If recognition, redemption, and resolution constitute the tragic trinity, then the plot of life as it is presented in the theatre of the world is neither tragic nor comic. Perhaps the divine playwright intended it as a tragedy; if so, he has either written it poorly or we have misunderstood his intentions, in quite the same wrong way that Horatio misunderstands Hamlet's agony:

Hamlet: report me and my cause aright
To the unsatisfied. . . .
                                    . . . tell my story.
Horatio: And let me speak to the yet unknowing world
            How these things came about: so shall you hear
            Of carnal, bloody, and unnatural acts,
            Of accidental judgements, casual slaughters;
            Of deaths put on by cunning and forc'd cause,
            And, in this upshot, purposes mistook
            Fall'n on the inventors' heads; all this can I
            Truly deliver. . . .
                                    . . . lest more mischance
            On plots and errors happen.

Well, the notion of a divine ironist is diverting; it is, however, hardly conducive to faith.

Whatever the doctrinal difficulties inherent in the *theatrum mundi* metaphor, these two variations share the assumption that the image of the world as a stage is a viable analogy which imposes shape and significance on the flux of human existence. The physical form of the playhouse and the parallel aesthetic form of the play which it houses, themselves the signs of controlled intelligence, combine to create a metaphor whose form in turn reaffirms controlled intelligence and thereby asserts coherence and stability, that is, the world makes sense and we can live in it.

                    But pardon, gentles all,
        That flat unraised spirits that hath dar'd
        On this unworthy scaffold to bring forth
        So great an object; can this cockpit hold
        The vasty fields of France? or may we cram
        Within this wooden O the very casques
        That did affright the air at Agincourt?

The answer of the poet is yes, for within that wooden O:

Theatrum Mundi: *Illusion as Reality*

> In little room confining mighty men,
>   Mangling by starts the full course of their glory.
> Small time, but in that small most greatly liv'd
>   This star of England: Fortune made his sword,
>   By which the world's best garden he achiev'd, . . .

When we recall the symbolic significance of the garden:

> In narrow room nature's whole wealth; yea, more—
> A Heaven on Earth; . . .

orderly life within, destructive chaos without, we may add another layer of meaning to the *theatrum mundi* metaphor: art imposes order on nature. Our metaphor, then, confirms the life of art as it consecrates the art of life.

But, despite all that, our metaphor is an uneasy one; it sustains an illusion by means of an art of illusion. For of all the art forms, the theatre is the one which most depends for its effectiveness on the strength of illusion: it is the representation of a contrived action on a raised platform by impersonators who speak an uncommon language in an artificial space-time continuum within a building deliberately designed to heighten that illusion through the devices of lighting, scenery, music, costume, makeup, distance, and seating arrangement; we have, in effect, a Clabber Girl regression of illusion. Indeed, we may thinks of the *theatrum mundi* metaphor as one of that intriguing class of devices which the artist uses when he wishes to blur the line between reality and illusion, along with mirror imagery, the play-within-the-play episode, the dream sequence, slowed-down and speeded-up montage (from Caligari to Hitler is much more than a clever title), caricature, and cartoon. The strain between what we know ought to be there and what we actually see breaks down our hold on our instinctive acceptance of our three-dimensional, perspective, space-time, cause and effect universe. The results of our ordinary processes of perception and logic are deliberately and systematically reversed, misdirected, and even repudiated, and we are thus startled into a fresh perception of experience but often at the cost of our confidence in that as well. The metaphor and like devices must by their nature carry with them the overtones of suspicion and anxiety: one can never be sure any more, either in the displaced or the new vision, for, having been tricked once, we feel sure we will be tricked twice. Once the actor has stepped out of his role, can we be sure that he really has returned to it; does the dream really end; if objects cast no shadows, are they really real; and if last year is either a dream of the past or a projection of the future, is there really no present? Ernest L. Stahl has acutely pointed out that Faust's assertion of his faith in an ordered universe:

> Does not the Heaven vault itself above us?
> Is not the earth established fast below?

is repudiated by Rilke in the eighth elegy:

> Always facing Creation, we perceive there
> Only a mirroring of the free and open,
> dimmed by our breath . . .
>
> And we, spectators always, everywhere,
> looking at, never out of, everything.
> It fills us. We arrange it. It collapses.
> We re-arrange it, and collapse ourselves.

In this sense, the *theatrum mundi* image may be regarded as an ancestor of the age of anxiety and the theatre of the absurd.

The world as a stage is, then, a pretty conceit but it is also a misleading one. For if the tale it tells is told by an idiot, then the shape of content is smashed, and without that shape, neither the form of the art nor the form of the metaphor which depends on that art can claim to have any meaning; art which should reveal the meaningfulness of form degenerates into artifice which conceals the meaninglessness of formlessness. What can be said to this double betrayal? One can rail:

Theatrum Mundi: *Illusion as Reality*

> When we are born, we cry that we are come
> To this great stage of fools.

One can pretend:

> Our revels are ended. These our actors,
> As I foretold you, were all spirits and
> Are melted into air, into thin air:
> And, like the baseless fabric of this vision,
> The cloud-capp'd towers, the gorgeous palaces,
> The solemn temples, the great globe itself,
> Yea, all which it inherit, shall dissolve
> And, like this insubstantial pageant faded,
> Leave not a rack behind. We are such stuff
> As dreams are made on, and our little life
> Is rounded with a sleep.

Or one can watch the idiot's tale:

> Now they are clapper-clawing one another; I'll
> go look on.

In the language of Beckett and of thermonuclear war alike, we are at ground zero; when Dante saw it, he cried out: "This was not life, and yet it was not death," but where he had Purgatory and Paradise still before him, Beckett is writing the last word in the last sentence of the last paragraph of the last chapter of the last book.

The reference to the image of the book is not accidental for I was thinking of the medieval love of the book symbol as Curtius has so warmly described it and even more of Panofsky's demonstration of the centrality of the book image as the controlling metaphor of medieval thought: the arrangement and articulation of the parts of the book are the visual manifestation of the arrangement and articulation of the arguments which are in their turn the arrangement and articulation of creation itself; the architecture of the argument is no less significant that the validity of the argument itself. From this point of view, the theatrical metaphor with its shifting scenes, its illusions and concealments, its shades and shadows, the ambivalence of its characters, the uncertainty of its denouements, and, above all, the intellectual self-denial of the playwright—do we not say that it is Hamlet who speaks, not Shakespeare—all these are in direct contradiction to the emotional and intellectual ambiance of the medieval mind which I make bold to characterize as an open, outdoor mind in contrast to the theatrical, indoor mind of the *theatrum mundi* metaphor.

The mutations of our metaphor derive from and signalize that intellectual crisis of the Renaissance which has become our heritage as well and which we have been no more successful in overcoming, that is, how to organize and absorb and subdue the flux of fact from the macrocosm (including the facts from within the microcosm itself) by a tiny part of that microcosm which has set itself up as its judge and master. If we go back to the *theatrum mundi* metaphor in its narrow sense as a mnemonic device, we now see that its fantastic articulation has burst asunder the medieval book; it is a symptom of failure of method, nor is it alone in this failure. In the same letter from which I quoted at the opening of these remarks, Panofsky defines the basic innovation of Renaissance thought in this way: ". . . the consistent destruction or obscurantism of *borderlines* which the Middle Ages had established and observed, while not as yet renouncing the use of the concepts previously defined by these borderlines. Wherefore the absence of the *Summa* in the Renaissance is more than a mere accident; it was replaced, on the one hand, by Rabelais' *Gargantua,* and on the other, by such truly amazing specimens of hodgepodge as, for example, Giulio Camillo's *Theatrum Mundi.*" "He first, I following," we have returned to the starting point of our inquiry.

(1961)

Yet Another Theory of the Renaissance

I FEEL CERTAIN THAT every student of the Renaissance who has read Panofsky's *Gothic Art and Scholasticism* must have had the same double response to it that I did: admiration, for the brilliance of its insight and synthesis; and envy, that what he did was done for the Middle Ages and not for the Renaissance. Selfishly, I have asked him more than once to devise a guide through the tangle of the Renaissance as clear and as helpful as his map of the Middle Ages but he has always smiled and turned my requests aside. As it is now well over ten years since the Wimmer lecture was given, it begins to occur to me that he does not intend to accede to them. Well, perhaps I have deserved Raphael's rebuke to Adam:

> Solicit not thy thoughts with matters hid: . . .
> Heaven is for thee too high
> To know what passes there; be lowly wise;
> Think only what concerns thee and thy being;
> Dream not of other worlds.

And, like Adam, I reply:

Gentle to me and affable hath been
Thy condescension, and shall be honoured ever
With grateful memory. . . .

But, this time, like Eve, though submiss, I persist, and my
remarks are intended, not to substitute for the paper Panofsky
will not write, but to provoke him to reproval, and so to
obtain his paper after all. For, as Eve asks:

Shall . . . to us be denied
This intellectual food?

If we accept Panofsky's two key terms, *manifestatio* and
concordantia, and all that he has shown they imply, as defining
the quality and mode of operation of the medieval mind, then
we must be prepared to admit that the Renaissance mind must
be characterized in virtually the same way, and that, in fact,
the Renaissance world view is the medieval world view pro-
longed in time. That Renaissance thought exhibits the same
hierarchical and stratified structure and content as does
medieval thought has been one of the main motifs of Renaissance scholarship since the reaction to Burckhardt first set in,
and even so ardent a defense of the originality of the Renaissance as Chabod's newly revised essay, "The Concept of the
Renaissance," suffers from its Janus-like criteria for differentiating the Renaissance from the Middle Ages; and, indeed,
his paper ends on a surprisingly ambivalent note, for if his
reinterpretation of the meaning and significance of the quarrel
between the ancients and moderns is to be accepted, then the
arguments which he advances for demarcating the Renaissance
from the Middle Ages become, instead, arguments for the
continuity of the Middle Ages in the Renaissance, a dilemma
into which I think Baron has recently gotten himself as well.
In whatever area of Renaissance thought we look, we find
more than enough examples of the persistence of the medieval
mode of thought. I am sure I need not belabor you with a long

list of citations; I will merely recall to you a single illustration from each of a representative range of disciplines. In aesthetics, Romei's *Courtier's Academy;* in alchemy, Paracelsus; in anatomy, Crooke's *Microcosmographica;* in criticism, Tyard's *Solitaire Premier;* in education, Elyot; in exegesis, Bocardus' commentary on *Genesis;* in emblem making, Estienne's *Art of Making Devices;* in embryology, Peter Severinus' *Idea Medicinae Philosophicae;* in the doctrine of the gentleman, Castiglione; in hieroglyphics, Valeriano's *Hieroglyphica;* in historiography, Raleigh; in jurisprudence, Fortescue; in the law of nature, Lloyd's *Brief Conference;* in linguistics, Agrippa's *De Occulta Philosophia;* in medicine, Fernel's *On Hidden Causes;* in music, Zarlino's *Institutione Harmoniche;* in mythologizing, Gyraldi's *De Deis Gentium;* in natural law, Hooker; in philosophy, Ficino's *De Vita;* in physics, Telesio's *De Natura;* in political economy, Starkey's *Dialogue;* in popular science, Digges' *Perfect Description;* in psychology, Lemnius' *Touchstone of Complexions,* in theory of the state, Forset's *Comparative Discourse;* in symbol formation, Pico's *Heptaplus;* and in theology, Goodman's *How Superior Powers Ought to be Obeyed.* The list can be extended to almost any length and any Renaissance specialist could easily add to it.

"All creatures of God," writes Lodowick Lloyd in his *Brief Conference of Divers Laws:*

as well in heaven as in earth, had laws given them after they were created, to be governed and ruled by: the sun, the moon, and the stars, to keep their perpetual motions and course in their places and regiments; so the seas have their limits and bounds, how far they should rule and reign. And though one star differeth from another in glory, in greatness and in brightness, yet are they governed by one perpetual law: so the seas, although the waves thereof be so lofty and proud, yet are they shut up within doors and commanded to keep in, and not to go further than the place to them by law appointed. By law also the elements are commanded to stay within their own regiments, without trespassing one of another.

"You knowe," Timothy Bright assures us in *A Treatise of Melancholy:*

God first created all things subject to the course of times, and corruption of the earth, after that hee had distinguished the confused masse of thinges, into the heavens, & the foure elements. This earth he had endued with a fecunditye of infinite seeds of all things: which hee comaunded it, as a mother, to bring forth, and as it is most agreeable to their nature, to entertaine with nourishment that which it had borne, & brought forth: whereby when he had all the furniture of this inferiour worlde, of these creatures, some he fixed there still, and maintaineth the seeds, till the end of al thinges, and that determinate time, which he hath ordained, for the emptying of those seedes of creatures, which he first indued the earth withall.

"The richest jewel in all the heavenly treasure," sings Sir John Davies:

> That ever yet unto the earth was shown,
> Is perfect concord, . . .

> Concord's true picture shineth in this art,
> Where divers men and women ranked be,
> And everyone doth dance a several part,
> Yet all as one in measure do agree,
> Observing perfect uniformity;
> All turn together, all together trace,
> And all together honor and embrace.

The most eloquent apostrophe to "this great worke which we call the world" is, to my mind, to be found in Romei's *The Courtier's Academy* when ". . . the Signior Patritio, a gentle man of Dalmatia, a man very learned, but especially in Platonicall philosophie," rises to the height of his discourse to say:

Proportion is the principal cause of beauty, throughout the universal frame, aswel of the world corporeal and sensible, as of the intelligible: considering that by proportion, it is created, and by the same preserved; therefore it deserveth the chiefest place in the beauty of the humane body, which is no other but a model of the great world. Except we should foolishly believe, that the worlde was made by chance, we must necessarily conceive, that with speciall providence, it was built by the divine architect, as also it is necessary to place in the same divine mind, the Ideal forme, as we have said of the world, by others termed the worldes Archtype, even as it is necessary, that the model and Ideal of the building, should be in the minde of the Architect. Now the principal and most perfect part, as well in the minde of divine, as humane Architect is proportion, because in it order and disposition are comprehended. . . . Proportion causeth harmonie in number, in bodies beautie, in humours health, in minde virtue; as contrariwise disproportion procureth in numbers discord, in bodies deformitie, in humours infirmity, and in the minde vice.

Such, then, was the eloquence which was inspired by the contemplation of the serenity and regularity of the frame of order, that goodly and wondrous Patterne which so moved Spenser, in which the Renaissance lived. My point, then, is that the medieval habit of thought, which I define as thinking analogically through correspondence, is the Renaissance habit of thought as well.

So far I have been on fairly obvious and safe ground. But if one of the main motifs of recent Renaissance scholarship has been, as I mentioned before, the exhibition of the persistence of the Middle Ages in the Renaissance, then another and equally leading theme has been the demonstration of the existence of a period subsequent to and different from the Middle Ages which, by a rather reluctant consent, is called the Renaissance. I should like to argue that if the Renaissance is the Middle Ages, it is the Middle Ages intensified and accelerated, indeed, so intensified and accelerated as to constitute a difference not merely of degree but of kind. To my definition of the medieval habit of thought as thinking analogically through correspondence, I should add this, that the medieval synthesis was a harmony between theory and fact. By this I mean that the Middle Ages possessed just enough information to fill its theoretical structure neatly and without strain, and that its theoretical structure was just large enough and supple enough to accommodate what was known, again neatly and without strain. Whitehead has spoken of the Middle Ages as forming ". . . one long training of the intellect of Western Europe in the sense of order." And Lovejoy, too, must have had the same impression of the texture of the medieval mind when he describes the cosmical scheme of the Middle Ages as having ". . . the essential qualities of a work of classical art"; and he goes on to say: "The world had a clear intelligible unity of structure, and not only definite shape, but what was deemed at once the simplest and most perfect shape, as had all the bodies comprising it." Bonaventura had affirmed it most tersely of all: *"Nihil in universo est inordinatum."* It is this sense of order which gives Dante his firm grasp on the cosmos as an articulated and integrated arrangement of reality: "All things howe'er diverse/ Have order among themselves."

The Renaissance, then, inherited from the Middle Ages a cabinet intricately but cleanly wrought, its many drawers filled tidily and appropriately, and into this cabinet it tried to stuff more than it was built to hold. The Renaissance knew the same kind of things the Middle Ages did, but it knew more, much more, of them. The Middle Ages knew the classics, but only those classics it needed; the Renaissance, too, knows the classics, but so many that the authorities contradict each other. The Middle Ages knew the map of the heavens, but only enough to confirm its cosmos; the Renaissance, too, studies the stars, but finds so many of them and so much more about them that the concentric circles break and burst asunder. The Middle Ages knew history, but only enough to accept the logic and justice of events; the Renaissance knows too many eras, too many peoples, too many customs, too much of the affairs of men, and destroys the divine sequence. The Renaissance avidity for experience becomes a passion which feeds on itself, and that intensification and acceleration, of which I spoke before, manifests itself in every field of thought and activity; it is as though one were watching a motion picture called "The Middle Ages" feverishly speeded up so that while the individual frames remain the same, one is witnessing another, and astounding, film altogether. This sense of the quickening of events in the spheres of history, economics, and politics in the Renaissance has been deftly caught out by Engels in a posthumous paper discovered only a few years ago, "The Decline of Feudalism and the Rise of the Bourgeoisie"; if, however, Marxist authority does not sit well, I refer to Ferguson's paper, "The Interpretation of the Renaissance: Some Suggestions for a Synthesis," in which he declares: "When we turn to the modern age, say by the beginning of the seventeenth century, the general complex of European civilization has changed so radically that it amounts to a change in kind rather than in degree."

Now, at its best, the medieval synthesis holds together; Panofsky has concisely described both the style of its architecture: "First, human reason can furnish direct and complete proof for whatever can be deduced from principles other than revelation, that is, for all ethical, physical, and metaphysical tenets including the very *praeambula fidei*, . . . Second, it can elucidate the content of revelation itself: by argument, . . . it can refute all rational objections against the Articles of Faith . . . and it can supply *similitudines* which 'manifest' the mysteries by way of analogy"; as well as the engineering of its architecture:

. . . if faith had to be 'manifested' through a system of thought complete and self-sufficient within its own limits, . . . it becomes necessary to 'manifest' the completeness, self-sufficiency, and limitedness of the system of thought. And this could be done only by a scheme of literary presentation that would elucidate the very processes of reasoning to the reader's imagination just as reasoning was supposed to elucidate the very nature of faith to his intellect. Hence the much-derided schematism or formalism of Scholastic writing which reached its climax in the classic *Summa* with its three requirements

77

of (1) totality (sufficient enumeration), (2) arrangement according to a system of homologous parts and parts of parts (sufficient articulation), and (3) distinctness and deductive cogency (sufficient interrelation)—all this enhanced by the literary equivalent of Thomas Aquinas' *similitudines:* suggestive terminology, *parallelismus membrorum,* and rhyme.

I know, of course, there are exceptions enough to the classic structure of medieval thought; there are such intellectual extremists as Joachim de Flora, Hildegard von Bingen, and that belated medieval Opicinus de Canistris, nor do I overlook the doctrinal excesses known as heresies. But heresy presupposes a norm from which it is a deviation, and the Renaissance had neither a norm nor a *Summa.* By virtue of the intensification and acceleration of its experience and its learning, the Renaissance was forced into excessive interrelation. To intensification and acceleration we must now add, therefore, fantastication.

The more the Renaissance knows, the less it can fit into its medieval framework, and, under the relentless pressure of that knowledge, the classic symmetry of medieval order is pushed and pummelled out of shape. Contrast, for example, the crisp topography of Dante with the fuzzy landscape of Spenser; with Dante, you read as though a map were spread out before you so that you know exactly where you are at each step; with Spenser, you are immediately and irretrievably lost, and, I suspect, deliberately so. I can best explain the difference between the medieval clarity of Dante and the Renaissance confusion of Spenser by applying to them the distinction which Coleridge made in the *Statesman's Manual* between allegory and symbol; symbol stands for Dante, allegory for Spenser. Coleridge writes:

Allegory is nothing but a translation of abstract notions into a picture-language which is itself nothing but an abstraction from objects of the senses; the principal being more worthless even than its phantom proxy, both alike unsubstantial and the former shapeless to boot. On the other hand, a symbol . . . is characterized by a translucence of the special in the individual, or of the general in the special, or of the universal in the general; above all by the translucence of the eternal through and in the temporal. It always partakes of the reality which it renders intelligible; and while it enunciates the whole, abides itself as a living part in that unity, of which it is the representative.

Wind quotes from a letter which Pico wrote a friend concerning his first essay in the philosophy of myths, his commentary on Benivieni's *Canzona D'Amore:* "If I am not mistaken, it will be intelligible only to a few, for it is filled with many mysteries from the secret philosophy of the ancients," and we owe to Wind, as well as to other members of the Warburg school, fascinating glimpses into the mazes of the Renaissance mind at work.

To take but one or two examples. To those who still think of the Renaissance as a revival of classical culture in which the Renaissance poets drank directly out of the clear wellspring of classical mythology, I recommend as an astringent corrective Panofsky's elucidation of the "complex and often very corrupt tradition," as he calls it, from which the Renaissance derived its notions of classical mythology; add to this Seznec's *The Survival of the Pagan Gods,* Yates' *French Academies,* Starnes and Talbert's *Classical Myth and Legend in Renaissance Dictionaries,* Gombrich's study of Botticelli, and Wind's *Pagan Mysteries in the Renaissance;* and you realize only too well that the Renaissance was far from seeing the classical world whole, and even then through a glass darkly.

To what lengths of fantastication the Renaissance mind can go can be seen in almost any one of the books I mentioned earlier. Sizzi writes: "There are seven windows in the head, two nostrils, and a mouth: so in the heavens there are two favourable stars, two impropitious, and Mercury alone undecided or indifferent. From which, and many other similar phenomena of nature, such as the seven metals, etc. which it were tedious to enumerate, we gather that the number of the planets is necessarily seven." "Easy it is to see," states Maplet in *The Dial of Destiny:*

that there is no one parte in all the whole proportion and workmanship of man's body, that is not ruled or disposed by some one Planet or other, to affectate that most of all other things which the superior force doth frame them and enclyne them unto: . . . As for example, To begin with *Sol* or the Sunne, it is apparent how he holdeth, governeth, and hath in possession the Braynes and forepart of the head, the heart, the marrow, the right Eye, the vitall Spirite or breath of life: likewise the Mouth, the tongue and all other the Organes or instruments of sense, or feeling; besides this, he chalengeth the hands, the feete, the Synewes, the Imagination, and the whole operation of the power phantasticall.

Under the influence of the Moon are the lungs, "a great portion of the Braine," the marrow of the backbone, the stomach, the left eye, and those organs dealing with excrement; to Saturn belongs the liver; and to Jupiter, the navel, the ribs, and the bowels; to Mars, the veins, the kidney, the chest, the back, and the buttocks; to Mercury, the spleen and the bladder; and to Venus the secret parts. I point to Forset's *Comparative Discourse of the Bodies Natural and Politique,* in which the technique of correspondences is carried out in incredible and sometimes loathsome detail. "The Soule," writes Forset, "also hath made choice of some other principall parts of the body, which he needfully useth and employeth in the ministeriall functions of life; which if they once either fayle in their offices, or decay in their essence, the body can neither continue living, nor performe his actions." He then describes the role of the lungs, lights, liver, heart, milt, gall, and kidneys and argues "that as these bee placed so helpfully in the body, with such succeeding each other in their works, as accordeth to an accomplishment of health and perfection in the whole: so there must bee in the publike weale, a wise and political

ordering of the good gifts and imployments of the chiefe statesmen, that their endeavors be discreetly sorted to the general
good." So far, so good, but when Forset goes on to compare
the body politic to the human body down to such details as the
kidneys and the toenails, then the analogy has cracked apart.
And I sympathize indeed with Miss Nicolson when she wearily
says: "A little of *The Purple Island* goes a very long way," for
she has just quoted from stanzas 33-34, Canto II, out of a
possible 12 cantos and 700 stanzas of analogy, Fletcher's
description of the stomach: "The Islands common Cook,
Concoction;/ Common to all; therefore in middle space/ Is
quarter'd fit in just proportion." Or, if this example seems too
contrived, we can, with Panofsky, sympathize with Ficino's
desire to prove "the full consonance" of Neo-Platonism,
Pseudo-Dionysius the Areopagite, Hermes Trismegistos,
Orphism, classical literature, Augustine, Dante, classical mythology, physics, astrology, and medicine with the Christian
religion; we can admire his learning and his invention; but we
still have to admit that the *Theologica Platonica* is a philosophical failure whose daring reach has been thwarted by the
flabbiness of its methodological grasp. I cite one final example,
and this is a familiar one. While he is waiting for the Ghost's
first appearance to him, Hamlet, who has not gone to school
for nothing, gives his pedagogical bent full rein by lecturing
on the motivations of men:

> So, oft it chances in particular men,
> That for some vicious mole of nature in them,
> As, in their birth—wherein they are not guilty,
> Since nature cannot choose his origin—
> By their o'ergrowth of some complexion
> Oft breaking down the pales and forts of reason,
> Or by some habit that too much o'er-leavens
> The form of plausive manners, that these men,
> Carrying, I say, the stamp of one defect,
> Being nature's livery, or fortune's star—

Luckily, the lecture is interrupted by the Ghost, otherwise the list might have been extended indefinitely. What I am getting at is that the list is a compendium of virtually all the available Renaissance theories of the motivations of men, and my quarrel with it is not with its scholarship, which is admirably complete, but with its logic, which is contradictory, since each of the motivations cancels out the other. The elegant shape of the medieval mind had become in the Renaissance, to quote its best exemplar and victim, ". . . rank and gross in nature." For Hamlet is the victim of too many obligations, too many choices, too many reasons—and too many motivations.

Within a relatively limited range of information, the mode of thinking analogically through correspondence can be made to operate successfully, successfully enough, indeed, to have brought about the creation of a *Summa,* a *Divine Comedy,* and a Chartres. But when the amount of material it must absorb rapidly increases both in volume and in range far beyond the limits of its structure, it breaks apart and loses its relevance. Meaning is encrusted over, and what was once clear, though perhaps complicated, is now obscure; at the best, it becomes fanciful; at the worst, it is preposterous. The shattering of the medieval world view is felt as a betrayal which expresses itself in an art of frenetic immoderation of ideas and imagery, that is, Mannerism, whose extravagance made even its own adherents cry out against it:

> Tell me no more of minds embracing minds,
> And hearts exchanged for hearts;
> That spirits spirits meet, as winds do winds,
> And mix their subtlest parts;
> That two unbodied essences may kiss,
> And then like angels, twist and feel one bliss. . . .

What the Renaissance lacked, then, was a method of handling what it knew. The medieval mode of thinking analogically through correspondences could no longer cope with the amount and variety of materials it was called on to incorporate within itself: the analogies became slipshod or overwrought and the correspondences ill-fitting or oversubtilized, with the result that the essential defect of the analogical mode of thought was cruelly exposed, though unintentionally—namely, that it is a system which proceeds by adding one to the other likenesses which are derived from the observation of outward appearances and having no more necessary relation to each other than that of superficial similarity. Nor could the other Renaissance claimant for synthesizing the new increase of knowledge do more: the Baconian method of induction is likewise merely additive and lacks the essential control of a principle of organization: the accumulation of facts will not of itself produce the generalizations by which those facts may be related and understood; Bacon may well be regarded as the first public relations man for science but he is in the sense I have been speaking of the last of the medievals. Is it Bacon the modern or Bacon the medieval who writes:

. . . I do certainly for my own part . . . incline to this opinion,—that beneath no small number of the fables of the ancient poets there lay from the very beginning a mystery and an allegory. It may be that my reverence for the primitive times carries me too far, but the truth is that in some of these fables, as well in the very frame and texture of the story as in the propriety of the names by which the persons that figure in it are distinguished, I find a conformity and connexion with the thing signified, so close and so evident, that one cannot help believing such a signification to have been designed and meditated from the first, and purposely shadowed out. For who is there so impenetrable and that can so shut his eyes to a plain thing, but when he is told that after the *Giants* were put down, *Fame* sprang up as their posthumous sister, he will at once see that it is meant of those murmurs of parties and seditious rumors which always circulate for a time after the suppression of a rebellion?

"The Mathematicians have found out by their observance of the beauteous and uniforme proportion of the body of man, and by the symetrie of the parts thereof," Forset informs us, "their true scantiliness and dimensions; yea by the laying of it in his full length, & then spreading the armes and legges to their widest compasse, they have contrived both the perfect square, and the exact circle." But, of course, the mathematicians neither do nor tell us such things, and it was the failure of the Renaissance either to develop the mathematics it needed or to appreciate what mathematics was being developed which brought about its intellectual downfall. Let me soften the harshness of my previous statement by rephrasing it in this way: I am not saying that the Renaissance did not possess the proper mathematical methods for dealing with phenomena; rather, what mathematics it had was either insufficiently developed for the range of observation it had to comprehend or was not altogether free enough from numerological mystification to be effective as a means of handling what was known. Even in the work of the most daring and original innovators of science there is an admixture of mysticism and mystification. This is especially true of Nicholas of Cusa and what are we to say of Copernicus' argument for the centrality of the sun: "But in the center of all resides the Sun. Who, indeed, in this most magnificent temple would put the light in another, or in a better place than that one wherefrom it could at the same time illuminate the whole of it? Therefore it is not improperly that some people call it the lamp of the world, others its mind, others its ruler. Trismegistus calls it the visible God, Sophocles Electra, the All-Seeing. Thus, assuredly, as residing in the royal see the Sun governs the surrounding family of the stars." In a similar vein is Bruno's argument for an infinity of worlds: "Why should we, or could we imagine that divine power were otiose? Divine goodness can indeed be communicated to infinite things and can be infinitely diffused; why then should we wish to assert that it would choose to be scarce and to reduce itself to nought . . . ? Why do you desire that centre of divinity which can extend indefinitely to an infinite sphere, why do you desire that it should remain grudgingly sterile rather than extend itself as a father, fecund, ornate and beautiful?" No wonder Kepler was moved to protest: "This very cogitation carries with it I don't know what secret, hidden horror; indeed, one finds onself wandering in this immensity, to which are denied limits and center and therefore also all determinate places." "Mathematics," as Whitehead defines it, "is thought moving in the sphere of complete abstraction from any particular instance of what it is talking about." It is therefore the very opposite of the analogical mode of thought which relates seemingly individual and specific likenesses to each other so as to constitute a significance of hitherto unperceived contiguous relationship. The mathematical mode of thought says that things equal each other, not because they have any necessarily observable physical characteristics in common, but because they are capable of being encompassed within the same abstraction. The first sees a delicious significance in the parallel between the roundness and softness of a peach and the mistress' cheeks; the other concerns itself with fruit and females. The analogical mode of thought is concrete, emotive, and anthropomorphic; the mathematical mode of thought is abstract, rational, and disengaged. I am not arguing the superiority of the one way of thought over the other, but I would put the difference in this way: the medieval audience knew that the magician had bought his trick hat from a reliable firm which guaranteed its product; it took its pleasure not in the surprise that rabbits should be pulled out of the hat, for it knew they were there before the show started; its enjoyment was derived from the dexterity with which the medieval magician-philosopher whipped out the rabbits. But for us the show takes place in a theatre whose address we do not know, performed by a magician who has had to construct his own hat and who is worried whether it will work, and we ourselves are not at all sure whether we should be delighted or dismayed by what comes out of the hat, if anything comes out at all, let alone rabbits.

But once the mathematical mode of thought gains the upper hand over the analogical mode, the Renaissance comes to an end, though historically the two modes overlap and compete with each other for almost two centuries more, and, as a matter of fact, they still continue to compete with each other to this day. From Descartes on, however, the mathematical mode has slowly but inevitably tipped the scales in its favor, and I do not suppose that even the most medieval-minded would now be willing to exchange the amenities of their homes today and everything which has gone into their making for a cloistered cell and everything which went into its making. If the line of argument I have been advancing has carried any conviction, then the tripartite division of world history into classical, medieval, and modern, with the Renaissance subsumed within it, a division which is a legacy of the Renaissance itself, must be changed into a quadrupartite division of world history into classical, medieval, Renaissance, and modern. And I would date the Renaissance, using literary figures as guideposts, as running from Petrarch to Samuel Johnson, for Johnson had more in common with the world view of Erasmus, and, I dare say, with Cicero, than Coleridge, who was already twelve years old when Johnson died, had with his. For once Coleridge began to read a poem not as a completed object outside of himself but as a work of creation in the process of becoming, then the mathematical mode of thought had finally succeeded in penetrating and overcoming the last stronghold of the analogical mode of thought and the modern era had begun.

Let me make one final comment on the aesthetic consequences of this momentous shift and with particular reference to Shakespeare. As the tenuous Renaissance synthesis begins to break under the weight of its own contradictions, a literature of despair not surprisingly makes itself heard. I do not mean to suggest by this that there is a simple one-to-one relationship between changes in the social order and changes in artistic style and content; there was a literature of despair before Donne, nor were all poets after Donne pessimistic. But shortly before the death of Elizabeth and surely after it the heart appears to go out of Elizabethan literature, nor can this be accounted for merely on the grounds that the conventional Elizabethan themes and techniques had been pretty well worked out by then; the motif of shocked betrayal is too persistent for that. And in the case of Shakespeare it seems to me that the new Christianizers of Shakespeare have by their attempts to read the middle and late comedies as Christian allegories clouded and obscured the brute fact that Shakespeare's tragic vision became incapable of sustaining itself in the face of changed circumstances and a shift in his own point of view. That shift seems to me to be signalized in the outright revulsion of *Troilus and Cressida,* in which the stupidity of both Greeks and Trojans is mercilessly exposed, and in the moral morasses of *All's Well That Ends Well* and *Measure for Measure,* the ambiguity of whose titles points up clearly enough the ambiguity of the moral worlds they depict. If the Duke of *Measure for Measure* is the God of mercy and justice, then Othello is a jealous fool, Lear a silly old man, Macbeth a poor host, Timon a bad loser, Antony a middle-aged lover, Coriolanus a stuffed shirt, and *Pericles, Cymbeline, The Winter's Tale,* and *The Tempest* fairy stories fit only for children. No, the Renaissance has begun to run out its course.

I am well aware that my remarks have been more descriptive than explanatory in nature, and that while I may have a little described the progress of a period of history across time I have given no reasons for its journey. In view of what happens to historians when they essay explanations, I should be very foolish indeed if I did not stop now, while I have the opportunity of being dismissed as having been nothing more objectionable than boring. Nevertheless, I am convinced that the value of any historical study depends in the long run on the adequacy of its theory of change and not alone, and surely not exclusively, on the accuracy of its description of what seems to have happened. To say that human nature does not really change and that whatever changes one thinks one perceives are thus only superficial is one kind of abdication of scholarly responsibility, just as the avoidance of the problem by a blindered preoccupation with the minutiae of data is another. It is the mind which tells the eye what it sees, and the mind sees by pattern and configuration before the observation actually occurs. In other words, the very pretense of objectivity is in itself a posture taken toward the question of purpose, an attitude toward history certainly no better, and perhaps worse, than explanations which fail to explain. As a matter of fact, no explanation really fails to explain, for if it does nothing else it explicates the explicator. History is a mirror which reflects the lineaments of the mind which produces it, or, if you prefer, it is a kind of oblique utopianism which reveals what one wants out of the present by what one does with the past; it is a guide through the labyrinth of the contemporary mind at any time. When the nineteenth century invented the image of the man of the Renaissance as an all-encompassing genius of superhuman energy, it reveals to us today its own dissatisfaction with the grubby motives and paltry behavior of its own men; when contemporary theologians of all faiths profess to find in the Renaissance the origin of sins of scepticism, scientism, and materialism which presumably infest us today, they are criticizing us—and themselves as well.

And yet, though the individual picture is incomplete and unfair both to the past and to the present, each has managed to uncover an aspect of the past which had hitherto been concealed. It is able to do so because each of us brings to the study of the past an individual and therefore unique awareness honed on the sharp edges of one's own experience; one sees the past in the refraction of the present; you rediscover only what you have already experienced, suffered from, and therefore know in the ultimate sense of the word. In other words, one makes models of events, and in this sense, history can lay claim to being considered a science; but, when it turns out that the model is after all a model of oneself, history becomes an art (I might add parenthetically that despite its pretensions, the models made by science seem to me suspiciously like models, not of the operations of nature outside of the mind, but models of the operations of the mind itself, so that it too may be considered as art, but I do not think that this argument will carry much weight with the foundations). But since no man can experience everything in and for himself, the models which history makes form in effect enlargements of vicarious experience, that is to say, the humanities, oddly enough, do (or more properly, can) humanize.

But I must return, however briefly, to the problem of change. To my mind, the best description of the way the Renaissance comes about is to be found in those pages of D'Arcy Thompson's *On Growth and Form* where he lists the steps in cellular division through the process of mytosis:

1. The chromatin . . . concentrates to form a skein or *spireme,* often looked on as a continuous thread, but perhaps discontinuous or fragmented from the first. It, or its several fragments, will presently split asunder; for it is essentially double, and may even be seen as a double thread, or pair of *chromatids,* from an early stage. The *chromosomes* are portions of this double thread, which shorten down to form little rods, straight or curved, often bent into a V, sometimes ovoid, round or even annular. . . . they keep apart from one another, as by some repulsion, and tend to move outward towards the nuclear membrane. . . .

2. Meanwhile a certain deeply staining granule known as the *centrosome,* has divided into two. . . . The two resulting granules travel to opposite poles of the nucleus, and there each becomes surrounded by a starlike figure, the *aster,* . . . immediately around the centrosome is a clear space, the *centrosphere.* Between the two centrosomes, or the two asters, stretches the *spindle.* . . . the spindle sets in the direction of least resistance. . . .

3. The definite nuclear outline is soon lost. . . . The lines of the spindle become visible, the chromosomes arrange themselves midway

between its poles, to form the *equitorial plate,* and are spaced out evenly around the central spindle, again a simple result of mutual repulsion.

4. Each chromosome separates longitudinally into two. . . .

5. The halves of the split chromosomes now separate from and apparently repel one another, travelling in opposite directions towards the two poles, for all the world as though they were being pulled asunder by actual threads.

6. Presently the spindle itself changes shape, lengthens and contracts, and seems as it were to push the two groups of daughter-chromosomes into their new places. . . .

7. On the central spindle, in the position of the equitorial plate, a 'cell-plate,' consisting of deeply staining thickenings, has made its appearance during the migration of the chromosomes. . . .

8. Meanwhile a constriction has appeared in the cytoplasm, and the cell divides through the equatorial plane.

Thompson adds two further interesting points: 1) that the whole process is of extreme slowness, at the rate of two years to a yard; and 2) that when the equitorial constriction begins, the protoplasm bursts into violent activity, the granules and fat-globules streaming in and out as the pustules of the cytoplasm rise and fall and move away.

This would be analogy enough for me, but Thompson goes on to relate the processes of cell division to the very processes of matter itself:

The whole, or nearly the whole, of these nuclear phenomena may be brought into relation with some such polarisation of forces in the cell as a whole as is indicated by the 'spindle' and 'asters' of which we have already spoken: certain particular phenomena, directly attributable to surface-tension and diffusion, taking place in more or less obvious and inevitable dependence upon the polar system. At the same time, in attempting to explain the phenomena, we cannot say too clearly, or too often, that all we are meanwhile justified in doing is to try to show that such and such actions lie *within the range* of known physical actions and phenomena, or that known physical phenomena produce effects similar to them. We feel that the whole phenomenon is not *sui generis,* but is somehow or other capable of being referred to dynamical laws, and to the general principles of physical science.

Thus, if I understand this correctly, this mode of behavior is universal in nature for parallel processes may be observed in psychology and myth, so that men and their actions being in nature too, their behavior must be subsumed within that pattern as well (nor is the argument invalidated by the possibility that the description of the process is nothing less than the shadowing forth of the operation of the mind itself). I should add but two steps to Thompson's description of the process. First, I would suggest that the force which motivates the process is not a single, isolatable entity but rather a part of the organization of the mechanism itself; the invader takes the form of depletion or surfeit from within or the intruder from without. Second, it seems to me that the process as Thompson pictures it occurs on the horizontal plane alone, as it were, thus permitting only an infinitude of repetition; I should tip the plane sideways and upwards to account for variation and innovation. To put it another way, to myth I would add mind; to Plato, Marx.

(1959)

The Myth and Ritual Approach to Shakespearean Tragedy

THE MYTH AND RITUAL approach to literature is now one of the high gods in the pantheon of contemporary criticism and numbers among its devotees not a few eminently respectable names. This was not always so, however, and even as Zeus himself had laboriously to struggle up the ladder of divine acceptance, so the myth and ritual approach to literature now grows fat on quarterly hecatombs. So much so indeed, that the very word myth has acquired a mana of its own, and has been elevated into a substitute—less precise, less bold, and, if I may say so, less honest—for religion, though in this guise it has given many the courage of their conversion. As with other methods for the study of literature, the myth and ritual approach has its values, and they are distinctive and useful, but it also has its limitations, for it is certainly not a panacea concocted to cure all critical complaints.

What I want to do in this paper is to describe the myth and ritual approach to literature as I understand it and to show what new light it can throw on Shakespeare's tragedies, and presumably to illuminate them afresh. For the purposes of this analysis, I take the myth and ritual pattern as fundamental and anterior to tragedy and I pass Shakespeare's tragedies over this pattern, as tracings over the original drawing, in order to reveal his changes, modifications, and alterations of it; that is to say, I try to distinguish the uniquely Shakespearean from the generally tragic. I do not wish to be understood as suggesting that the myth and ritual pattern is either the *ur*-tragedy from which all others descend or the ideal tragedy toward which all others tend. But variation and difference cannot be separated except in terms of a fixed object arbitrarily put at rest, though it too is in motion and changes and is changed by the very process of observation.

Certainly I am not the first to suggest such a correlation; on the contrary, many critics have seen the connection and have in fact gone beyond the tragedies to the later plays in an effort to prove that the pattern of rebirth and reconciliation is fundamental to virtually the whole of Shakespeare's plays. "Birth, struggle, death, and revival," the late Theodore Spencer wrote, "these are not only the themes of the individual final plays, they are the themes which describe the course of Shakespeare's work as a whole, from his earliest plays through *King Lear* to *The Tempest*." E. M. W. Tillyard has said of the last plays: "Regeneration emerges dominant from the total tragic pattern" and he sums up this pattern as a ". . . general scheme of prosperity, destruction, and re-creation. The main character is a King. At the beginning he is in prosperity. He then does an evil or misguided deed. Great suffering follows, but during this suffering or at its height the seeds of something new to issue from it are germinating, usually in secret. In the end this new element assimilates and transforms the old evil. The King overcomes his evil instincts, joins himself to the new order by an act of forgiveness or repentance, and the play issues into a fairer prosperity than had first existed." And summing up nearly two decades of devotion to Shakespeare, G. Wilson Knight describes what he has found to be: ". . . the habitual design of Shakespearean tragedy: from normalcy and order, through violent conflict to a spiritualized music and then to the concluding ritual." So that if we add to this testimony the recent interpretations of the middle plays, particularly *Measure for Measure,* in the light of the doctrine of atonement, we see that the bulk of Shakespeare's plays has been found to conform to the myth and ritual pattern.

While the myth and ritual pattern so used makes, if I may say so, a Christian Olympian out of Shakespeare, it does so only at the expense of the myth and ritual pattern and of the substance of the plays themselves. It is my contention that while the last plays of Shakespeare do indeed carry forward the tragic pattern established in *Hamlet, Othello, King Lear,* and *Macbeth,* they neither heighten nor deepen it but on the contrary reject and even destroy it. In fact, I would go so far as to argue that the tragic pattern in the tragedies themselves is scarcely maintained with equal strength over each of the plays. For, on the basis of a comparison between the myth and ritual pattern as I have described it in *Tragedy and the Paradox of the Fortunate Fall* and the tragedies, I think that Shakespeare's tragic vision, which he was able to sustain but tentatively in *Hamlet,* most fully in *Othello,* barely in *King Lear,* and hardly at all in *Macbeth,* failed him altogether in the last plays, and that this failure is manifested by the use of the elements of the myth and ritual pattern as mere machinery, virtually in burlesque fashion, and not as their informing and sustaining spirit. The instinct of the critics in applying the myth and ritual pattern to the plays has been sound but their superimposition of the pattern on the plays has been inexact and, I suspect, prompted more by religious rather than by critical motives, with the result that both the method and the plays have been falsified.

If I begin with some diffidence, it is because I am always acutely aware that the myth and ritual pattern, upon which the myth and ritual approach to literature must be founded, is as uncertain in its origins as it is unrealized in actuality. I have tried to account for the persistence and power of the myth and ritual pattern by retracing it generally to that initial impact of experience which produced the archetypes of belief, and specifically, to the archetype of rebirth as crystallized out of the archetype of belief. Unfortunately, no real proof of this process is possible, for the events which generated the primary shock of belief are now too deep and too dim in the racial memory of man to be exhumed by archaeological means, though the psychoanalytic probings of Freud have cleared a path through this labyrinth with reluctant confirmation coming from the anthropologists and classicists. Similarly, we must not forget that there is really no such thing as the myth and ritual pattern *per se;* at best, it is a probable reconstruction of many varieties and variations of a number of beliefs and actions so closely related to each other that it is reasonable to construct—reconstruct would be a misleading word here—an ideal form of the myth and ritual pattern more comprehensive and more realized than any variations of it which we actually possess.

The myth and ritual pattern of the ancient Near East, which is at least six thousand years old, centers in a divine king who was killed annually and who was reborn in the person of his successor. In its later development, the king was not killed, but went through an annual symbolic death and a symbolic rebirth or resurrection. Starting out as a magical rite designed to ensure the success of the crops in climates where the outcome of the struggle between water and drought meant literally the difference between life and death, the pattern was gradually transformed into a religious ritual, designed this time to promote man's salvation, and finally became an ethical conviction, freed now of both its magical and religious ritual practices, but still retaining in spiritualized and symbolic form its ancient appeal and emotional certitude. Because it begins with the need to survive, the pattern never loses its force, for it is concerned always with survival, whether physical or spiritual. So far as can be ascertained at present, the pattern had a double growth, one along the lines of the ancient civilizations of the Near East, the Sumerian, the Egyptian, the Babylonian, both South and North, the Palestinian, first with the Canaanites, and then with the Hebrews and from thence into Christianity; the other along the lines of the island civilizations of the Aegean, from Crete to the mainland of Greece, from thence to Rome, and once more into Christianity, the two streams of development flowing into each other and reinforcing themselves at this crucial juncture.

Despite the differences between the religions of the ancient Near East, as, for example, between those of Egypt and Mesopotamia, and between that of the Hebrews and of the others, nevertheless they all possessed certain significant features of myth and ritual in common. These features, in their turn, stemmed from the common bond of ritual, characteristic in one form or another, of all together, though, as I have said, none possessed completely all the elements, which varied in some degree from religion to religion. In this single, idealized ritual scheme, the well-being of the community was secured by the regular performance of certain ritual actions in which the king or his equivalent took the leading role. Moreover, the king's importance for the community was incalculably increased by the almost universal conviction that the fortunes of the community or state and those of the king were inextricably intermingled; indeed, one may go so far as to say that on the well-being of the king depended the well-being of the community as a whole. On the basis of the evidence covering different peoples at different times, we know then that in the ancient Near East there existed a pattern of thought and action which gripped the minds and emotions of those who believed in it so strongly that it was made the basis on which they could apprehend and accept the universe in which they lived. It made possible man's conviction that he could control that universe for his own purposes; and it placed in his hands the lever whereby he could exercise that control.

From an analysis of the extant seasonal rituals, particularly the new year festivals, and from the coronation, initiation, and personal rituals of the ancient Near East, it is possible to make a reconstructed model of the basic ritual form. Essentially, the pattern contains these basic elements: 1) the indispensable role of the divine king; 2) the combat between the God and an opposing power; 3) the suffering of the God; 4) the death of the God; 5) the resurrection of the God; 6) the symbolic recreation of the myth of creation; 7) the sacred marriage; 8) the triumphal procession; and 9) the settling of destinies. We must remember, however, that the dying-rising of God theme constitutes but one illustration, so to speak, of the greater cycle of birth, death, and rebirth. The many and various rites connected with birth, with initiation, with marriage, and with death in the case of the individual, as well as the rites concerned with the planting, the harvesting, the new year celebrations, and with the installation ceremonies of the king in the case of the community, all these rites repeat, each in its own way, the deep-rooted and abiding cycle of death and rebirth. Not only do these rituals symbolize the passage from death to life, from one way of life to another, but they are the actual means of achieving the change-over; they mark the transition by which, through the processes of separation, regeneration, and the return on a higher level, both the individual and the community are assured their victory over the forces of chaos which are thereby kept under control.

The purpose of these rituals is by enaction to bring about a just order of existence in which God, nature, and man are placed in complete and final rapport with one another; they are both the defence against disorder and the guarantee of order. In the myth and ritual pattern, then, man has devised a mighty weapon by which he keeps at bay, and sometimes even seems to conquer, the hostile forces which endlessly threaten to overpower him. In the early stages of the development of the myth and ritual pattern, however, the best that man could hope for was an uneasy truce between himself and chaos, because the cycle merely returned to its beginnings; the God fought, was defeated, was resurrected, was momentarily triumphant, and thus ensured the well-being of the community for the coming year, but it was inevitable that in the course of the year he would again be defeated and would again have to go through his annual agony. Thus, nothing new could be expected nor was anticipated, and year after year man could hope for no more than a temporary gain which he was sure would soon be turned into an inevitable loss. To achieve genuine faith, therefore, was an act of courage difficult and infrequent to attain, and it is no wonder that we detect in the myth and ritual pattern of the ancient Near East before the Hebraic-Christian tradition takes over, too strong a reliance on the mere machinery of ritual, ultimately leading not to faith but to superstition, as well as the melancholy notes of despair and pessimism. But the Hebraic-Christian tradition in the very process of adapting the pattern, transformed it, for by virtue of its unique and tenacious insistence on the mercy and judgment of its transcendent God, it introduced a new and vital element to the pattern, that of the dialectical leap from out of the endless circle on to a different and higher stage of understanding. But the crucial moment in this transformation of the myth and ritual pattern comes when man, by himself, undertakes on his own to make the leap; to him remains the decision and his is the responsibility; by making the leap, he makes himself. The Hebraic-Christian tradition utilized the cycle of birth, life, death, and rebirth to conquer chaos and disorder, but it made its unique contribution to the pattern by giving man the possibility of defeating chaos and disorder by a single, supreme act of human will which could wipe them out at one stroke. In so doing, it preserved the potency of the pattern and retained its ancient appeal, and, at the same time, ensured its continued use by supplying the one element it had hitherto lacked to give it its permanent role as the means whereby man is enabled to live in an indifferent universe: it showed that man can, by himself, transcend that universe.

This, then, is the myth and ritual pattern as I understand it. What are its implications for tragedy? To start with, I would suggest that in the myth and ritual pattern we have the seedbed of tragedy, the stuff out of which it was ultimately formed. Both the form and content of tragedy, its architecture as well as its ideology, closely parallel the form and content of the myth and ritual pattern. But having said that, I must also say that the myth and ritual pattern and tragedy are not the same. Both share the same shape and the same intent but they differ significantly in the manner of their creation and in the methods of achieving their purposes. The myth and ritual pattern is the group product of many and different minds groping on many and different levels over long and kaleidoscopic periods of time under the stimulus of motivations quite different from those which produce tragedy. I am not suggesting anything like the formerly accepted communal origin of the ballad for we know that myth in its form as the complement to ritual must have been devised by the priest-astrologer-magicians of the ancient world. The intent of the myth and ritual pattern is control, its method that of mimetically reproducing the rhythm of birth, death, and birth again to gain that control. But imitation here means, not acting alike, as we think of the term, a parallel and similar yet at the the same time a distinct and different attitude and behavior toward the thing imitated, but rather the interpenetration of and union with the imitator, the thing imitated, and the imitation, all three being one and the same thing.

Tragedy, on the other hand, is a creation compounded of conscious craft and conviction. If we describe the myth and ritual pattern as the passage from ignorance to understanding through suffering mimetically and at first hand, then we must describe tragedy as the passage from ignorance to understanding through suffering symbolically and at a distance. To speak of symbolic meanings is already to have made the leap from myth to art. In the myth and ritual pattern, the dying-reborn God-king, the worshippers for whom he suffers, and the action of his agony are identical; in tragedy, the tragic protagonist undergoes his suffering at an aesthetic distance, and only vicariously in the minds of his audience. And for that reason does Aristotle tell us that tragedy is an imitation of an action. You participate in a ritual but you are a spectator of a play.

Moreover, tragedy reconstitutes the myth and ritual pattern in terms of its own needs. Of the nine elements which make up the myth and ritual pattern as I have described it, four have been virtually eliminated from tragedy, namely, the actual death of the God, the symbolic recreation of the myth of creation, the sacred marriage, and the triumphal procession; two elements, the indispensable role of the divine king and the settling of destinies, are retained only by implication and play rather ambiguous roles in tragedy; while the remaining three, combat, suffering (with death subsumed), and resurrection, now give tragedy its structure and substance. I have already noted that one of the characteristics of the myth and ritual pattern is its adaptability, its ability to change shape while retaining its potency, and we should therefore not be surprised to find the same process at work in its relation to tragedy. What is revealing, however, is the direction of change for we find, first, that the theme of the settling of destinies which is the highest point in the myth and ritual pattern, the goal of the struggle, since without it the passion of the God would be in vain and chaos and disorder would be triumphant, this theme, so elaborately explicated in the ritual practices of the ancient Near East, is no more than implied in tragedy, just as the correspondence between the well-being of the king and the well-being of the community, again so detailed in ritual, is only shadowed forth, as a condition to be aimed at but not to be achieved in reality.

Second, we discover that even greater emphasis is placed on the small moment of doubt in tragedy than in the myth and ritual pattern itself. In the rituals of the ancient Near East, at the point between the death of the God and his resurrection, all action is arrested as the participants fearfully and anxiously wait for the God to be revived. After the din of combat, this quiet moment of doubt and indecision is all the more awful for there is no assurance that the God will be reborn: "For a small moment have I forsaken thee." "But," continues Isaiah, "with great mercies will I gather thee." It is no wonder that the small moment is followed in the pattern by creation, the sacred marriage, and the triumphal procession as the peoples' expression of joy that the death of the God has not been in vain and that for another year at least "the earth remaineth, seedtime and harvest, and cold and heat, and summer and winter, and day and night shall not cease." And, clearly spelling out the implications of the second change made by tragedy in the myth and ritual pattern is the third, the freedom of choice of the tragic protagonist and the responsibility for the consequences of making that choice. For in that small moment of doubt and indecision, when victory and defeat are poised in the balance, only the moral force of man wills him on in action to success. The tragic protagonist acts in the conviction that his action is right and he accepts the responsibility for that action; for him to do less than that means the loss of his stature as a moral, responsible agent. The tragic occurs when by the fall of a man of strong character we are made aware of something greater than man or even mankind; we seem to see a new and truer vision of the universe.

But that vision cannot be bought cheaply. It cannot be bought by blind reliance on the mere machinery of the myth and ritual pattern and it cannot be bought by fixing the fight, as Handel's librettist fatuously puts it:

> How vain is man who boasts in fight
> The valour of gigantic might,

And dreams not that a hand unseen
Directs and guides this weak machine.

Better the indifferent Gods of Lucretius than the busybody *deus ex machina* of Vine Street and Madison Avenue. Only the deliberate moral choice of the tragic protagonist confronted by two equal and opposite forces and fully aware of the consequences of his choice can bring off the victory, and then only at the expense of pain and suffering: "He was despised, and rejected of men; a man of sorrows, and acquainted with grief." But suffering can be made bearable only when at the same time it is made part of a rational world order into which it fits and which has an understandable place for it:

I called by reason of mine affliction unto the Lord,
And he answered me;
Out of the belly of hell cried I,
And thou heardest my voice.
For thou didst cast me into the depth, in the heart of the seas,
And the flood was round about me;
All thy waves and thy billows passed over me;
And I said, I am cast out from before thine eyes; . . .
The waters compassed me about, even to the soul;
The deep was round about me;
The weeds were wrapped about my head.
I went down to the bottoms of the mountains;
The earth with her bars closed upon me for ever;
Yet hast thou brought up my life from the pit, O Lord my God . . .
They that regard lying vanities
Forsake their own mercy.
But I will sacrifice unto thee with the voice of thanksgiving;
I will pay that which I have vowed.
Salvation is of the Lord.

Salvation is indeed of the Lord, but Jonah must deliberately look to the holy temple and must remember the Lord of his own free will; *then* salvation is of the Lord.

Tragedy therefore occurs when the accepted order of things is fundamentally questioned only to be the more triumphantly reaffirmed. It cannot exist where there is no faith; conversely, it cannot exist where there is no doubt; it can exist only in an atmosphere of sceptical faith. The protagonist must be free to choose, and though he chooses wrongly, yet the result of the wrong choice is our own escape and our enlightenment. Yet nothing less than this sacrifice will do, and only the symbolic sacrifice of one who is like us can make possible our atonement for the evil which is within us and for the sins which we are capable of committing. Nevertheless, in western thought, if man is free to choose, in the end he must choose rightly. He is free to choose his salvation, but he is punished for his wrong choice. Man is free, but he is free within the limits set for him by his condition as a man. So great is the emphasis placed on freedom of choice in tragedy that the settling of destinies, which in the myth and ritual pattern is the tangible reward of victory, recedes more and more into the background and the messianic vision implicit in the settling of destinies is personalized and humanized in tragedy in the form of heightened self-awareness as the end of the tragic agony. In short, what I have been saying is that the myth and ritual pattern pertains to religion which proceeds by assertion, tragedy to literature which proceeds by assessment.

To sum up, then, the structure of tragic form, as derived from the myth and ritual pattern, may be diagrammed in this way: the tragic protagonist, in whom is subsumed the well-being of the people and the welfare of the state, engages in conflict with a representation of darkness and evil; a temporary defeat is inflicted on the tragic protagonist but after shame and suffering he emerges triumphant as the symbol of the victory of light and good over darkness and evil, a victory sanctified by the covenant of the settling of destinies which reaffirms the well-being of the people and the welfare of the state. But in the course of the conflict there comes a point where the protagonist and the antagonist appear to merge into a single challenge against the order of God; the evil which the protagonist would not do, he does, and the good which he would, he does not; and in this moment we are made aware that the real protagonist of tragedy is the order of God against which the tragic hero has rebelled. In this manner is the pride, the presumption which is in all of us by virtue of our mixed state as man, symbolized and revealed, and it is this *hybris* which is vicariously purged from us by the suffering of the tragic protagonist. He commits the foul deed which is potentially in us, he challenges the order of God which we would but dare not, he expiates our sin, and what we had hitherto felt we had been forced to accept we now believe of our free will, namely, that the order of God is just and good. Therefore is the tragic protagonist vouchsafed the vision of victory but not its attainment:

> But the Lord was wroth with me for your sakes, and would not hear me: and the Lord said unto me, Let it suffice thee; speak no more unto me of this matter.
>
> Get thee up into the top of Pisgah, and lift up thine eyes westward, and northward, and southward, and eastward, and behold it with thine eyes: for thou shalt not go over this Jordan. (Deuteronomy 3: 26-27)

Seen from this point of view, *Hamlet* is a particularly fascinating example of the relationship between the myth and ritual pattern and tragedy because it shows within the action of the play itself the development of Shakespeare's awareness of tragedy as a heightened and secularized version of the pattern. Hamlet begins by crying for revenge which is personal and ends by seeking justice which is social. Shakespeare deals with the problem of the play: how shall a son avenge the injustice done his father, by presenting it to us in four different yet related ways simultaneously, each consistent within its pattern of behavior, yet each overlapping and protruding beyond the other, like the successive superimpositions of the same face seen from different angles in a portrait by Picasso. First, there is Hamlet-Laertes who, incapable of seeking more than revenge, dies unchanged and unfulfilled, no better nor no worse than when he had begun. Then there is Hamlet the Prince, caught midway between revenge and justice, who passes from ignorance to understanding but too late. Third, there is Hamlet-Fortinbras who avenges his father's wrongs by joining the warring kingdoms into a single nation under his able rule. And finally, containing all these Hamlets, is Hamlet the King, idealized by his son into the perfect king whom he must replace. From this dynastic destiny stems Hamlet's ambivalence towards his father: he loves him for the man he wants to be himself and hates him for the King who stands in the way of the Prince and for the father who stands in the way of the son. Seeking his father's murderer, Hamlet finds himself. The same necessity holds Hal and Hamlet alike, but where Hal sees a straight line between his father and himself:

> You won it, wore it, kept it, gave it me;
> Then plain and right must my possession be. . . .
> 　　　　　(*II Henry IV*. IV.v.222-23)

and is therefore sure of himself and of his actions, Hamlet finds himself in a labyrinth whose walls are lined with trick doors and distorting mirrors: "O cursed spite,/ That ever I was born to set it right!"

Hamlet's ambivalence is reflected in the fragmentation of his character; there are as many Hamlets as there are scenes in which he appears and each person in the play sees a different Hamlet before him. But of the contradictions in his character, two stand out as the major symptoms of his incompleteness. The first is Hamlet's yearning to be able to act, not for the sake of action alone, but rightly, in the clear cause of justice, for while no tragic protagonist acts more frequently and more vigorously than does Hamlet, he is more and more perplexed to discover that the more he would do good, that is, cleanse

Denmark by avenging his father's death, the more evil he in fact accomplishes; hence his envy of Fortinbras' ability to act resolutely and without equivocation (IV.iv.). Second, though he is nominally a Christian, yet in the moments of sharpest crisis Hamlet turns instead to the consolations of Stoicism: "If it be now, 'tis not to come; if it be not to come, it will be now; if it be not now, yet it will come; the readiness is all. Since no man has aught of what he leaves, what is't to leave betimes?" (V.ii.231-35). And it is not enough: his mission succeeds only by mischance, his cause is still not understood, and with his dying breath he calls on Horatio, the true Stoic, to tell his story to the unsatisfied. Hamlet's vision is still clouded at his death: "Things standing thus unknown," Horatio's own version of the events is surprisingly but an advertisement for a tragedy by Seneca (V.ii.391-97), and there is something too cold and callous in the way Fortinbras embraces his fortune. In short, the myth and ritual elements have not been completely assimilated into the tragedy; the suffering of the tragic protagonist is neither altogether deserved nor altogether understood by him, the rebirth is not quite inevitable nor necessary, and the settling of destinies in the person of Fortinbras is somewhat forced and mechanical. The genuine sense of tragic loss is somewhat vulgarized into regret: Hamlet has been too fascinating.

In *Othello*, Shakespeare mixed his most perfect amalgam of the myth and ritual elements with tragedy. Where in *Hamlet* he was almost too fecund and profusive in characterization, invention inundating integration, in *Othello* he ruthlessly simplified and organized; if *Hamlet* is linear, proceeding by the method of montage and multiple exposure, *Othello* is monolithic and nuclear: the opposites of good and evil in human nature are forcibly split and then fused together in the fire of suffering. By overvaluing human nature, Othello destroys the balance between good and bad which is the condition of man; by undervaluing human nature, Iago brings about the same destruction from the equal and opposite direction. Each in his own way is an incomplete man: where Othello responds emotionally, Iago reasons; where Othello feels that men are better than they are, Iago knows that they are worse; each, in short, believes only what he wants to, and they are alike only in that both lack tolerance and understanding. Othello must be made to realize that the perfect love which he demands: "My life upon her faith!" "And when I love thee not,/Chaos is come again," is nothing more than the perfect hate which Iago practices:

> *Othello.*   Now art thou my lieutenant.
> *Iago.*   I am your own for ever. (III.iii.478-79)

If Iago is motivated by pride, will, and individualism, so then is Othello in his own way. Iago is the external symbol of the evil in Othello, for everything that Othello would stand for is negated and reversed in Iago: the subvertor of the order of God whose coming is after the working of Satan, the man who rejects principle, and who denies virtue, love, and reputation. To him, ideals are but a mask which conceals the sensuality, the brutality, and the greed for money, power, and sex, which he believes constitute man's true nature.

As the opposites of character in Othello and Iago meet and merge in Act III, scene iii, Othello becomes for the moment Iago: he reverts to paganism and calls on the stars for help, he orders his friend murdered, he spies on and humiliates and at the last repudiates his wife: "She's like a liar, gone to burning hell." But this is for him the bottom of the pit, and, by a supreme effort of will, he purges the Iago from within him; and in that awful moment of self-awareness, he recreates himself as he might have been, he realizes his potential as a human being. Having by his rashness put the well-being of the people and the welfare of the state in jeopardy, as Brabantio had foretold, perhaps better than he knew:

Mine's not an idle cause: the duke himself,
Or any of my brothers of the state,
Cannot but feel this wrong as 'twere their own;
For if such actions may have passage free,
Bond slaves and pagans shall our statesmen be.

(I.ii.95-99)

Othello is inevitably punished. And Iago is defeated by the one force which he is incapable of understanding, the power of principle. What he fails to see is that Othello's love for Desdemona is the symbol of Othello's faith in the goodness and justice of the world. What Othello seeks, therefore, when that faith is called into question, is not revenge, which is Iago's goal, but the cleansing of evil and the reaffirmation of goodness and justice: "It is the cause, my soul." From the depth of his self-awareness, bought at so dear a price, there emerges the theme of the settling of destinies, not embodied in the person of a successor, but filling as it were with its vision the entire stage, the sign of evil purged and the good restored: the image of man in his full stature as responsible man: "Speak of me as I am." "And when man faces destiny," Malraux writes, "destiny ends and man comes into his own."

Both *Hamlet* and *Othello* possess three features in common which by contrast are not present in *Lear* and *Macbeth*. First, both *Hamlet* and *Othello* are, for the Elizabethan audience, contemporary plays laid in contemporary or nearly contemporary settings. No great historical distance separates them from their audience as it does in *Lear* and *Macbeth* which are laid in pre-Christian England and Scotland. Second, both *Hamlet* and *Othello* operate within the Christian framework, recognized and apprehended as such by the audience for which they were written. But in *Lear* and *Macbeth* the pagan background is insistent. From the depth of their suffering Lear and Gloucester can appeal no higher than to the heathen gods: "As flies to wanton boys, are we to th' gods,/ They kill

us for their sport" (IV.vi.80). In *Macbeth,* the witches play
the same role as do the gods in *Lear:*

> But 'tis strange;
> And oftentimes, to win us to our harm,
> The instruments of darkness tell us truths,
> Win us with honest trifles, to betray 's
> In deepest consequence. (I.iii.122-26)

Finally, the theme of the settling of destinies, present directly
in *Hamlet* and indirectly in *Othello,* fades away in *Lear* and
disappears altogether in *Macbeth.* These changes reveal a
significant shift in Shakespeare's use of the myth and ritual
pattern and seem to be symptomatic of his increasing inability
to bear the burden of the tragic vision. Having confronted
the face of evil in *Othello* with an intensity unmatched even
by the man staring at Death in Michelangelo's "Last Judgment" and having in the face of that evil been able to reassert
the good, Shakespeare seems to have fallen back exhausted
so to speak, the effort of holding off evil weakening with each
successive play.

Lear begins with the abdication of responsibility already
accomplished; that a king could even contemplate, let alone
achieve, the division of his kingdom must have struck an
Elizabethan audience with fear and horror. By his own act,
Lear deliberately divests himself of power and retains only
the trappings of power which in turn are one by one inexorably stripped from him until he stands naked on the heath
in the rain. The waters of heaven give him wisdom but his
insight into the hypocrisy of this great stage of fools comes to
him only in his madness and he realizes at last that clothes—
the symbols of his *hybris*—make neither the king nor the man.
Having been purged of the pride of place, he sees himself
as he is:

I am a very foolish fond old man,
Fourscore and upward, not an hour more nor less;
And to deal plainly,
I fear I am not in my perfect mind.

(IV.vii.60-63)

But this moment of illumination, of heightened self-awareness, so like Othello's, occurs not at the end of Act V where
it would normally be expected but at the end of Act IV.
Having said: "Pray you now, forget and forgive; I am old
and foolish" (IV.vii.85), what is left for Lear to say, yet Shakespeare forces the action on to the shambles of the Grand
Guignol of Act V, completely cancelling the calming and
cleansing effect of the tragic vision already attained with Lear's
self-awareness. The play ends not with the hope that this
suffering has not been in vain but with the defeatism of Kent's
"All's cheerless, dark, and deadly" and Edgar's "The oldest
have borne most; we that are young shall never see so much,
nor live so long." The order of nature has been turned topsy-
turvy; the old who cannot bear suffering have endured too
much of it; the young who should be able to bear it are too
weak. But at least *Lear* gives us the consolation of the settling
of destinies, mishandled and misplaced as it is; there is none
in *Macbeth*.

The action of *Macbeth* begins with the figure of the bloody
man and ends with the figure of the dead butcher, and nothing
between mitigates the endless horrors of the progression from
one to the other. Macbeth accepts the evil promise of the
witches' prediction because they so neatly match the evil
ambition already in him. Nor does his desire for the crown
even pretend that it is for the well-being of the people and
the welfare of the state, that excuse which gives some color
to Bolingbroke's ambition: "I have no spurs/ To prick the
sides of my intent," Macbeth confesses to himself, "but only/
Vaulting ambition." The country suffers under Macbeth's
iron rule: "Things bad begun make strong themselves by ill"
(III.iv.55) says Macbeth, and Malcolm confirms him:

> I think our country sinks beneath the yoke;
> It weeps, it bleeds; and each new day a gash
> Is added to her wounds. (IV.iii.39-41)

More—while Malcolm stands behind Macbeth as Fortinbras stands behind Hamlet, can we seriously accept him as the doctor who can:

> . . . cast
> The water of my land, find her disease,
> And purge it to a sound and pristine health. . . .
> (V.iii.50-52)

What are we to make of a potential successor to the throne whose own ambivalence towards himself confounds even his strongest supporter? Is Macduff—are we—really persuaded that Malcolm is in fact capable of exhibiting "The king-becoming graces,/ As justice, verity, temp'rance, stableness,/ Bounty, perseverance, mercy, lowliness,/ Devotion, patience, courage, fortitude" (IV.iii.91-94)? Surely his black scruples, coupled with his innocence and inexperience, bode ill for Scotland, whatever the outcome, so that when at last Malcolm is hailed King of Scotland, and, like Hal and Fortinbras, emerges as the symbol ot the settling of destinies, our eyes do not see the vision of peace rising from suffering and our ears hear only the echo of:

> . . . for, from this instant,
> There's nothing serious in mortality.
> All is but toys; renown and grace is dead;
> The wine of life is drawn, and the mere lees
> Is left this vault to brag of. (II.iii.96-101)

repeated in the dying close of Macbeth's reply to Seyton. The witches have indeed triumphed:

> He shall spurn fate, scorn death, and bear
> His hopes 'bove wisdom, grace, and fear;

And, you all know, security
Is mortals' chiefest enemy. (III.v.30-33)

Man's security, for which he has fought so feverishly, the
guarantee of rebirth, has at the very last moment been snatched
away from him. Tragedy may be much more and much different from what I have been suggesting here, but one thing it
cannot be and that is a tale signifying nothing.

The disintegration of the tragic pattern which we have
seen take place in the major tragedies is paralleled in the three
middle comedies and comes to its culmination in the four last
plays. In the period of eight years during which he was writing
the tragedies from *Hamlet* to *Timon of Athens,* Shakespeare
wrote three comedies: *Troilus and Cressida, All's Well That
Ends Well,* and *Measure for Measure.* The latter two strike
us immediately as being the only two ironic titles in the
Shakespeare canon. "She knew her distance and did angle for
me"—Bertram's protest well catches Helena's strategy and one
may very well wonder how a marriage so described (V.iii.212),
and in a bare one hundred lines later converted into "I'll
love her dearly, ever, ever dearly" (V.iii.311), can indeed end
well. It has always seemed to me that Shakespeare failed to
write the best scene in the play in which Bertram and Helena,
out of reach of the King's interference, and out of the public
gaze, get down to brass tacks and have it out; I am sure that
Helena would not under those circumstances second Kath-
erina's fervent "Fie, fie" to headstrong women. Like *Lear,*
Measure for Measure begins with the abdication of kingly
responsibility: "It was a mad fantastical trick of him to steal
from the state, and usurp the beggary he was never born to"
(III.ii.98-100). Having allowed Vienna to go to the dogs for
some fourteen years as he himself acknowledges, the Duke,
who would eat his cake and have it too, puts on Angelo the
the burden of cleaning up the mess. Yet surely Angelo is the
worst possible deputy to choose, for as the Duke himself observes of Angelo's character:

> Lord Angelo is precise,
> Stands at a guard with envy, scarce confesses
> That his blood flows, or that his appetite
> Is more to bread than stone; hence shall we see,
> If power change purpose, what our seemers be.
>
> (I.iii.50-54)

The extremes of licentiousness and rectitude clash with the expected results: the exemplar of rectitude is shown to have at least two feet of clay and the exemplar of licentiousness shows a tolerance—"Something too crabbed that way, friar" which the disguised Duke will not accept: "It is too general a vice, and severity must cure it" (III.ii.104-07). The Duke's reply shows how far a distance we have travelled from the cakes and ale of *Twelfth Night*. Nor does Isabella's defense of her chastity in the face of her brother's anguished appeal: "Sweet sister, let me live" strike me as exhibiting the quality of compassion so characteristic of the high comedies and tragedies; indeed, Emilia's realism stems from a deeper wisdom than the cloistered virtue of Isabella can plumb. And again, one cannot help wondering how the relationship between Angelo and Mariana, scarcely on a very firm footing at best, is going to be improved by the ducal decree: "Look that you love your wife." The Duke notes that Angelo perceives he is safe; he seems not to notice, however, that Angelo says nothing to Mariana. Nor can one help observing that in the midst of all the *brouhaha*, the Duke has managed to keep a sharp and steady eye on Isabella and rewards himself for his fine performance in the role of *deus ex machina* by snagging Isabella for himself. Since the Duke has suffered nothing and learned nothing, one can well imagine what the next fourteen years will be like in Vienna.

I am prepared to admit that the interpretation of these two plays as ironic commentaries on their own titles may, in the light of the most recent criticism of them, fail to carry conviction, but I cannot go along with the view, best summed up by Professor Coghill's declaration with reference to *Troilus and Cressida,* that "Knowledge of the medieval tradition behind Shakespeare has made rubbish of the recent sentimental view of his supposed disgust and disillusion with life." Certainly every artist works within tradition but it is what he does with it which distinguishes him from tradition and gives him his uniqueness and significance. *Troilus and Cressida* is Iago's *chef d'oeuvre* for it assumes the worst of human nature and proves it: ". . . our raging motions, our carnal stings, our unbitted lusts, whereof I take this that you call love to be a sect or scion . . . is merely a lust of the blood and a permission of the will." Professor Coghill has rightly called Ulysses the Machiavel, Ajax a braggart, Achilles a gangster, Thersites bastardly, and Cressida inconstant, but if Troilus stands for truth in love, his passion drives him to madness; and if Hector stands for chivalry in battle, he witlessly lets Troilus talk him to his death. When Diomedes gives the lie to Marlowe:

> She's bitter to her country, Hear me, Paris:
> For every false drop in her baudy veins
> A Grecian's life hath sunk; for every scruple
> Of her contaminated carrion weight,
> A Trojan hath been slain (IV.i.68-72),

Paris half-heatedly protests: "You are too bitter to your countrywoman," hardly the kind of reply we would expect from a man who has just been called a lecher and his mistress a whore. Aeneas winks an eye at Troilus' philandering, Calchas betrays his people, and like father like daughter, Cassandra cries in vain, and Pandarus bestows his name on the second oldest profession, and are these not Trojans too? Who can distinguish, as Professor Coghill suggests we can, which are the noble hearts who perish in contention with the scum of the earth; *Troilus and Cressida* is sonnet 129 realized on the stage. "Lechery, lechery; still wars and lechery; nothing else holds fashion" (V.ii.196-97). Thersites' judgment holds; this is the way the world ends; unlike Eliot, Shakespeare does not sentimentalize.

From 1600 to 1608, then, Shakespeare seems to have swung from assertion to denial of the myth and ritual pattern and back again: first *Hamlet,* then *All's Well that Ends Well* and *Troilus and Cressida,* back to *Othello* and again to *Measure for Measure,* and from them to *Lear* and *Macbeth.* But as we watch the needle on the dial swing back and forth, we see that more and more it inclines toward the zero mark and in the end rests there. In no other plays of Shakespeare do the elements of the myth and ritual pattern occur so frequently as they do in the last four plays, but their very profusion is a sign of the breakup of the pattern in Shakespeare. Never does the sea storm so often and so violently, never is magic music heard so much, never do so many magicians practice their art, never are there so many mock deaths in so many guises followed by so many rebirths, never does the conflict between age and youth, between winter and summer, between the old and the new— "Thou met'st with things dying, I with things new-born"— break out so frequently and in so many different forms, never are there so many reconciliations, reformations, and marriages as take place in these plays. They remind me of nothing so much as Mozart's *Magic Flute* which abounds in much the same grotesque mockeries of the myth and ritual elements. But the measure of distance between *The Magic Flute* and *The Marriage of Figaro* is precisely the same as that between the high comedies and the late romances; the spirit is gone, leaving only the dry bones of stunning technique. If we look at the history of the myth and ritual pattern, we shall find that at those times when a breakdown of faith in the efficacy of the pattern has occurred, and it has happened more than once, there is a corresponding preoccupation with the mere machinery of the pattern at the expense of its spirit. The less faith one has, the more desperately one relies on the exact and sterile performance of ritual for its own sake; superstition takes the place of belief. Mill's concluding remarks on the relation of liberty to the state apply here as well: "... a state which dwarfs its men, in order that they may be more docile instruments in its hands even for beneficial purposes will find that with small men no great things can really be accomplished; and that the perfection of machinery to which it has sacrificed everything will in the end avail it nothing, for want of the vital power which, in order that the machine might work more smoothly, it has preferred to banish." When the freedom of choice of the tragic protagonist is at the last coffined by the orthodoxy of conformity, the myth and ritual pattern is no longer operative, the small moment has run out, and he who dared confront Othello with Iago would have us content with:

> We are such stuff
> As dreams are made on, and our little life
> Is rounded with a sleep.

The configuration of Shakespeare's thought was for the most part sympathetic to the shape of the myth and ritual pattern. But having raised the pattern to the heights of its most moving and significant expression, Shakespeare was unable to hold it there for long. But this does not mean that we must regard him as less than, say, Sophocles or Milton, neither of whom seems to have given way to doubt, nor does it mean that the myth and ritual pattern is inadequate either to its purposes or as a means of elucidating tragedy. On the contrary, the application of the pattern to Shakespeare's plays discriminates between them with nicety, it intensifies our awareness of the unique qualities of the individual plays, and it enables us to respond to Shakespeare on a most profound level of understanding. Recent critics of Shakespeare have enjoyed many a laugh at the expense of their predecessors who labored to box Shakespeare's plays under the neat labels in the workshop, in the world, out of the depths, and on the heights—to use Dowden's terms—but I cannot see that they themselves have done anything more than to say the same thing in perhaps more fashionable language. But the myth and ritual approach converts a Progress into a Calvary.

Shakespeare paid for the cost of the tragic vision by its loss. He looked long and directly into the face of evil; in the end, he shut his eyes. Writing of another artist who found himself in the same dilemma, Sir Kenneth Clark says: "The perfect union of Piero's forms, transcending calculation, rested on confidence in the harmony of creation; and at some point this confidence left him." As it seems to me, at some point Shakespeare too lost his confidence in the harmony of creation. I do not know when Shakespeare reached that point but I think that it perhaps came at the moment of his greatest expression of faith in the harmony of creation, in *Othello,* when he realized that he had left Iago standing alive on the stage. When in the bottommost circle of Hell, Virgil steps aside from Dante and reveals to him that creature fairest once of the sons of light: "Behold now Dis!" the poet is moved to cry out: "This was not life, and yet it was not death." So in the end Iago:

> Demand me nothing; what you know, you know.
> From this time forth I never will speak word.

The rest is silence.

(1957)

The Branch that Grew
Full Straight

Anyone who undertakes to defend *The Golden Bough* today must concede before he can confound. He must concede that Frazer falls just short of magnitude and far short of magnanimity; he is neither embattled nor heroic nor passionate nor tragic; and the absence of these qualities shows itself in the magisterial blandness of his style. He must concede that Frazer never set foot in the field so far as his anthropological work is concerned, though quite the opposite is true of his classical studies; even as late as 1921, Frazer could still assert that the collection of data should be kept quite apart from the task of examining, comparing, and evaluating the evidence; should not, in fact, be entrusted to the observers in the field but is best done by others in their libraries at home or at their universities; I suppose by this he meant himself, though in all fairness we ought to remember such testimonials from field-workers as Malinowski's: "The letters which I received from Frazer during my sojourns in New Guinea and Melanesia helped me more by suggestion, query and comment than any other influence." He must concede that if with Darwin, Marx,

Freud, and Einstein, Frazer helped shape the modern mind, he is patronising toward Darwin, McCarthyite concerning Marx, arrogant to Freud, and simply ignorant about Einstein.

Nor is this all he must concede. He must bow his head, though not so low as Raglan would demand, under such a charge as: "Frazer was a great scholar and a great writer, but, as we all are, he was a man of his age, and that age remained the Victorian. He was also emphatically a Linnaean. He spent most of his life in collecting and sorting out facts and anecdotes about the superstitions of savages. He was not very critical in his use of authorities, and since he liked adding items from old and obscure writers to his collection, he often used unreliable material when better was available. . . . In the result, the picture of the savage world which he paints is misleading in the extreme. . . . The savage of Frazer and his disciples is a creature of fiction." And he must acknowledge the force of Frankfort's argument that there are many significant differences in the handling of the death and resurrection theme by the various peoples of the ancient Near East. Admitting the possibility of a myth of a dying god which would contain features common to the myths of Egypt, Syria, and Mesopotamia, Frankfort nevertheless asserts that Frazer's dying god is ultimately depicted as a mortal in whom the spirit of fertility is for the moment incarnate, and who dies a violent death. But such a concept, he thinks, is foreign to the myth of the dying god in the ancient Near East; he is not incarnate in a human being and is not killed but dies in the regular round of the seasons; more, there is uncertainty as to whether the dead god will be found and even more whether he will be resurrected; and the community does not passively await his resurrection but rather goes out in frantic search for him, often symbolized in the mourning and search undertaken by his wife and mother. Again, Osiris ranks below the Sun God, nor is he the child of the goddess who saves him; Adonis is not thought of as a creator; Horus does not help Osiris in the same way in which Nabu and Ninurta aid Marduk and Eulil; Osiris is not merely a dying god, he is actually a dead god who never returned, as did Tammuz, to the land of the living, and his place was taken there by Horus; there are variations in the relations of these gods to plant life, to animals, and to water; and finally, there are many disparities between the various cultic practices associated with the gods. "The gods as they confront us in the religions of the ancient Near East," Frankfort concludes, "express profoundly different mentalities."

Yet, for all this, it still cannot be denied that along with Darwin, Marx, Freud, and Einstein, Frazer does remain a major molder of the modern mind. But, when we ask ourselves how this came about, how in fact the work of such different and difficult writers was able to stir—even to inflame—the imaginations, not only of the intellectual class, which is much more open to the winds of doctrine than it likes to pretend, but also of great masses of ordinary men who are much more resistant to ideas, and especially to ideas which call out for change, then we realize that we are dealing with a much more profound problem than accounting for a mere shift in attitude through persuasion by reason, assuming this ever really does take place. For if we look at the books of these men as incitements to the imagination and provocations to passion, we are struck by the realization that if ever writing was less calculated to arouse, to excite, indeed, to convert men of all classes and conditions, it is surely their work.

Darwin writes serviceable and sturdy English, but he writes ponderously, and he was himself well aware of the inadequacies of his style. His concern is with the accumulation of detail which in the end overwhelms, but he seldom permits himself the luxury of the sweeping generalization or the flashing phrase; even his great catch-phrases lie half-hidden in the steady flow of his evidence. *The Communist Manifesto* is, to be sure, a deliberate instigation, but I strongly suspect that Engels' hand is the stronger there, for he at least writes a swift, clean, figured prose. But these qualities are certainly missing from *Das Kapital*, which is elephantine in its size, tenacious-ness, and deliberation; it is faulted as a piece of prose, not by propaganda, which is at least irritating, but by a pedantry which is relentlessly dull, and never was a book less fitted to make the heart beat faster nor to set the myriad feet of millions of men to marching. Frazer's writing is carefully artful, for he was a conscious stylist who took as his models the Authorized Version—the allusions are deliberately worked in, especially in the purple passages—Addison, some Gibbon, a little Browne, and certainly the tradition of Latinate English. The tone of his writing is majestic, calm, yet somehow artificial, like the contrived majesty and calm of Elgar's big works; he leans over backward to avoid argument and commitment; he is as chary of generalization as though he were spending it; and the carefully artful occasionally slips down into Brobdingnagian archness. Freud does write well, in a nervous—in the Latin sense—style, but his narration is often better than his exposition and there are occasions where one would willingly trade a fascinating account of a case-history for a clearer statement of a theoretical point; in addition, his thought changes and grows and deepens, so that there are many and subtle and complex Freuds with whom to contend. As to Einstein, and I am here speaking of him as a scientist and not as a citizen of the world, candor compels me to confess utter ignorance, and I must take the word of my scientific friends on his greatness. Obviously then, we cannot explain the striking effects of these men on stylistic or purely intellectual grounds alone.

I would suggest that the source of power behind the mundane prose is in each instance a vision, a way of looking at the phenomena of existence, a controlling and unifying metaphor on the grandest scale so vivid, so dramatic, so immediately convincing, both emotionally and intellectually, that we cannot help being caught up by this new sudden awareness, this startlingly fresh insight into the meaning of existence, this astounding bringing together of the disparate and lifeless fragments of experience into a pattern of order and meaning, and giving it all our most fundamental assent. And I would go on to suggest that the source of power behind the new vision is in each instance again the force of that ancient myth and ritual pattern of birth, death, and rebirth, now expressed in terms of the language, the orientation, and the needs of our own times and circumstances, and therefore once again made freshly relevant. Nor need we assume the deliberate intent on the part of these men to restate the pattern in contemporary accents; on the contrary, for too much self-consciousness would smear the pattern by imposing on it a merely artificial pseudo-relationship. Yet, without intending to, each man in his own way has been able to work his way back to the ultimate fructifying source of the Western tradition, and, as before, as in virtually every moral and intellectual crisis of the past, to re-affirm its message: that, in the face of an indifferent, even hostile, universe, man can live, and live meaningfully.

In the case of Darwin, my friend, Stanley Hyman, has convincingly shown that ". . . *The Origin of Species* caught the imagination of its time as a dramatic poem, and a dramatic poem of a very special sort," in point of fact, as a tragedy, with the struggle of existence as the *agon* and *sparagmos,* and natural selection or survival of the fittest as the *anagnoresis* and *epiphany.* "It is interesting to contemplate a tangled bank," writes Darwin in the very last paragraph of *The Origin of Species:*

clothed with many plants of many kinds, with birds singing on the bushes, with various insects flitting about, and with worms crawling through the damp earth, and to reflect that these elaborately constructed forms, so different from each other, and dependent on each other in so complex a manner, have all been produced by laws acting around us. These laws, taken in the largest sense, being Growth with Reproduction; Inheritance which is almost implied by Reproduction; Variability from the indirect and direct action of the conditions of life, and from use and disuse; a Ratio of Increase so high as to lead to a Struggle for Life, and as a consequence to Natural Selection, entailing Divergence of Character and the Extinction of less-improved forms. Thus, from the war of Nature, from famine and death, the most exalted object which we are capable of conceiving, namely, the production of the higher animals, directly follows. There is grandeur in this view of life, with its several powers, having been originally breathed by the Creator into a few forms or into one; and that, while this planet has gone cycling on according to the fixed law of gravity, from so simple a beginning endless forms most beautiful and most wonderful have been, and are being evolved.

Thus the myth and ritual pattern, the cycle of birth, struggle, defeat, resurrection, and triumph is the very program and process of nature itself.

If, for the God-king-hero of myth who regularly goes through this same cycle, we simply substitute the proletariat, then Marxism becomes a secularized version of the myth and ritual pattern now expanded to encompass the vicissitudes of the mass of people themselves instead of their surrogate alone. "As soon as this process of transformation has sufficiently decomposed the old society from top to bottom," Marx thunders:

as soon as the labourers are turned into proletarians, their means of labour into capital, as soon as the capitalist mode of production stands on its own feet, then the further socialisation of labour and the further transformation of the land and other means of production into socially exploited and, therefore, common means of production, as well as the further expropriation of private proprietors, takes a new form. That which is now to be expropriated is no longer the labourer working for himself but the capitalist exploiting many labourers. This expropriation is accomplished by the action of the immanent laws of capitalistic production itself, by the centralisation of capital. One capitalist kills many. Hand in hand with this centralisation, or this expropriation of many capitalists by a few, develop, on an ever extending scale, the co-operative forms of the labour-process, the conscious technical application of science, the methodical cultivation of the soil, the transformation of the instruments of labour into instruments of labour only usable in common, the economising of all means of production by their use as the means of production of combined, socialised labour, the entanglement of all peoples of the world in the net of the world-market, and this, the international character of the capitalistic regime. Along with the constantly diminishing number of the magnates of capital, who usurp and monopolise all advantages of this process of transformation, grows the mass of misery, oppression, slavery, degradation, exploitation; but with this too grows the revolt of the working-class, a class always increasing in numbers, and disciplined, united, organised by the very mechanism of the process of capitalist production itself. The monopoly of capital becomes a fetter upon the mode of production, which has sprung up and flourished along with, and under it. Centralisation of the means of production and socialisation of labour at last reach a point where they become incompatible with their capitalist integument. This integument is burst asunder. The knell of capitalist private property sounds. The expropriators are expropriated.

Again, the myth and ritual pattern is the program and process of history itself, and, as Engels wrote in 1888 of *The Communist Manifesto,* its fundamental proposition that in every epoch the prevailing mode of economic production and its corresponding social organization forms its ultimate basis so that the whole history of mankind is a history of class struggles which has finally reached the stage where the proletariat cannot emancipate itself from the bourgeoisie without at the same time emancipating society at large from all exploitation and class struggle, this proposition, Engels declares, ". . . is destined to do for history what Darwin's theory has done for biology."

Thus, the two greatest forces operative outside of and on man, nature and history, were brought by Darwin and Marx within the purview of the myth and ritual pattern; it remained for Freud first to apply that pattern to the inner life of man, and then to weld psychology, biology, and history into a consistent and unifying concept whose program and process were once again the myth and ritual pattern. In one sentence in *Moses and Monotheism* Freud summed up his contribution to psychoanalysis: "Early trauma-defence-latency-outbreak of the neurosis-partial return of the repressed material: this was

the formula we drew up for the development of a neurosis."
And then, in a magnificent leap, he went on to relate the inner
life of man to history itself: "Now I will invite the reader to
take a step forward and assume that in the history of the
human species something happened similar to the events in the
life of the individual. That is to say, mankind as a whole also
passed through conflicts of a sexual-aggressive nature, which
left permanent traces, but which were for the most part warded
off and forgotten; later, after a long period of latency, they
came to life again and created phenomena similar in structure
and tendency to neurotic symptoms." The first two parts of
Moses and Monotheism were published in 1937, but as early
as 1911, when Freud was avidly reading Darwin, Robertson
Smith, and Frazer—note his sources—he had already stated:

I am of the opinion that the time will soon be ripe for us to extend
a principle, the truth of which has long been recognized by psycho-
analysts, and to complete what has hitherto had only an individual
and ontogenetic application by adding its anthropological and phylo-
genetically conceived counterpart. 'In dreams and in neuroses' so
our principle has run, 'we come once more upon the *child* and the
peculiarities that characterize his modes of thought and his emotional life.' 'And we come upon the *savage* too,' thus we may complete our proposition, 'upon *primitive* man, as he stands revealed to
us in the light of archaeology and of ethnology.'

Thus the primal law of nature, of history, and of the inner life
of man is that ontogeny recapitulates phylogeny but with this
added and significant difference, that of the dialectical transformation of the highest sequence before into the lowest stage
of the next higher sequence.

Darwin, Marx, Freud—what, then, is Frazer's claim to a
place on this roster (I must perforce omit Einstein)? Simply
this, that is was Frazer who first set the myth and ritual pattern
on a firm historical foundation, who traced its tortuous movements, and, above all, gave it shape and coherence. For *The*

Golden Bough is not a mere conglomeration of unrelated facts, fables, and fancies, a Hearstian warehouse of myth, but a carefully structured organization of data, collected from the most heterogeneous sources, whose variety and multiplicity are poured into a single, solid form which supports the thesis that:

... we may illustrate the course which thought has hitherto run by likening it to a web of three different threads—the black thread of magic, the red thread of religion, and the white thread of science, if under science we may include those simple truths, drawn from observation of nature, of which men in all ages have possessed a store. Could we then survey the web of thought from the beginning, we should probably perceive it to be at first a chequer of black and white, a patchwork of true and false notions, hardly tinged as yet by the red thread of religion. But carry your eye further along the fabric and you will remark that, while the black thread and white chequer still runs through it, there rests on the middle portion of the web, where religion has entered most deeply into its texture, a dark crimson stain, which shades off insensibly into a lighter tint as the white thread of science is woven more and more into the tissue. To a web thus chequered and stained, thus shot with threads of diverse hues, but gradually changing colour the farther it is unrolled, the state of modern thought, with all its divergent aims and conflicting tendencies, may be compared. Will the great movement which for centuries has been slowly altering the complexion of thought be continued in the near future? Or will a reaction set in which may arrest progress and even undo much that has been done? To keep up our parable, what will be the colour of the web which the Fates are now weaving on the humming loom of time? Will it be white or red? We cannot tell.

So, too, Freud ended his *The Future of an Illusion* on a note of gloomy apprehension, nor are Darwin and Marx simple-minded exponents of a jejune idea of progress either. Rather their tell-tale metaphors bring to mind ebb and flow, change and corruption, flowering and decay, the inter-penetration of life and death: Darwin's tangled bank, Marx's entangled net, Freud's: "The picture which life presents to us is the result of the working of Eros and the death-instinct together and against each other," and Frazer's woven web. Hyman has acutely characterized the great Tangled Bank of Life image of Darwin as ". . . disordered, democratic, and subtly interdependent as well as competitive, essentially a modern vision," and I am sure he will not object if I apply his terms to the images of the others as well.

Frazer, then, is not quite the pedant he has been made out to be, nor the naive evolutionist as some see him, nor yet the indifferent and rationalistic denigrator of the peoples he spent a lifetime studying. Frazer saw the difference between the myths of Osiris, Tammuz, Attis, and Adonis, and he indicated them, contrary to Frankfort's criticism, but he also saw more, and that more is the measure of his achievement: he saw man engaged in a most heroic attempt to work out for himself his place in a hostile universe; he sympathized with that attempt as only one who had followed it in all its bitter and frustrating detail alone could; and he evolved out of the mass of his evidence the tragic drama of man making himself over, no less. He saw it as a tragic drama because he could perceive the false starts, the wrong turns, and the bestiality and cruelty of man toward man; he could also see that in the long run the attempt was doomed to failure, not only because the methods were perhaps hopeless in the face of the problem (for reality is ultimately unknowable) but also because the aim itself was bound to be fruitless (the universe does remain indifferent); but it was a tragic drama in another sense, too, for out of the struggle he could see that man might learn what he was capable of becoming (even though, with Freud, he suspected that man would not).

Like Freud, Frazer rejoiced in the accomplishments of his discipline, calling the new comparative study of the beliefs and institutions of mankind another Renaissance; like Freud, he had the courage to face up to the fact that in the revealing light of his new science ". . . weak spots in the foundations on which modern society is built" are ruthlessly exposed, and surely he had religion in mind when he wrote that line; and like Freud, he declared as his justification: "Whatever comes of it, wherever it leads us, we must follow truth alone." It is true, however, that Frazer occasionally used pejorative language when he wrote of primitive man; he was rather over-fond of the phrase "our rude forefathers"; but in the main he was neither insensitive nor unsympathetic and sought to understand the mental processes of primitive man within their own terms; indeed, in the second volume of *Spirits of the Born and of the Wild,* he goes so far as to declare the savage "a better reasoner than his civilised brother." In short, Frazer neither judged nor condemned: magic was the best that man could do in primitive circumstances, just as religion was the best that man could do under later circumstances, and just as science can do under present circumstances: each seeks the same goals, but along different paths, yet it is certain that neither magic nor religion nor science possesses the ultimate answers.

The foundation upon which the elaborate edifice of *The Golden Bough* is raised is the homogeneity of the human mind. In the Preface to the first volume of *Balder the Beautiful,* Frazer assessed the value of his own work: "My contribution to the history of the human mind consists of little more than a rough and purely provisional classification of facts gathered almost entirely from printed sources. If there is one general conclusion which seems to emerge from the mass of particulars, I venture to think that it is the essential similarity in the working of the less developed human mind among all races, which corresponds to the essential similarity in their bodily frame as revealed by comparative anatomy." This principle is more fully explained in his appreciation of William Robertson Smith:

Now when, laying aside as irrelevant to the purpose in hand the question of the truth or falsehood of religious beliefs, and the question of the wisdom or folly of religious practices, we examine side by side the religions of different races and ages, we find that, while they differ from each other in many particulars, the resemblances between them are numerous and fundamental, and that they mutually illustrate and explain each other, the distinctly stated faith and circumstantial ritual of one race often clearing up ambiguities in the faith and practices of other races. Thus the comparative study of religion soon forces on us the conclusion that the course of religious evolution has been, up to a certain point, very similar among all men, and that no one religion, at all events in its earlier stages, can be fully understood without a comparison of it with many others.

Thus it would appear that Frazer is a Uniformitarian in strict opposition to the Diffusionists; you will recall Raglan's attack on Frazer on this point. However, the sentence right after the one which I just quoted from the Preface to *Balder* goes on to read: "But while this general mental similarity may, I believe, be taken as established, we must always be on guard against tracing to it a multitude of particular resemblances which may be and often are due to simple diffusion, since nothing is more certain than that the various races of men have borrowed from each other many of their arts and crafts, their ideas, customs, and institutions." Thus, sensibly and characteristically, Frazer compromised the question, as he did again in his allocution at the Sorbonne after he had been granted an honorary doctorate: ". . . je crois que, tandis que beaucoup des resemblances qu'on trouve dans les idées, dans les arts, dans les institutions de tribus différentes s'expliquent par la theorie d'emprunt, certaines autres se sont produites indépendamment les unes des autres, grâce à la similitude de l'esprit humain, qui partout, pour répondre aux mêmes besoins de la vie, sait trouver des inventions à peu près pareilles." And then he went on to formulate the rule: ". . . à l'égard des découvertes faites par l'homme, la probabilité d'une origine unique pour chacune d'elles varie en proportion inverse de la complexité des idées qu'elle implique."

But to continue along this line of discussion would bog

us down in sterile controversy over the limitations of Frazer's anthropological scholarship and theory which I have already admitted; besides, the arguments pro and con uniformity versus diffusion have been sufficiently rehearsed by Malinowski and Toynbee, to mention no others. I am sure that it is no secret by now that I am not interested in Frazer the anthropologist but in Frazer the myth-maker, for it is as a mythmaker that he has succeeded in capturing the creative imagination of our time. This is not the place for a long list of names but I think I can safely say that there is hardly a writer or critic of consequence from Yeats on down who has not, to a lesser or greater degree, directly or indirectly, simply by living in the post-Frazerian climate of opinion, derived from Frazer that deep perspective in time and culture which is the particular mark of the contemporary consciousness. Just as Darwin suddenly plunged man deep into the remotest geological past, as Marx thrust him deep into the very guts of the historical process, as Freud flung him along the deep and endless corridors of the psyche, as Einstein hurled him into the fearsome deeps of a new space and a new time, so Frazer exposed the savage hidden deep in his past—and present. Frazer was right in speaking of a Renaissance, for as the first Renaissance irreparably opened the crack between microcosm and macrocosm by revealing a new earth, a new heaven, and a new man, so the second Renaissance forced the gap even more yawningly apart and the frontiers of nature and man, scarcely as yet assimilated, into even more fearsome dimensions and directions. Man was now seen as no more than a by-product casually thrown off by vast natural forces whose purposes were incomprehensible to him, if indeed there were any at all; at the mercy of forces, both within and without himself, over which he had no control, or, if he did, seemed to be used only for evil ends; the discarded plaything of nature and history alike.

So by their work, Darwin, Marx, Frazer, Freud, and Einstein forced man once again painfully to face up to the immensity, the indifference, and the evil of a universe which neither he nor his gods had made and on which, therefore, he could lay no claim. But if they left him with doubt and terror, they at the same time gave him the means of meeting that doubt and terror: they gave him the vision of man immersed in the very processes of nature and history, an integral part of them, and belonging to them, neither superior to, nor at odds with, nor inferior to, but *in* nature and history. Just as Darwin bound man to his physical past, Marx to his historical past, Freud to his psychological past, and Einstein to his cosmic past, so Frazer bound him to his cultural past; and the unity of nature, history, and man, once broken, was once more re-forged. It is this vision, bought at no small price, as we know, which accounts for the immediacy and intensity of their appeal. You have not read in *The Golden Bough* for very long when, from out of its meticulously structured sentences, so Handelian in tone and vocabulary, there emerges, vivid, exciting, arousing our fears and hopes, engaging our compassion, provoking our anger, irritating, exhilarating, degrading, ennobling, the drama of man struggling to survive, and winning that struggle. Like the dying-reborn god of his own making, he engages in conflict with the powers of darkness, death, and evil; he is defeated; he suffers; he dies; he is reborn triumphantly; and he celebrates that victory in a new vision; and then the cycle is repeated on ever higher levels of achievement. Frazer has thus created the myth of the myth.

It will be objected that I have devoted as much attention, if not more, to the work of Frazer's peers than to Frazer himself, but that is precisely the point: he did, in his own way, what they did in theirs, and it is this accomplishment which gives him the right to be set beside the others. And I suppose that if the prophets and the poets were the seers of the past, it is fitting that the scientists should be the seers of the present. Yet, speaking as a curmudgeonly humanist, an academic dodo wandering around the computers and cyclotrons which now dominate the American campus as football stadia did a decade or so ago, I like to think that what makes Darwin, Marx,

Frazer, Freud, and Einstein so meaningful to us is not their science, which we must admit can now be pretty well punctured in varying degrees, but their prophecy and their poetry which are impervious to attack because they recall to us the old, harsh truth which their Epigoni would lull us into forgetting, that: "Good and evil we know in the field of this world grow up together almost inseparably. . . . And perhaps this is that doom which Adam fell into of knowing good and evil, that is to say, of knowing good by evil." The myth and ritual pattern tells us how and ". . . where that immortal garland is to be run for," but it tells us, too, that it must be run ". . . not without dust and heat," for ". . . that which purifies us is trial, and trial is by what is contrary." Not without dust and heat is the trial to be won—this is the meaning of the myth and ritual pattern, and this is what Darwin, Marx, Freud, Einstein, and Frazer with them, tell us again. Raglan and Malinowski rather dismiss Frazer as the last of the Victorians and I dare say the same charge can be laid against Freud and Einstein (Toynbee, too?), but in the sense in which I am treating them, they are timeless.

Only two years separated the birth of Freud from the birth of Frazer, and only two years separated their deaths, and it would be fitting if somehow Frazer's animosity toward Freud could now be softened. Freud ends his *Civilization and Its Discontents* with this statement:

The fatal question of the human species seems to me to be whether and to what extent the cultural process developed in it will succeed in mastering the derangements of communal life caused by the human instinct of aggression and self-destruction. In this connection, perhaps the phase through which we are at this moment passing deserves special interest. Men have brought their powers of subduing the forces of nature to such a pitch that by using them they could now very easily exterminate one another to the last man. They know this—hence arises a great part of their current unrest, their dejection, their mood of apprehension. And now it may be expected that the other of the two 'heavenly forces,' eternal Eros, will put forth his strength so as to maintain himself alongside of his equally immortal adversary.

Frazer, too, ended *The Golden Bough* on a note of mingled gloom and hope, and I am sure that, with Freud, he too would stand by the side of eternal Eros.

(1961)

The Hard Vision of Freud

"THE CASE HISTORIES I describe," Freud once observed, "read like short stories." And, as a consequence, short stories read like case histories. Yet if Freud gave much to literature, he received as much from it. He was a constant and critical reader who brought to the enjoyment and understanding of literature the sophisticated taste of the European humanist. Not only did he read widely but his comments on his reading range from the easy familiarity of allusion to formal, full-scale exposition and analysis. In response to an invitation from the Italian scientific journal *Scientia*, Freud wrote an essay, "The Claims of Psycho-Analysis to Scientific Interest," published in 1921, in which he demonstrated the applicability of psychoanalysis to other fields of study. Of the eight disciplines he considers, the humanities take up four: philology, philosophy, history of civilization, and the theory and history of art. His published work and letters constitute an uninterrupted exemplification of the application of psychoanalysis to the humanities and testify to his deep devotion to literature.

I have found in his work quotations from and allusions to the major writers of Greece, Rome, Italy, France, Spain, Germany, Austria, Switzerland, Norway, Russia, England, and the United States. He was particularly fond of English literature; writing to his fiancee Martha in 1882, he praises the English character and the English way of life, and he tells her that his sojourn in England ". . . had a decisive influence on my whole life. . . . I am taking up again the history of the island, the works of the men who were my real teachers—all of them English or Scotch; and I am recalling what is for me the most interesting historical period, the reign of the Puritans and Oliver Cromwell with its lofty monument of that time—*Paradise Lost,* where only recently, when I did not feel sure of your love, I found consolation and comfort." If you will pardon the pride of a teacher of English, I note that he refers to Shakespeare, Bacon, Milton, Samuel Johnson, Fielding, Sterne, Burns, Scott, Byron, Dickens (his favorite), Disraeli, Thackeray, George Eliot (by whom he was especially impressed), J. S. Mill (whose essays he translated), Darwin, Huxley, Pater, Herbert Spencer, Kipling, Samuel Butler, Lang, Robertson Smith, Frazer, Arthur Evans, Havelock Ellis, and Shaw (whom he did not like). As to American authors, there are references to Wendell Phillips, Bret Harte, William James, and, above all, to Mark Twain. Jones tells us that in September of 1898 Freud attended a lecture by Twain and greatly enjoyed it; and in *Wit and Its Relation to the Unconscious,* Freud, stating that "Economy of sympathy is one of the most frequent sources of humoristic pleasure," goes on to remark that "Mark Twain's humor usually follows this mechanism," and tells three Twain stories to illustrate his point. In addition, Freud wrote a number of papers and books which deal directly with literary and artistic problems: "Psychopathic Characters on the Stage," "Delusion and Dream," "The Relation of the Poet to Day-Dreaming," "The Antithetical Sense of Primary Words," *Leonardo da Vinci and a Memory of His Childhood,* "Contributions to the Psychology of Love," "Formulations Regarding the Two Principles of Mental Functioning," "Great Is Diana of the Ephesians," "The Occurrence in Dreams of Materials from Fairy-Tales," "The Theme of the Three Caskets," *Totem and Taboo,* "The Moses of Michelangelo," "Some Character-Types Met with in Psycho-analytic Work," "Dostoevsky and Parricide," *Moses and Monotheism;* in the course of these and other works, there are to be found extended critiques of *Oedipus, The Merchant of Venice, Richard III, Hamlet, Macbeth, King Lear,* Hebbel's *Judith and Holofernes,* Meyer's *Die Richterin,* Jensen's *Gradiva, The Brothers Karamazov,* and *Rosmersholm.* Finally, Jones informs us that for Freud "An evening spent at a theatre was a rare event. It had to be something of special interest to him, such as a performance of a Shakespeare play or a Mozart opera before he could tear himself away from his work." I cannot conclude this rather solemn listing without adding that despite a considerable knowledge of Shakespeare and of Shakespearean scholarship, Freud fell for the Oxford theory of Shakespearean authorship of the doubly unfortunate Looney, and, despite the most solicitous efforts of James Strachey, persisted in this delusion. As late as 1930, on the occasion of receiving the Goethe Prize for Literature he was still capable of declaring: "I have . . . ceased to believe that the author of Shakespeare's works was the man from Stratford." Homer nodded, Freud dreamt.

Of the effect of literature on Freud, then, there can be no doubt. Nor can there be any doubt at all of the influence of Freud on literature. The unfolding of his thought is a fascinating and ennobling spectacle. Starting from the letters to Fliess in 1887 and continuing through almost one hundred books and papers, we can see how Freud expanded and widened the range of his observation: he begins with the immediate and intense but necessarily limited data of self-analysis and then, notch by notch, he stretches the frame of his reference, from the observation of himself to the observation of his patients and from thence, escaping the confines of his own historical and social milieu, he gradually encircles the whole range of human experience, from the earliest and most primitive, derived from his study of anthropology and the history of religion, to the most recent and sophisticated, as expressed in art and literature. From the raw material of his observation, Freud hammered out both a view of the nature of human nature and a language capable of articulating that view which profoundly affected the subject matter, the style, and indeed the very orientation of modern literature. This is not the place to demonstrate the indebtedness of modern literature to Freud, and besides it has been done in scholarly fashion by F. J. Hoffman in his *Freudianism and the Literary Mind,* but one has only to think of Joyce, D. H. Lawrence, Auden, Sherwood Anderson, O'Neill, Kafka, Gide, Koestler, and Mann, to mention no others, to realize how powerfully and boldly Freud redirected the course of literature. I am certainly not saying that before Freud writers were incapable of character analysis; on the contrary, he has shown how deeply and truly they probed. But since him, no writer can be innocent of the mechanism of motivation; what Freud did was to give him a conceptual and terminological framework within which he structures his character delineation, while leaving him free to assess the moral significance of action within that framework as his own insight dictates. If the excitement of the discovery of the twenties and thirties has quieted down by now, it is only because his influence has been so completely absorbed by writers and readers alike that it has become a natural and accepted constituent of our *Weltanschauung;* along with Darwin, Marx, Frazer, and Einstein, Freud is an indispensable element of the intellectual air we breathe, without which the life of the mind today would simply not be possible. As Auden has written: "To us he is no more a person/ Now but a whole climate of opinion."

Yet, so rich and vital is Freud's thought that, I am confident, its influence, far from being exhausted, has still to exert its full force; more, I believe that the most profound layers of his thought remain to be penetrated and brought into use. To support this belief, I should like to call attention to two aspects of the Freudian ideology whose bearing on criticism and on literature have yet to be determined and whose impact may turn out to be more fundamental than Freud's initial impingement on literature, deep though that went. There are, it seems to me, two divergent and perhaps even antithetical modes of thought by which Freud operated, two processes of mind which differ in method, object, intent, and effect. The first I call his scientific or operational point of view, which is descriptive, objective, analytical, and altogether free from moral intrusion. The other is philosophical, emotionally involved, and deeply concerned with moral judgment. To the first we owe the studies of hysteria, of dreams, of the psychopathology of everyday life, of wit, of sexuality, and the first lectures on psychoanalysis; to the other such books as *Beyond the Pleasure Principle, The Ego and the Id, The Problem of Anxiety, The Future of an Illusion,* and *Civilization and Its Discontents;* the transition point seems to be marked by *Totem and Taboo* and "Thoughts for the Times on War and Death." I should have been more diffident in putting forward this view of Freud had I not found in Jones an illuminating passage dealing with what he calls Freud's "obstinate dualism": "This was of course most pronounced in his basic classifications: love-hunger; ego-sexuality; auto-eroticism-heteroeroticism; Eros-Thanatos; life-death, and so on. . . . It is as if Freud had a difficulty in contemplating any topic unless he could divide it into two opposites, and never more than two. That there was a fundamental conflict between two opposing forces in the mind was for him a basic fact." Freud, then, thought dialectically, in opposites, addressing different problems in different modes of apprehension.

Freud's scientific mode of thought is directed at discovering the laws of movement of the mind; rejecting the conventional body-mind division, he thinks of the psychic processes as a continuum whose motions he conceives it his business to describe operationally. As he explains in his last work, *An Outline of Psychoanalysis,* psychoanalysis makes a fundamental hypothesis, namely, that ". . . there are physical or somatic processes which accompany the mental ones and which must admittedly be more complete than the vital series, since some of them have conscious processes parallel to them both but others have not. It thus seems natural to lay the stress in psychology upon those somatic processes, to see in *them* the true essence of what is mental and to try to arrive at some other assessment of the conscious processes." And he goes on to say that the processes with which psychology is concerned ". . . are in themselves just as unknowable as those dealt with by the other sciences, by chemistry or physics, for example; but it is possible to establish the laws which these processes obey and to follow over long and unbroken stretches their mutual relations and interdependences—in short, to gain what is known as an 'understanding' of the sphere of natural phenomena in question." Thus, the basic concepts of psychoanalysis are of the same order and validity as those of the natural sciences: they are statements of relationships between phenomena in motion. It is revealing that Jung attributes to Freud the mechanistic-causal standpoint and ascribes to himself the energic viewpoint, a deliberate misinterpretation, if not a reversal, of the very approach to phenomena which entitles Freud to the name of scientist.

Properly to estimate the further potential contribution of Freudianism to criticism, it is necessary to look for a moment at its present state, and, as no paper on criticism can be considered complete without some reference to Aristotle, I shall do my literary duty now. Criticism owes to Aristotle a triple legacy willed through the *Poetics,* the *Ethics,* and the *Rhetoric:* first, the pursuit of the history of literature as the history of genres; second, the understanding of character within moral categories; and third, the analysis of expression in terms of the devices of rhetoric. Each of these approaches to literature has come, in our day, perilously close to a crisis of methodology which has forced criticism into unpathed waters: away from the work of art as the mere addition of rhetorical parts to the work of art as an organism; away from the work of art as finished form, as end product only, to the work of art as the fruition of the creative process, that is, from being to becoming; and away from genetic chronicle to the unfolding of the history of the mind, both of the individual and of the group, behind the work of art. This parallel triple shift is, in its turn, the Coleridgean legacy to criticism which now stands in need of a method and vocabulary which can describe objectively the mode of operation peculiar to literature, namely, the process of image and symbol formation. For while Coleridge was vouchsafed the Pisgah-sight of a new criticism, he was unable, for historical and personal reasons, to lead it into the promised land. That has now been done by Freud, who, when he described the mode of operation of the dream-work, named its parts, and demonstrated how it can be applied successfully to other fields in his book on wit, showed us how the Coleridgean insight can be profitably exploited. Anyone who has attempted to study the genesis and development of a poem from its first conception through to its printed form by means of letters, notebooks, manuscripts, and corrections, that is to say, the actual creative work of the poet, will grasp and welcome the enlightening relevance of the Freudian categories of the dream-work to the creative process. Moreover, as Freud himself insisted, the same process is equally applicable—and I quote his own list—to mythology, philology, folklore, folk psychology, and religion. But of these areas of study, only two, mythology and religion, have to any degree been explored by the Freudian method of symbol analysis, and these almost exclusively by Freud himself and by the first generation of his disciples, Abraham, Ferenczi, Jones, Rank, Reik, and Roheim. Indeed, speaking in the light of my own work on myth, I am fully persuaded that the mythopoeic mind, which stretches in an unbroken line from the myth and ritual pattern of the ancient Near East to the poet at work at his desk today, and which is to the rational, scientific mode of thought as the submerged bulk of the iceberg to its surfaced tip, can be understood only in terms of the dream-work. I regret that many students of myth tend to look down on Freud as an intruder in their field, but they forget that the union of anthropology and psychoanalysis, which is the foundation upon which the modern study of myth now rests, was sealed by Freud; he was among the very first to grasp the significance of Frazer's work from which he audaciously drew the conclusions which Frazer either did not see or did not dare to express. I wish I could say that Frazer returned the compliment of Freud's interest, but, unfortunately, the only reference in Frazer which I can find which appears to refer to psychoanalysis is a nameless and simultaneous slap at Freud and Jane Harrison. Instead of following this line of symbol analysis, however, psychoanalytic criticism has veered, mistakenly I think, toward pathography, that is, the identification of characters in literature as examples of the Freudian typology, and, as Freud himself was conspicuously unsuccessful with this method (it is after all tautological), it is no wonder that later Freudians should do no better. Nor has criticism taken advantage of the opening which Freud gave it; outside of Prescott, Baudouin, and Burke, I do not recall any critics who have employed the Freudian analysis of symbol formation in any systematic fashion. Yet this method, the creation of Freud's scientific mind, can stand to criticism in the same relation as mathematics to physics: as the dispassionate expression of relationships between impersonal phenomena. To see human behavior, so warm, so various, so enmeshed in passion, and especially to look at literature and art which have always been rightly regarded as among the highest forms of spiritual utterance, in this controlled and directed way requires of the mind a discipline of steel, and this is the scientific side of Freud's hard vision. He once said to Abraham: "You are right in saying that the enumeration in my last paper may give the impression of claiming a place beside Copernicus and Darwin." This is merely accurate: he dealt with the mind in exactly the same way as they had dealt with the phenomena of nature, and, in some ways, he needed greater courage because the hazards he faced were greater; that he showed that courage we know.

But there is another aspect of Freud's hard vision, the philosophical. At the end of *The New Introductory Lectures on Psychoanalysis* he remarks that psychoanalysis is not in a position to create a *Weltanschauung,* nor need it do so, for it can subscribe to the scientific *Weltanschauung.* Yet even a scientific *Weltanschauung* must have no pretensions since scientific thought is incomplete, unsystematic, and negative. But this dismissal has been preceded by a whole series of other rejections: he has already told us that he has never been a therapeutic enthusiast, and he has excoriated religion in words more scathing than Marx's; "Its doctrines carry with them the stamp of the times in which they originated, the ignorant childhood days of the human race. Its consolations deserve no trust. Experience teaches us that the world is not a nursery. . . . it seems not so much a lasting acquisition, as a parallel to the neurosis which the civilized individual must pass from childhood to maturity"; and he condemned philosophic relativism and Marxism as well. In their place, he substitutes an apocalyptic vision of man's relation to the world outside and within himself which complement and supplement each other. Within, the picture is this:

The proverb tells us that one cannot serve two masters at once. The poor ego has a still harder time of it; it has to serve three harsh masters, and has to do its best to reconcile the claims and demands of all three. These demands are always divergent and often seem quite incompatible; no wonder that the ego so frequently gives way under its task. The three tyrants are the external world, the super-ego and the id. When one watches the efforts of the ego to satisfy them all, or rather, to obey them all simultaneously, one cannot regret having personified the ego, and established it as a separate being. It feels itself hemmed in on three sides and threatened by three kinds of danger, towards which it reacts by developing anxiety when it is too hard pressed. . . . In this way, goaded on by the id, hemmed in by the super-ego, and rebuffed by reality, the ego struggles to cope with its economic task of reducing the forces and influences which work in it and upon it to some kind of harmony; and we may well understand how it is that we so often cannot repress the cry: 'Life is not easy.'

And without, the picture is this: "It would seem that aggression when it is impeded entails serious injury, and that we have to destroy other things and other people in order not to destroy ourselves, in order to protect ourselves from the tendency to self-destruction. A sad disclosure, it will be agreed, for the Moralist." But this is not all the Moralist must see: "And now the instincts," Freud writes, "in which we believe separate themselves into two groups; the erotic instincts, which are always trying to collect living substances together into ever larger unities, and the death instincts which act against that tendency, and try to bring living matter back into inorganic condition. The co-operation and opposition of these forces produce the phenomena of life to which death puts an end." So Freud wrote in 1933 in philosophical terms, but he had already drawn up a more specific indictment:

Psychoanalysis has concluded from a study of the dreams and mental slips of normal people, as well as from the symptoms of neurotics, that the primitive, savage, and evil impulses of mankind have not vanished in any individual, but continue their existence, although in a repressed state—in the unconscious, as we call it in our language—and that they wait for opportunities to display their activity. It has furthermore taught us that our intellect is a feeble and dependent thing, a plaything and a tool of our impulses and emotions; that all of us are forced to behave cleverly or stupidly according as our attitudes and inner resistances ordain. And now just look at what is happening . . . , at the cruelties and injustices for which most civilized nations are responsible, at the different ways in which they judge of their own lies, their own wrong-doings, and those of their enemies, at the general loss of clear insight; then you must confess that psychoanalysis has been right in both its assertions.

The date of this statement? December 28, 1914.

"All that he did was to remember/ Like the old and be

honest like children," says Auden of Freud. But, as I recall it,
the child who drew attention to the emperor's nakedness was
not commended for his honesty, and it appears to be all too
true that we praise those who see life as we would like it to
be, soft and easy, and scorn those who see it as it is. There is
no consolation or comfort in Freud: he proffers neither pallia-
tive nor nostrum. "For my part," he wrote to Putnam, "I have
never been concerned with any comprehensive synthesis, but
always with certainty alone." Freud's certainty concerning the
human condition, the picture of man, beset within, battered
from without, always at the mercy of inner and outer forces
over which he has no control, immeasurably stronger than he
is, and against which he so pitifully struggles in vain, a
Sisyphus ceaselessly and eternally swallowing and pushing a
double stone, this picture is not new, nor did Freud intend it
to be thought of as something hitherto unperceived, for he well
knew it had been proclaimed long before him:

> Once a man fostered in his house
> a lion cub, from the mother's milk torn. . . .
> In the first steps of its young life
> mild, it played with children
> and delighted the old. . . .
> But it grew with time, and the lion
> in the blood strain came out; it paid
> grace to those who had fostered it
> in blood and death for the sheep flocks,
> a grim feast forbidden.
> . . . only the act of evil
> breeds other to follow,
> young sins in its own likeness. . . .
> But Pride aging is made
> in man's dark actions
> ripe with the young pride
> late or soon when the dawn of destiny
> comes and birth is given
> to the spirit none may fight or beat down,

The Hard Vision of Freud

> sinful Daring; and in those halls
> the black visaged Disasters stamped
> in the likeness of their fathers.

This is the tragic vision; it is the hard vision of Freud. I have been glad to see that the occasion of his centenary has been the signal for a determined counterattack against the revisionists of Freud who had almost succeeded, Uranus-like, in emasculating his strength. But it is this very strength which indissolubly links him to the tradition of tragedy, and, if his language is different from that of the poets, it is only because he had to restate their revelation in a way which we could best understand. It matters very little whether his scientific or philosophic side will prevail; they both stem from the same hardness of vision; in either case his immortality is assured.

(1956)

"A Very Curious and Pains-
taking Person"— Robert
Graves as Mythographer

T HE CRITIC WHO undertakes to deal with Robert Graves'
The Greek Myths must, from the very beginning, decide
which of two widely divergent approaches to it he will take,
for it will not be by the simple arithmetic of adding up the
errors he finds but by his commitment to his choice that he
will shape his judgment of the work. Unfortunately, his option
is made doubly difficult for him, first, by the ambiguous nature
of the book itself, which, ostensibly a companion to the Penguin Classics in the form of a dictionary of classical mythology, is in fact a bold recasting of the corpus of Greek myth
into a new and exciting but questionable mold, and then by
Graves' own methodological ambivalence as manifested in his
treatment of his materials, for while superficially he appears
to follow the practices of conventional classical scholarship on
myth, his real concern is with fitting his subject within a
theoretical framework decidedly at variance with the present
position of that scholarship. Yet, unless there is at the outset

a sympathetic understanding between the author's ultimate intention and the reader, unless one makes certain that the book is being read for what it is, and not for what it is not, *The Greek Myths* stands in danger of being misunderstood and therefore condemned. But, overshadowing even these considerations is this question: if *The Greek Myths* is intended for readers who are interested in myth but who are not conversant with the many and vexing problems of origin, authenticity, and interpretation with which the study of myth is now embroiled, should so individual and unconventional a book be given the wide and untechnical acceptance which publication by Penguin Books makes virtually certain?

Both Graves and his publisher make the somewhat exaggerated claim that ". . . not for over a century, since Smith's *Dictionary of Classical Mythology* first appeared, has the attempt been made to provide for the English reader a complete 'mythology'," the implication being that *The Greek Myths* is to be regarded primarily as ". . . a mythological dictionary on modern lines large enough in its scope for all normal requirements of the student and general reader." The two volumes, numbering nearly 800 pages in the Penguin format, cover in systematic fashion the myths of the Greek gods and heroes, starting with the several variants of the Greek creation myths and ending with the deeds of Odysseus. As Graves tells us, his method has been ". . . to assemble in harmonious narrative all the scattered elements of each myth, supported by little-known variants which may help determine the meaning, and to answer all the questions that arise, as best I can, in anthropological or historical terms." Structurally, there are three parts to the book so arranged that each of the 171 sections consists, first, of Graves' own retelling of the myth in all its details; second, a list of the sources, mainly classical and patristic, of his reconstructed narratives; and finally, an examination and explanation of the myth, utilizing parallels drawn from the myths of other peoples; historical, archaeological, and anthropological data; iconography; and, above all, the application of Graves' own method of myth interpretation. Graves' industry is never in doubt; he has painstakingly unsorted and collated the jumbled coil of sources from which the myths must be disentangled and has combined them into smooth and integrated narratives; his learning is formidable and gracefully carried; and indeed the book as a whole is an astonishing achievement for one man alone to have accomplished. Surely one of the masters of contemporary English prose, Graves has retold the myths in a crisp and laconic style which brings out and enhances their flavor; his language has the supple strength of the Greek.

Taken at its face value, then, *The Greek Myths* appears as a work of conventional scholarship, to be examined on the basis of the accuracy and completeness of its scholarship, as one would examine, say, H. J. Rose's *Handbook of Greek Mythology.* Graves himself would seem to second this procedure: "Not for the first time," he writes, echoing a complaint previously made in *The White Goddess* and *The Nazarene Gospel Restored,* "I will find the scholarly specialists combining to criticize me on parts of detail which they have made their own, though not combining to suggest an alternative general hypothesis." Though the book has not, at this writing, been extensively reviewed in the classical journals, one can anticipate the criticisms which the scholarly specialists, as though in response to Graves' challenge, will make of it. In the first place, they will question his narrative syntheses; they will ask whether he is right in giving equal weight of authority to his varied and unequal sources in order to attain his goal of a harmonious and full retelling of the myths. They will wonder if the aesthetic necessities of narrative form have not in effect over-ridden the bounds of scholarly discrimination between sources. It is instructive, for example, to compare Graves' version of the Hyacinthus myth with Guthrie's analysis of it in his *The Greeks and Their Gods;* Graves has brought together perhaps a little too forcefully the contradictory motifs of which the myth is built up for the sake of rounding off the tale, and

Miss Mellink's study, *Hyakinthos*, gives a clearer view of the myth as seen in the light of its historical unfolding. I should say, in partial defense of Graves, that the problem of determining the degrees of authority of the sources of myth is still unsettled; even Rose falls into the error of multiple quotation from a variety of unequal sources, to fill out the narrative of a myth. Again, and this is somewhat unexpected, the very complexity of the layers of origin and meaning embedded in the Dionysus myth, which in part accounts for its fascination, is perforce smoothed over in Graves' rendering which has something of the tepid taste of a mythological representation by Angelica Kaufmann. Next, since Graves is in the habit of making historical and anthropological assertions without documenting them, his critics will naturally ask for the evidence on which he bases his statements, particularly where his bland assurance glosses over scholarly disagreement and uncertainty; we can expect another exchange of letters between frustrated reviewer and exasperated author of the kind which followed the *New Statesman and Nation* review of *The Nazarene Gospel Restored*. I cite two examples chosen at random: "A question remains: was the double-S really the monogram of Sisyphus. The icon illustrating the myth probably showed him examining the tracks of the stolen sheep and cattle . . ." and "The myth of Enalus and Phieis is probably deduced from an icon which showed Amphitrite and Triton riding on dolphins." One is almost persuaded of the actual existence of the first icon and of the effect of the other until one is arrested by the "probably." If the first icon exists, what is it and where is it reproduced? This is not a petty question since Graves is fond of referring to iconographic representations of myths but hardly ever with the necessary identification, and while in a book of this sort the meticulous documentation which characterizes, for example, Nilsson's use of iconographic evidence is not to be expected, it is not churlish to ask for the pertinent bibliographical information, particularly since the terrain here is far from being mapped. And does the icon precede the myth; does, in practice, a myth derive from its depiction, or are not icons of myths rather representations of ritual actions already performed? But Graves has himself exposed this mythogenetic sleight of hand in the introduction where he has previously defined true myth ". . . as the reduction to narrative shorthand of ritual mime performed on public festivals, and in many cases recorded pictorially on temple walls, vases, seals, bowls, mirrors, chests, shields, tapestries, and the like."

The claim that the conclusions of modern anthropology and archaeology are embodied in *The Greek Myths* is substantiated by the text so far as archaeology is concerned but is less warranted with regard to anthropology. Graves' espousal of the matriarchal origin of society is surely out of line with the findings of contemporary anthropology, and, outside of an occasional reference to African or Australian tribal practices, the evidence from anthropology is not systematically employed. I am myself uncertain as to how the evidence from anthropology can be properly used to elucidate early myth, and Graves himself would appear to share this uncertainty, for while he professes to answer questions about myth in anthropological terms he declares earlier that: "A true science of myth should begin with a study of archaeology, history, and comparative religion . . ."; intentionally or not, he has here omitted reference to anthropology. On the other hand, he handles the archaeology of Greece with skill and authority and has related the Minoan-Mycenaean monuments to Greek myth with care and in illuminating detail. But while he shows that he is alert to the value of the parallels which can be drawn between Greek myths and those of the ancient Near East, he does not, disappointingly, exploit them to the fullest advantage. Perhaps it is because of the placing of the notes directly after each myth, but the progressive movement westward of the myth patterns from the fertile crescent to the eastern and southern shores of the Mediterranean and thence across the islands in the Aegean Sea and the Sea of Crete to the Greek mainland is not shown in action and is thereby robbed of its relevance to Greek myth. Instead, Graves is much more excited by the parallels which can be made with post-Hellenic, non-Latin European myths, and especially with Celtic myths, which, since he regards them as indigenous in origin, he employs to clarify obscurities in the corresponding Greek myths. This procedure is in accord with his belief that ". . . despite differences of race and climate, the religious system of the neolithic and Bronze Ages in Europe seems to have been remarkably homogeneous." But again, scholarly opinion on this point is much more divided than Graves' easy statement would suggest, and it was precisely because he thought that Frazer had failed to discriminate sharply between the myths and ritual practices of the peoples of the ancient Near East that Frankfort attacked the methodology of *The Golden Bough* in *Kingship and the Gods.*

While errors in detail might be picked out in *The Greek Myths,* no particular purpose would be served to list them here; such errors are unavoidable in a work of this scope; and I am sure that they will not impugn Graves' attainments as a classicist. Rather, since the full weight of scholarly disapproval will fall on Graves' general hypothesis within which he has placed his examination of the Greek myths, his point of view needs to be objectively summarized. Graves has himself succinctly defined his thesis in the foreword to *The White Goddess:*

My thesis is that the language of poetic myth anciently current in the Mediterranean and Northern Europe was a magical language bound up with popular religious ceremonies in honour of the Moon-Goddess, or Muse, some of them dating from the Old Stone Age, and that this remains the language of true poetry—'true' in the nostalgic modern sense of 'the unimprovable original, not a synthetic substitute.' The language was tampered with in late Minoan times when invaders from Central Asia began to substitute patrilinear for matrilinear institutions and remodel or falsify the myths to justify social changes. Then came the early Greek philosophers who were strongly opposed to magical poetry as threatening their new religion of logic, and under their influence a rational poetic language (now called the Classical) was elaborated in honour of their patron Apollo and imposed on the world as the last word in spiritual illumination: a view that has prevailed practically ever since in European schools and universities, where myths are now studied only as quaint relics of the nursery age of mankind.

This thesis is in turn the base on which *The Greek Myths* is founded.

The study of Greek mythology, Graves insists, ". . . should begin with an understanding of the matriarchal and totemistic system which obtained in Europe before the arrival of patriarchal invaders from the east and north. One can then follow its gradual supercession first by a matrilineal and then by a patrilineal sacred monarchy, at last by a fully patriarchal system—as the migrant tribe with its phratries and clans gave place to the regional state with its towns and villages." These social changes are reflected in the changes of content and meaning of the myths themselves, a development which begins with the worship of the Great Goddess and ends with the *Iliad*. "Early Greek mythology is concerned," Graves states, "with the changing relations between the queen and her lovers, which begin with their yearly, or twice-yearly, sacrifices; and end, at the time when the *Iliad* was composed and kings boasted: 'We are far better than our fathers!', with her eclipse by an unlimited male monarchy." Thus Graves has irrevocably committed himself to the matriarchal theory of social and myth origins; the influence of Bachofen and Briffault is unmistakable and is acknowledged by Graves. At the same time, his definition of true myth, already quoted, derives from the theory of the ritual origin of myth which, as Hyman has shown by an analysis of Harrison's *Themis,* consists of three postulates: first, that myth arises out of rite, and not the reverse; second, that it is ". . . spoken correlative of the acted rite"; and third, that it is *sui generis*. By proposing that mythological research should follow the lines suggested ". . .

by such indefatigable and humane scholars as Sir James Frazer, A. B. Cook, F. M. Cornford, Jane Harrison, E. R. Dodds," Graves acknowledges his debt to the ritual school as well. Finally, by his insistence that all myths are derived from and are variants of *the* single poetic theme, ". . . the antique story," as Graves calls it in *The White Goddess,* "which falls into thirteen chapters and an epilogue, of the birth, life, death and resurrection of the God of the Waxing Year; the central chapters concern the God's losing battle with the God of the Waning Year for love of the capricious and all-powerful Threefold Goddess, their mother, bride and layer-out," he may be said to belong as well to the school which believes in the monomyth, the single pattern of death and rebirth within which all myths are embraced and of which they are but variants.

Now, it is possible for these three views to coexist, if not quite at peace with each other, then at least in a state of suspicious neutrality. But Graves is not content with working with them alone; he has added yet another approach and this one is altogether incompatible with the others, and especially with the ritual school. For when he roundly declares in *The Greek Myths:* "A large part of Greek myth is politic-religious history," he reveals himself an out-and-out euhemerist, and to make sure that there is no mistaking him on this point, he uncompromisingly rejects the psycho-analytical approach to myth as altogether unfounded in fact, for otherwise the logic of his position *vis-à-vis* the first three views would have forced him in the end to turn to the psycho-analytic method of mythogeny. Once the euhemeristic bias is detected, the notes to *The Greek Myths* can be seen as constituting a single-minded and sustained attempt to relate the motifs which cluster about the myths, and therefore the myths themselves, to real and actual historic events, and it is to this end that the full force of his learning is brought to bear. Here are some typical statements: "Except for the matter of the imprisoned winds, and the family incest on Lipara, the remainder of the myth concerns tribal migrations"; "The myth of Erechtheus and Eumolpus concerns the subjugation of Elyusis by Athens, and the Thraco-Libyan origin of the Eleusinian Mysteries"; "This myth concerns ecclesiastical politics in Northern Greece, and the Peloponnese: the suppression, in Apollo's name, of a pre-Hellenic medical cult, presided over by Moon-priestesses at the oracular shrines of local heroes reincarnate as serpents, or crows, or ravens"; "This myth records the early arrival in Greece of Helladic colonists from Palestine, by way of Rhodes, and their introduction of agriculture into the Peloponnese"; "The Federalization of Attica"; "The myth of Demeter and Poseidon records a Hellenic invasion of Arcadia."

Yet the proponents of the ritual school have time and again argued that it cannot usefully coexist with the euhemeristic approach; as Hyman has said, ". . . myths are never the record of historical events or people, but freed from their ritual origins they may attach to historical events or people . . .; they never originate as scientific or aetiological explanations of nature, but freed from their ritual origins may be so used." This crucial distinction Graves signally fails to observe, and over and over again we find in the notes the two points of view placed side by side without any sense of contradiction, as in the explanation of the Daedalus myth: "In one sense the labyrinth from which Daedalus and Icarus escaped was the mosaic floor with the maze pattern, which they had to follow in the ritual partridge dance; but Daedalus' escape to Sicily, Cumae, and Sardinia refers perhaps to the flight of the native bronzeworkers from Crete as the result of successive Hellenic invasions." Greek mythology, Graves assures us, is ". . . no more mysterious in content than are modern election cartoons," and though he scorns Socrates for having, as he says, turned his back on poetic myths, it is by employing Socrates' own method of rational inquiry that Graves, "the very curious and painstaking person" postulated by Socrates as the success-ful mythographer, has been able to reconcile myth with prob-ability.

How are we to account for Graves' methodological inconsistencies? I am afraid that the contradiction can be explained only by a paradox. Despite his devotion to the classics and the classical themes, Graves' habit of mind is, for all that he disclaims it, essentially romantic. The difference between the classical poet and the true poet, he insists in *The White Goddess,* is a difference in attitude toward the White Goddess; the classical poet asserts himself her master but the true test of a poet's vision is ". . . the accuracy of his portrayal of the White Goddess and of the island over which she rules." The final chapters of *The White Goddess* are devoted to showing how and why the worship of the White Goddess was attacked and beaten down in Western society; they set forth the evidence in detail which Graves is able to offer only in abrupt and shorthand form in *The Greek Myths.* In essence, Graves argues that once the concept of a patriarchal God and of a theocratic society gained domination over Western thought and institutions, the poet lost his sense of the White Goddess; "the ancient, intuitive language of poetry: the life, death, and resurrection of the Spirit of the Year, the Goddess' son and lover" was all but forgotten. Apollo symbolizes for him the triumph of reason, law, science, order, and conformity over the orgiastic freedom of the worship of the White Goddess, for, as he says, ". . . as soon as Apollo the Organizer, God of Science, usurps the power of his Mother, the Goddess of inspired truth, wisdom and poetry, and tries to bind her devotees by laws—inspired magic goes, and what remains is theology, ecclesiastical ritual, and negatively ethical behaviour." The climax of his protest comes in a simple declaration: "This is an Apollonian civilization."

Such, then, is Graves' fundamental point of view, without which understanding and judgment of *The Greek Myths* would be incomplete and unfair. This sketch will, I think, justify to the student of the history of the interpretation of myth my characterization of Graves' attitude toward myth as essentially romantic. The influence of German romantic speculation about myth is unmistakable; one hears in Graves echoes of Nietzche and behind him of Herder, Heyne, Schelling, F. Schlegel, and Schiller: the opposition between the Dionysian and the Apollonian; the intimate relationship between poetry, myth, and religion; the evocation of the power, depth, and mystery of myth; the warfare between popular paganism and official Christianity; the office of the poet as celebrant of the hidden mysteries; these, combined with Graves' conviction that the worship of the White Goddess, though hounded out of the center of official Western thought and practice, survived, concealed and disguised, at its fringes (hence, his absorption with Celtic myth, with riddles and anagrams, with cryptography and etymology, though, surprisingly enough, he makes no use of Murray and Spence), and his passionate, even abandoned devotion to the Fatal Woman, "La belle Dame sans merci" (a reading of his recent lyrics as autobiography would show that Graves is far from indulging in fancy; their reiterated theme is ". . . a sole woman's fatefulness"), this rich complex of ideas and feeling is, I believe, the source of his attitude toward myth. On its surface, then, *The Greek Myths* presents an appearance of serenity, created by the discipline of its scholarship, its uncompromising rationalism, its determination to reduce the mysteries of myth to common sense, and its straightforward style; these qualities combine to produce an effect which can only be called, ironically enough, Apollonian. But below the cool and smooth facade seethe Graves' passions, barely held in check, as I fear they were not in *The White Goddess* and *The Nazarene Gospel Restored,* by the structural requirements of the dictionary form. *The Greek Myths* has thus the aesthetic property peculiar to Graves' poetry, that of passion congealed in form, and it is this character which gives it its distinction and quality.

I supposed that I am now expected to render an unfavorable verdict on the book. Recall, however, the question which I raised at the beginning of this critique; I asked, whether so individual and unconventional a book should be the means

by which a large and unprofessional readership should make
its acquaintance with Greek myth. My answer is yes, for when
the errors and the bias of methods are subtracted from the
work as a whole, what remains far outweighs them. The objections which I have raised are, after all, primarily the concern of specialists, but they do not, and this seems to me the
single most determining factor, affect the real value of *The
Greek Myths* which, by its enthusiasm for myth, its lucid
style, and its unshakable conviction that myth is still alive
and still meaningful, cannot fail to reach the reader and
capture his interest. In the face of the adverse circumstances
of our times, to maintain the tradition of myth is a service
in comparison with which other considerations must be secondary.

There is in English literature an old and honorable line of
scholar-poets who were able to fuse the discipline of scholarship with the love of literature into a poetic amalgam singu-
larly endowed with strength and grace. The chief of these is
Milton whose powerful scholarship, firmly embedded in the
fertile mixture of the classical and Christian traditions, was
the tap-root which nourished and invigorated both his po-
lemics and his poetry. Hardly the man to accept the lazy
verdict of conventional opinion, his independence of mind
drove him to reshape and thereby to revitalize the theological
and mythological traditions within which he worked; with
the sharp edges of his occasional obstinacies now rounded off
by the passage of time, the essential Miltonic qualities stand
out clearly: the vigor of mind, the freshness and skill in the
manipulation of traditional materials, the abiding concern
with their significance and application, and, above all, the
ineradicable certainty that learning and art are not to be
hidden away untried but are to be used and tested in the fire
of living experience. I am not suggesting that Graves is another Milton but he has the Miltonic pride—he has rightly
described himself as "nobody's servant"—and he has the
Miltonic attitude toward the role of learning and art, with

the result that his poetry has, though in much less degree of course, the quintessential Miltonic quality of passion in form. I therefore count ourselves as fortunate that we can see the Greek myths through the eyes of a scholar-poet of his stature. However much we may disagree with his vision, we have been forced to look at the myths once more and we have thereby renewed them and made them live again. It is worth recalling the incredible sources which previous students of myth had to rely on; the romantic poets, for example, had to find the gold of myth in the vast rubble heaped up by such mythographers as Bryant, Davies, Stukeley, and Wilford; and though one may not care for Graves' methods of work, he has given us freely and abundantly of his labor, and more, he has asked us to share his love.

Since writing this critique, I have come across two specialist reviews, one by the American classicist, Kevin Herbert, in *The Classical Journal,* LI (1956), pp. 191-92, and the other by the Scots authority, H. J. Rose, in *The Classical Review,* LXIX (1955), pp. 208-09. Graves' fears concerning the scholarly reception of *The Greek Myths* are amply confirmed; though Herbert does try to see the book in the light of Graves' hypothesis, he rejects it out of hand; Rose is merely merciless.

(1956)

The Twisted Cue

I T IS DISHEARTENING to realize that after almost a century of continuous performance the libretti of W. S. Gilbert are still not taken seriously. The reason for this failure is not hard to find: the wit of the words and the charm of the music to which they are set divert the reader from the more profound and significant meanings which lie hidden in the texts. Other instances of similar distraction caused by the attractiveness of surface texture over inner depth will clarify this point; the lush lure of Spenser's imagery which stunts his readers' growth in mental health; the glow of poetry in the final plays of Shakespeare which obscures their celebration of the resurrection and renewal in Christian ritual; the simple grace of Herrick's "Corinna's going a-Maying" which quiets the clash between the pagan and Christian world views going on within it; the polished ease of Gray's "Ode on a Distant Prospect of Eton College" which makes the reader miss the substantive object first geometrized and then turned into a rate of motion in such phrases as "chase the rolling circle's speed" instead of "roll the hoop"; the overpowering style of Conrad's *Lord Jim* which glosses over its Manichean heresy; and the elemental simplicity of Hemingway's *The Old Man and the Sea* in which such a seemingly natural act as the old man's passing of the spear of the fish to the boy actually represents in a kind of double phallic symbol the mutability of virility and the immortality of continuity, that is, the replacement of the old and dying god by the young and virile god who himself will be replaced, and so on in an endless cycle of death and renewal. It is along the line of this strategy of criticism that I propose to examine the libretti of W. S. Gilbert in an effort, first, to disclose in them the presence of the paradigms of ritual, and, second, and more significantly, to portray them as exemplars of Christian belief. In so doing, I hope at the same time to reveal their hitherto undetected source.

If we abstract from the plots of the libretti of the leading operettas their quintessential action (taken in the Aristotelian sense of the term), we find their basic pattern of action to consist of some such arrangement as this. The protagonist is a young man of unknown or apparently low birth who falls in love with, and is in turn loved by, a young lady of high or even royal station. To gain the young lady's love and hand in marriage, he undergoes a series of trials and tests; in particular, his way to consummation is blocked by an older woman who uses every device at her command (devices often diabolic in their conception and execution) to prevent the achievement of his goal; we shall return to the significance of this older woman later on. At the moment of his deepest despair, when he is on the verge of loss of love or banishment or even death, his true identity is disclosed, often by the same older woman who has hitherto tried to prevent his marriage, and he is revealed to have been as highly born as his lady and assuredly worthy of her in every respect. The play ends with their marriage and its attendant celebrations.

This basic plot structure is clearly seen in the vicissitudes of Ralph Rackstraw in *H.M.S. Pinafore,* in Frederic in *The Pirates of Penzance,* in Strephon in *Iolanthe,* in Sir Ruthven Murgatroyd in *Ruddigore,* in Nanki-Poo in *The Mikado,* in Colonel Fairfax in *The Yeomen of the Guard,* and in Luiz in *The Gondoliers.* The most representative illustration is to be found in *The Mikado.* Disguised as a wandering minstrel, Nanki-Poo seeks the love of his lady Yum-Yum who is, however, betrothed to her guardian Ko-Ko, the Lord High executioner; at the same time, Nanki-Poo is under the order of the Mikado to marry Katisha, an elderly lady of the Court, and it is to flee this sentence that he has assumed the guise of a Second Trombone and has come to the town of Titipu to join with his true love. When the Mikado decrees that an execution is to take place in Titipu, the town having been quite derelict in its duty in this respect, a victim must be found, and, in despair over the frustration of his love, Nanki-Poo volunteers to be executed. As a reward for his civic enterprise, he is permitted to marry Yum-Yum for a period of a month, and the marriage is in fact about to be celebrated when Katisha bursts in to stop it; at the same time, she almost discloses his true identity. The approach of the Mikado is now announced, and, on his arrival, he is informed that an execution has been duly performed. Though he says that he would have been truly interested in so expeditious an execution, the main purpose for his visit to Titipu is to find his son, reported to be there. When he discovers that it is the Heir Apparent himself who has been the leading figure in the execution, he angrily orders those responsible for the fiasco executed as well. But Nanki-Poo is alive and married to Yum-Yum, and he assumes his rightful station; his other problem is solved when it is discovered that Katisha has married Ko-Ko. All difficulties having been surmounted, the play ends with the rites of the marriage celebration. I should add that the reversal of fortune of the protagonist is perhaps more sharply handled in *H.M.S. Pinafore* and in *The Gondoliers;* in *The Pirates of Penzance, Ruddigore,* and *The Yeomen of the Guard,* the reversal takes the form of freeing the protagonist from a false position or an unfair obligation; Gilbert has masterfully diversified his plots to bring out the great variety of treatment to which the basic action can be fruitfully submitted. The two basic requirements of the drama, reversal of the situation and recognition, are thus fully met.

In *The Hero with a Thousand Faces,* Joseph Campbell

has given a most succinct description of the structure of action of the mythological hero's alternations of fortune in the form of a symbolic journey as follows:

The mythological hero, setting forth from his common-day hut or castle, is lured, carried away, or else voluntarily proceeds, to the threshold of adventure. There he encounters a shadow presence that guards the passage. The hero may defeat or conciliate this power and go alive into the kingdom of the dark (brother-battle, dragon-battle: offering, charm), or be slain by the opponent and descend in death (dismemberment, crucifixion). Beyond the threshold, then, the hero journeys through a world of unfamiliar yet strangely intimate forces, some of which severely threaten him (tests), some of which give magical aid (helpers). When he arrives at the nadir of the mythological round, he undergoes a supreme ordeal and gains his reward. The triumph may be represented as the hero's sexual union with the goddess-mother of the world (sacred marriage), his recognition by his father-creator (father atonement), his own divinization (apotheosis), or again—if the powers have remained unfriendly to him—his theft of the boon he came to gain (bride-theft, fire-theft); intrinsically, it is an expansion of consciousness and therewith of being (illumination, transfiguration, freedom). The final work is that of the return. If the powers have blessed the hero, he now sets forth under their protection (emissary); if not, he flees and is pursued (transformation flight, obstacle flight). At the return threshold the transcendental powers must remain behind; the hero re-emerges from the kingdom of dread (return, resurrection), the boon that he brings restores the world (elixir).

This ideal version of the monomyth is substantiated in many ways by Lord Raglan's study of the myth of the hero, in which, from an analysis of the stories of Oedipus, Theseus, Romulus, Heracles, Perseus, Jason, Bellerophon, Pelops, Asclepios, Dionysos, Apollo, Zeus, Joseph, Moses, Elijah, Watu Gunung, Nyikang, Siegfried, Llew Llawgyffes, Arthur, and Robin Hood, he arrives at a pattern made up of the following incidents, all or most of which occur in the life of the hero:

1. The hero's mother is a royal virgin;
2. His father is a king, and
3. Often a near relative of his mother, but
4. The circumstances of his conception are unusual, and
5. He is also reputed to be the son of a God.
6. At birth an attempt is made, usually by his father or his maternal grandfather, to kill him, but
7. He is spirited away, and
8. Reared by foster-parents in a far country.
9. We are told nothing of his childhood, but
10. On reaching manhood he returns or goes to his future kingdom.
11. After a victory over the king and/or a giant, dragon or wild beast,
12. He marries a princess, often the daughter of his predecessor, and
13. Becomes king.
14. For a time he reigns uneventfully, and
15. Prescribes laws, but
16. Later he loses favour with the Gods and/or his subjects and
17. Is driven from the throne and city, after which
18. He meets with a mysterious death,
19. Often at the top of a hill.
20. His children, if any, do not succeed him.
21. His body is not buried, but nevertheless
22. He has one or more holy sepulchres.

Lord Raglan rightfully suggests that the considerable number of coincidences points to a ritual pattern as the origin of the myth of the hero and he notes that the three principal incidents in the life of the hero, his birth, his accession to the throne, and his death, correspond to the three principal *rites de passage*, at birth, at initiation, and at death. A somewhat similar pattern is depicted by A. M. Hocart in *Kingship* on the basis of his investigation of the Fijian, Brahamanic Indian, modern Cambodian, ancient Egyptian, Hebrew, Roman, Byzantine, Abyssinian, and European coronation ceremonies. This pattern is corroborated in turn by Tor Irstam's study of the coronation rites in the central belt of Africa, by G. Widengren's analysis of the Canaanite enthronement ritual, by R. Patai's study of the rites in the installation ceremonies of the Hebrew Kings, and by S. H. Hooke's description of the ideal myth and ritual pattern of the ancient Near East. And indeed, in the Annex II to V. V (ii) (a) titled, "Christus Patiens," in the sixth volume of *A Study of History,* Toynbee goes so far as to show no less than seventy-eight points of similarity between the life of Christ and the lives of a number of pagan heroes. The picture is thus completely filled out in all of its confirming details: the protagonist of the drama descends from and owes his power to move us to his incarnation as the dying-reborn god-hero-king of ancient myth and religion; he is our surrogate through whose sufferings and triumphs we are vicariously purged and redeemed.

We must not, however, expect the structure of religious ritual to be reproduced literally and exactly in the structure of drama which, in the course of its descent from and development of religious ritual, has omitted, telescoped, expanded, and thus changed the elements of religious ritual into a more compact and meaningful (from the point of view of formal aesthetic requirements) shape. We may therefore assert with some confidence that the basic action structure of the libretti of W. S. Gilbert is in the long run ultimately derived from the pattern of action of religious ritual and it is the immanent power and thrust of this pattern, infused and diffused through them, which gives them both their architecture and their capacity to move audiences, even when both artist and audience may be quite unaware of its presence in them. Nevertheless, we must raise these two questions: from what source did W. S. Gilbert most directly derive this pattern, and, was it from this source that the specific Christian coloring of the libretti comes?

I would suggest that Gilbert's source is Spenser's *The Faerie Queene.* Now, it is true that nowhere does Gilbert specifically allude to Spenser either in his libretti or in his letters. At the same time, it is equally true that Gilbert was extraordinarily attracted to the concept of the Fairy Land. The locale of two of the operettas, three of the verse plays, and many of the Bab Ballads is wholly and explicitly Fairy Land. Moreover, Gilbert, like Spenser before him, uses the Fairy Land as a symbol of the golden age, both as a criterion of judgment of contemporary manners and aspirations and as an ideal to be attained. To be sure, this is circumstantial evidence, but when Gilbert's libretti are read in the light of *The Faerie Queene,* when we place side by side the narratives of the adventures of, let us say, the Redcrosse Knight, with a typical Gilbert protagonist, let us say, Luiz in *The Gondoliers,* then the pattern of action will be seen to be startlingly and surely not coincidentally alike. In both cases, the pattern of action takes the form of the adventures of a young man of seemingly humble birth who sallies forth to do battle for the love of his lady; he encounters (physically and spiritually) enemies both without and within him (again physically and spiritually); he is apparently defeated by his own defects of character but learns through his actions and their reactions on and in him the lessons of Christian humility, obedience, and love; he overcomes his final great adversary; and, in the end, has earned the right to be proclaimed, and to be treated as, a true Christian knight. Thus the mythological journey of the hero has been allegorized into the pattern of Christian triumph over temptation and of resurrection over fall. G. Wilson Knight has written of Shakespeare: "Though his drama is no passive reflection of Christian dogma it certainly does very often, in matters both infernal and paradisal, demonstrate, not indeed the truth of the dogma, but the truth of *that* the truth of which the dogma exists to establish." The same may be said of Spenser, and, therefore, of Gilbert as well.

Revealing as this similarity is, it may be objected that it is rather too general, too capable of universal and therefore non-discriminating application. There is, however, one other point of comparison which is to my mind clear-cut and convincing. I have already referred to the mysterious older woman who plays such a key role in Gilbert's libretti. This figure takes the form of Little Buttercup in *H.M.S. Pinafore,* Ruth in *The Pirates of Penzance,* Iolanthe in the opera of the same name, Lady Blanche in *Princess Ida,* Katisha in *The Mikado,* Dame Hannah in *Ruddigore,* and Inez in *The Gondoliers.* This figure plays a double role in the action: on the one hand, she is often an obstruction in the path of success of the protagonist; on the other hand, she is just as often the revealer of truth whose story finally clears the way for him. She is thus in her dual role the reincarnation of the Great-Terrible Mother of ancient religion and myth; she is Lilith-Eve, Isis-Osiris, Asherath-Anath-Ashtaroth, Athene-Aphrodite, Mary-Mary, vampire-wife, temptress-sister, the Great Goddess, in short, in her two-fold character of witch-mother, seductress-protectress. The anthropological, archaeological, mythological, and psychological evidence for the power and persistence of the idea of the Great Mother in the ancient world has been fully set forth by Bachofen in *Das Mutterrecht,* Bruno Bettelheim in *Symbolic Wounds,* Robert Briffault in *The Mothers,* Frazer throughout *The Golden Bough* and especially in *Adonis Attis Osiris,* Freud in *Totem and Taboo* and *Moses and Monotheism,* Arnold van Gennep in *The Rites of Passage,* S. Giedion in *The Eternal Present: The Beginnings of Art,* Jung in virtually every one of his papers and books, Gertrude R. Levy in *The Gate of Horn,* Margaret Murray in *The God of the Witches,* Erich Neumann in *The Origins and History of the Consciousness* and in the fuller *The Great Mother,* and by Otto Rank in *The Myth of the Birth of the Hero.* Mircea Eliade who has treated the archetype of the Great Mother with learning and discernment in several of his books well sums up its double character in *Myths, Dreams and Mysteries:* "To men of the traditional cultures . . . all life was a hierophany, a manifestation of the sacred. Creation—at every cosmic level—presupposed the intervention of a holy power. Accordingly, the divinities of life and of fertility represented sources of holiness and of power, and of this their androgyny was confirmatory. But *androgyny extends even to divinities*

who are pre-eminently masculine, or feminine. This means
that androgyny has become a general formula signifying *autonomy, strength, wholeness;* to say of a divinity that it is androgyny is as much as to say that it is the ultimate being, the
ultimate reality." The penetration of the archetype into myth
and thence into literature has been documented by Joseph
Campbell in *The Hero with a Thousand Faces,* Mario Praz
in *The Romantic Agony,* Lord Raglan in *Jocasta's Crime,* but
above all by Robert Graves who attests to the potency of the
goddess in his own person and poetry, that poet, who with
crookedly broken nose, furrowed cheeks, and coarse grey hair,
". . . still stands ready, with a boy's presumption,/To court
the queen in her high silk pavilion."

But nowhere in modern literature, to my knowledge at least,
has the theme of the duplex female been more elaborated
than in *The Faerie Queene.* It is true that the white devils
and insatiable countesses of Jacobean drama still excite the
reader with horror; the Romantic period proliferated, as Praz
tells us, the Matilda of Lewis, the Velleda of Chateaubriand,
the Salammbô of Flaubert, the Carmen of Mérimée, the Cecily
of Sue, the Conchita of Pierre Louys, the Cleopatra of Gautier,
in addition to the Mater Lachrymarum of De Quincey and
the "La Belle Dame sans merci" of Keats; and later in the
century there are in England Swinburne, Pater, and Wilde;
in Italy D'Annunzio; and in France Baudelaire, Huysmans,
and Laforgue. But in none of these are the changes of the
theme rung with such variety, subtlety, and range of symbolic
significance as in *The Faerie Queene.* For every Una, there
is a Duessa; just as Nature destroys, so she creates; and if the
challenge to Zeus and the reign of law is made by woman
in her guise as Change, so she is put down by woman in her
other guise as Nature:

> Then forth issewed (great goddesse) great Dame Nature,
> With goodly port and gracious majesty, . . .
> Yet certes by her face and physnomy,

Whether she man or woman inly were,
That could not any creature well descry: . . .

This great grandmother of all creatures bred,
Great Nature, ever young yet full of eld,
Still mooving, yet unmoved from her sted,
Unseene of any, yet of all beheld, . . .

No student of Spenser has more penetratingly perceived the ambivalent (and thus simultaneously the androgynous) role of woman in *The Faerie Queene* than has A. C. Hamilton when he writes in *The Structure of Allegory in "The Faerie Queene"*:

The simultaneous awareness of the power of virtue and the wretchedness of life drives the poem into metaphor. Consequently its central visions are always twofold: Una is veiled, woman's beauty is combined with the serpent's tail in Error and Duessa, the glorious Lucifera as the fallen Faery Queen, Florimell and the false Florimell, Amoret bound, Venus with the snake wound around her feet, Isis and the crocodile. By exploring these visions the poem moves towards an image of man seen perfected in Arthur and also the image of Nature. As Arthur appears in the various knights, Nature appears in her various forms, from that original vision of the Faery Queen and the primary vision of Una to Belphoebe, Amoret, Florimell, Britomart, Colin's damsel surrounded by the graces and maidens, until Nature herself appears in the Mutability Cantos. We see this unfallen Nature herself in opposition to fallen Nature, her counterpart in the twofold vision. Since this nature is both without and within man, we see unfallen man in the images of virtue at one with nature opposed to fallen man in the images of vice. Once we see that opposition on all levels, Nature is redeemed, and therefore man. It is in this sense that Spenser delivers in his poem a golden world.

I believe that this tradition of the two-fold image of woman yielding up in the end the two-fold vision of Nature and therefore of man's redemption through suffering operates with sufficient force to account for its presence in Gilbert's libretti, and I am therefore sure that it is not at all necessary to attribute it to personal, psycho-analytical reasons as does Hesketh Pearson when he observes of Gilbert: "The other aspect of his work that appears to be related to impressions of the period of his youth is the mockery he makes in his operas of ageing females. Though this has some connection with his strong attraction for pretty women, held in check by an equally strong moral sense, the origin is possibly to be found in his total lack of sympathy with his mother, amounting in time to active dislike, his feeling revenging itself on all women whose age and insensitiveness called her to mind." Whatever the reason, this archetypal ambivalence, whose descent from myth through Spenser to Gilbert we have just traced, does play a most crucial part in the libretti. Thus, when we place Fidessa's letter to the King of Eden, intended to prevent the betrothal of the Redcrosse Knight to Una:

> "To thee, most mighty king of Eden fayre,
> Her greeting sends in these sad lines addresst . . .
> And bids thee be advized for the best,
> Ere thou thy daughter linck in holy band
> Of wedlocke to that new unknowen guest:
> For he already plighted his right hand
> Unto another love, and to another land.
>
> To me, sad mayd, or rather widow sad,
> He was affyaunced long time before,
> And sacred pledges he both gave, and had,
> False errant knight, infamous, and foreswore!"

side by side with Katisha's plaint:

> Your revels cease! Assist me, all of you!
> I claim my perjured lover, Nanki-Poo!
> Oh, fool! to shun delights that never cloy!
> Come back, oh, shallow fool! Come back to joy!

> The hour of gladness
> Is dead and gone;
> In silent sadness
> I live alone!
> The hope I cherished
> All lifeless lies,
> And all has perished
> Save love, which never dies!
> Oh, faithless one, this insult you shall rue!
> In vain for mercy on your knees you'll sue.
> I'll tear the mask from your disguising.
>
> My wrongs with vengeance shall be crowned!
> My wrongs with vengeance shall be crowned!

when we place these situations side by side, then, the links in the chain have been closed and the knot between myth, Christianity, Spenser, and Gilbert has been tied.

Gilbert, like Spenser, delivers a golden world, yet again, as in Spenser, we cannot escape hearing in him a note of melancholy, an overtone of despair. The very fact that Spenser left his grand structure uncompleted is a melancholy thing in itself; considering that there are already signs of loss of strength and imagination in Books V and VI, we cannot help wondering what the remaining sixteen books would have held for us. Similarly, after *The Gondoliers* and the break with Sullivan, Gilbert turned out libretti of the order of *The Mountebanks* and *His Excellency,* and even the renewed collaboration with Sullivan could produce nothing better than *Utopia, Limited* and *The Grand Duke.* Even in the most golden operettas, the Sophoclean note is struck:

> Is life a boon?
> If so, it must befall,
> That Death, whene'er he call,
> Must call too soon. . . .

The Twisted Cue

Is life a thorn?
  Then count it not a whit!
  Man is well done without it;
Soon as he's born
  He should by all means essay
  To put the plague away; . . .

Nor is it even certain that art itself can triumph over time:

  Is it, can it be,
  Nature hath this decree,
    Nothing poetic in the world shall dwell?
  Or that in all her works
  Something poetic lurks,
    Even in colocynth and colomel?
                    I cannot tell.

"I cannot tell"—this, perhaps, is the final answer of the poet.
No wonder, then, that art and criticism and life itself, all alike,
are played:

  On a cloth untrue,
  With a twisted cue,
  And elliptical billiard balls!

(1963)

Between Bennington and
Bloomington

THE DISCUSSION BETWEEN Lord Raglan and Stanley Edgar
Hyman, advocating the ritual point of view, and Stith
Thompson, as their critic, over the question of the extent of
the applicability of the ritualist formula makes the symposium
on myth in the October-December, 1955, issue of the *Journal
of American Folklore* stimulating and significant reading. As
I understand the discussion, Raglan and Hyman believe that
all forms of expression have been shown, or will in time be
shown, to have arisen in ritual, while Thompson argues that
the diversity and variety of peoples, of myths, and of circumstances are so great that no monistic approach can possibly
satisfy their range and scope. This is an issue of such consequence, both to folklore itself and to those studies which are
more and more drawing upon folklore for materials and direction, that further consideration of the problems involved is
surely not out of place. The differences between the two approaches are accurately summed up in the questions which
Thompson indicates each sets for itself: the ritualists ask,
"where do myths come from?"; their opponents ask, "where
does each individual myth come from?" I should add that

Thompson does not single out the ritual view as the only approach to myth which commits the monistic error; he condemns the psychological approach in even stronger terms (though here he slips from methodological disagreement to moral disapproval); but, by and large, his paper is directed mainly to a critique of the ritual view.

To look at myth from the point of view of a student of literature is to look at it in quite another way than does the folklorist, but it is conceivable that this different angle of approach may provide a fresh and therefore suggestive view of the problem under consideration. As such a student, I am basically and primarily concerned with the literature of the Western tradition, which, as I understand it, begins with the expression of the peoples of the ancient Near East which is in turn adapted and reshaped by Hebrew, Greek, and Christian thought, and is then transmitted to Northern Europe which makes its own modifications in it; that is, the progressively westward and northward movement of ideas and forms from the fertile crescent to the Mediterranean to the Atlantic. This area is the matrix of our civilization, and from it have come the problems and their possible solutions, in every form of expression, which continue to agitate us to this day. When we think, we think in terms of the distinctive form of logic which was evolved within the confines of that area; when we deal with the relations between men, we deal with them as they were uniquely shaped in that area; and when we express ourselves, we use the characteristic forms and modes of expression which were invented and developed in it. Whatever else has happened outside that area as I have described it, within its confines it is characterized by a relatively homogeneous concert of shared assumptions, attitudes, beliefs, and manner of action. If this is obvious, then it needs to be stated again, because it has been forgotten by both sides in the ritual controversy. Both sides seem to me to make the same error: because they want to claim so much territory, they neglect the very area which, from my point of view, is of the most significance.

The ritualists are convinced that any form of expression of any people can in the last analysis be made to originate in ritual; their opponents argue that there are so many forms and so many peoples that no such reduction can be made. Thompson observes with a note of triumph in his voice that ". . . the story which is cited in Raglan's paper exists in not fewer than a thousand known versions," and I suppose he would think that two thousand would be doubly convincing. This is carrying Baconian method to its ultimate absurdity, and both sides, in their zeal for completeness, ought to remember that the *Instauratio Magna* was never completed, nor, given Bacon's ideological presuppositions, could it ever have been completed. We have awakened from the Baconian dream which so haunted nineteenth-century science, and we have finally had to admit to ourselves that the number of swallows which make a summer must in the end be a statistical approximation. What I am saying is that it is neither possible nor necessary that each and every piece of evidence be collected before a single generalization can be made; what is possible and particularly necessary is that both the evidence and the generalizations be consistent within a carefully and clearly delimited area of relevance and that both the problems and their possible solutions be kept within a framework circumscribed by the needs of our most significant experience. To me, this means that the ritual theory should be tested not in Africa or the America of the Indians or in Australia but within the limits of the Western tradition as I have defined it. I do not see why Raglan or Hyman feel compelled to go outside that tradition to make their case, but it is just when they do that Thompson catches them out of bounds. Yet when he does, he is as much off the field of play as they are. And when both teams do manage to play on the same field, Thompson is forced to admit that under the rules of proper play he cannot catch the ritualists off base.

As a matter of fact, Hyman has admitted as much, without actually saying so. For if we examine his list of books which have carried forward the ritual approach, we find that virtually without exception they are concerned with the explication of monuments within the Western tradition. It is this very concentration which has given the ritual approach such a persuasive and pervasive influence over the study of that tradition. I know of no student of the classics who would now completely reject the Harrison-Murray-Cornford approach, whatever criticisms in detail have been made of it; even so sceptical a writer as Guthrie has said, in *The Greeks and Their Gods:*

For those of us to whom it has not been given to live in that age [when Jane Harrison was working], it would be unprofitable to pretend to an enthusiasm which has passed us by. We have missed much, but must take what profit we can from our position as epigoni. . . . This does not mean ignoring the solid and lasting work which will always be associated with such names as Rohde, Cornford, Murray and A. B. Cook. . . . It should mean only a shifting of the balance, a change of emphasis, a rearrangement which brings some things to the fore and pushes others a little more into the background.

And it was as recently as 1950 and 1952 that some of Cornford's most stimulating papers appeared in *The Unwritten Philosophy and Other Essays* and *Principium Sapientiae,* both, incidentally, with prefaces by Guthrie. Similarly, it is virtually impossible to deal with the history of the religions of the ancient Near East and with the impact of those religions on Christianity without the guidance of the ritual approach; Hyman has mentioned only a few of the names he could have listed had he more space at his disposal; and I strongly suspect that the problems posed by the Dead Sea Scrolls will be solved mainly through the application of the ritual approach. The legacy of the so-called Cambridge school has been more than a legacy of method; it has been abiding absorption in the well-springs and streams of the Western tradition.

When Thompson says that ". . . if one is examining the myths and folktales of a group of South American Indians, he will find that he is moving in a considerably different world from that which he encounters in the stories of the Indians of the North Pacific Coast or the natives of Polynesia," he is right; and I would go beyond even that to say that when one is examining the myth and ritual pattern developed by and in the Western tradition, one is moving not only in a different world, but in a unique world, unique in the precise amount of its difference from the myths and folktales of the South American Indians and of the Indians of the North Pacific Coast and of the natives of Polynesia. And even if the ritualists were able to prove the universal applicability of ritual origin, they would then be faced with an obstacle far greater than any Thompson has been able to put before them. They would then have to explain why, if all forms of expression everywhere originate in ritual, did the myth and ritual pattern of the Western tradition develop as richly and in the direction that it has. For it seems to me beyond contention that this pattern has shown itself capable of growth and adaptation on such a scale and to such levels of spiritual significance as to far transcend any other pattern in any other culture. Arrogant though this statement is, it is a qualitative judgment I am ready to defend, and I have only to recall the materials I dealt with in connection with the preparation of *Tragedy and the Paradox of the Fortunate Fall* and to compare them with the myths of other peoples in other areas to reconfirm this position. But lest it prejudice the point I am trying to make, I am willing to put that judgment aside, and phrase the question in this way: how do you account for the differences between the products of ritual origin within the Western tradition and the products of ritual origin outside it? Their desire to get everything in, though for opposite reasons, has prevented both sides from facing up to the problem of difference. But to the student of literature, the discrimination of difference is an ever-demanding responsibility.

Two further objections to the ritual point of view need to be considered. The first is that the universal applicability of ritual origin seems to presuppose a universal and similar system of social organization at exactly the same level of development everywhere and at the same time. The alternative to this hypothesis would have to be that, if inequalities in the development of social organization do exist, then ritual origin is actually a stage in social development which occurs at different times in different places as changing conditions make it possible. The second objection is that the ritual view must assume the existence of a universal mythopoeic mind which operates in the same way under the stimulus of the same needs and conditions. In a letter to me, in reply to these objections, Hyman has written: "(1) We assume only that every culture has ceremonial traits or had them, out of which myths, etc., derive, with no necessary evolutionary parallelism; and (2) I do not know anything about mythopoeic minds, but only that similar rites come out of similar psychological needs (man as a biological constant) and will be misunderstood in similar stories." These are strong and cogent defenses, and while they bring us closer home than does Thompson's approach, which, by insisting that each case is a separate problem with a separate solution, does not even permit us to start out, they do not quite bring us all the way. The problem of the relation of expression to the given state of social organization at any time, never a comfortable one at best, is particularly vexatious to the ritual point of view since it scratches its smooth universality with the sharp edges of diversity and variety. Similarly, if similar rites come out of similar psychological needs, as I am certain they do, then, unless one is willing to posit an ultimate *ur*-myth and ritual from which all other myths and rituals are descended, however changed and corrupted with the passage of time they may become, and this brings us dangerously close to the miasmas of the Jungian mystique, how can we account both for similarity and difference within the same methodological framework? I cannot help feeling that the ritualist compulsion toward universality has, for the time being at least, thrown unnecessary stumbling-blocks in its path.

In effect, then, both sides seem to me to commit the same methodological error: they assume that expression has its own history apart from and independent of the needs and circumstances of the men who give rise to it. But there is after all no reason for expression to change of its own accord; it changes only as a consequence of pressures exerted on it from outside itself, that is, in response to changes in men. But neither side shows any awareness of the problem of change; rather, they appear to me as rival academic imperialisms, ever reaching out for more and more conquests, the salient difference between them being that the ritualists would enlist all new territories under a single banner while their opponents would insist that each new province should fly its own flag. Yet once the problem of change is admitted, then the problem of difference is raised; and once difference is admitted, then the problem of difference in quality is raised.

But perhaps folklore as a science is not supposed to concern itself with qualitative judgments; again, such judgment is another major responsibility of students of literature. As such a student, I can never be grateful enough to those scholars whose work on myth and ritual led me to what I believe are the ultimate origins of tragedy and the tragic effect. But I had always to beware of confusing myth with literature; a work of art is after all something far different from its source, no matter how much of its power it may draw from and owe to it. The student of literature must discriminate between origin and artifact, just as he must discriminate among the artifacts themselves, and Hyman's warning that ". . . literature is analogous to myth, we have to insist, but is not itself myth," cannot be repeated often enough, though here I must confess that some overzealous students of myth and literature need the warning more than do the ritualists. It is in fact this sensitive awareness of the relationship between myth and literature which is the particular merit of the ritualist point of view. To return to Hyman's list once more: every work of importance in it is directed by way of myth to the understanding of literature. Myth is never made an end in itself but is a means to a greater end, the illumination of literature.

My comments have perhaps meandered along devious paths. I began by emphasizing the differences between the ritual point of view and its critics only to indict both for committing the same errors, of failing to delimit their studies to the area of greatest importance to the Western tradition, of failing to distinguish between cultures qualitatively (the corollary to this error would be the failure to distinguish qualitatively between comparable products of different cultures), and of failing to provide a satisfactory theory of change. Yet, in the end, I enrolled in the army of the ritualists. Perhaps folklorists are no longer surprised by the inconsistencies of students of literature. However, I am impelled to say in our defense that though literary history was once dominated by the analogy to biological collection and classification, that domination has since been overthrown; but if any scientific analogy is needed to justify our methods today, it would have to be the field theory of contemporary physics. In any case, I have put on record my bias in favor of the ritual point of view for whatever it may be worth in this assessment of the claims of both approaches.

(1956)

Dialectics as Tragedy

WHILE THE PHILOSOPHICAL assumptions upon which Joseph Wood Krutch's *The Modern Temper* was based have been pretty well rejected by now, his position in the field of aesthetics, and particularly on the problem of tragedy, is still widely retained. This is of course an inconsistency which has only to be stated for the contradiction to be seen, but it is necessary to examine the reasons why the Krutchean view that it is impossible to write tragedy today because there exists no ethos upon which it can be based cannot now be held.

I start by accepting Krutch's own definition of tragedy as an attitude of mind essentially optimistic, that is to say, based on a view which holds that man is ultimately capable of finding salvation. And furthermore, like Krutch, I shall look to Marxism to supply the ethical foundation upon which tragedy can be created, but, and here I depart from Krutch, I shall try to show that Marxism is not a philosophy of barbarism, as he so mistakenly calls it, but on the contrary, that it is the contemporary inheritor of the great western traditions of humanism, Christianity, and democracy, the sources from which we draw our values and standards.

Now, the use of Marxism as a method of historical and literary analysis is, for all that it is unaccepted, nonetheless a recognized technique of study. But the process by which Marxism may be used as a body of ideas and feelings forming the stuff out of which may be created art capable of arousing aesthetic response, especially that peculiar to tragedy, needs more careful examination than it has usually been given. I should like in this paper to examine Marxism for its possibilities in inspiring an attitude of mind and feeling resulting ultimately in the creation of tragedy. It is important to realize at the outset that I am not treating Marxism as an articulated and demonstrable set of logical propositions dealing with economics, but rather as a source of inspiration, a guide to the interpretation of experience, as a way, in short, of coping with ethical and religious problems. Just as it would be foolish to subject the Greek concept of fate or the Christian belief in the City of God or the Renaissance idea of individualism to formal analysis or to look to them for detailed and accurate information, when in fact one actually sees them, as Krutch puts it, as ". . . a profession of faith, and a sort of religion; a way of looking at life by virtue of which it is robbed of its pain," so I propose that we study Marxism, not for its possible contributions or errors in economics or sociology or history, all of which are legitimate matters of investigation in their own way, but for its mythological and inspirational and religious qualities without which no tragedy can be written.

In Greek tragedy, the central figure is afflicted with *atasthalia,* a hardening of the character as it were, the result of excessive pride and overbearing will. This strong individual is overwhelmed by a power greater than himself, which he cannot cope with, and which inevitably sweeps him on to his destruction. Yet even this interpretation of tragedy is too simple, too likely to degenerate into the Renaissance notion of tragedy as the fall of a great man dashed from prosperity to adversity by the turn of the "frail and inconstant Fortune" of Bandello ". . . who in a moment hoisteth a man up to the highest degree of her wheel, and by and by, in less space than the twinkling of an eye, she throweth him down again so low, as more misery is prepared for him in one day, than favour in one hundred years." We must look further for a more adequate explanation of tragedy.

In the pattern of classical tragedy, the leading character falls because of some excess, but the presumption which marks this excess must be understood as reflecting more than a personal disability. The fall of a great man through pride of will or the desire for power, while affecting enough, is at the most pathetic; certainly it is not tragic. We are swept away by the violence of personal passion, we are saddened by the uselessness of the destruction of one whom we pity, but we do not go beyond. Surely nothing could be more affecting than the hapless end of Romeo and Juliet, but the range of our emotional response is limited, nor are we prompted to reach out, to question, to wonder. The tragic occurs when by the fall of a man of strong character we are made aware of something greater than that man or even mankind; we seem to see a new and truer vision of the universe. It is to be admitted that the tragic hero suffers for his *hybris,* and we, the spectators, suffer too, but we are willing to suffer; indeed we take pleasure in the suffering, if only that suffering is made intelligible to us. But suffering can be made bearable only when it is made a part of a rational world order into which it fits and which has an understandable place for it. Something of the calm which comes when suffering has been shown not to have been in vain is apparent in Adam's speech at the end of *Paradise Lost:*

> Henceforth I learn that to obey is best,
> And love with fear the only God, to walk
> As in his presence, and in him sole depend,
> Merciful over all his works, with good
> Still overwhelming evil, and by small
> Accomplishing great things.

Here is to be found, I think, the core of the great tradition of tragedy, the mark by which it may be recognized: Not that we are to accept Milton's God, but the sense of assurance which is born of the serenity of rational order is the gift of the blind poet. In the way in which I am using the word, then, tragedy occurs when the accepted order of things is fundamentally questioned only to be the more triumphantly reaffirmed; the epic, in contrast, merely affirms but does not criticize, so that from this point of view, *Paradise Lost* is a tragedy.

To the Greeks, the natural order of things which made the affairs of the cosmos intelligible to men was termed *Dike* and the very conception of an order of things presupposed the necessity that every object in the universe occupy its rightful place, attempting neither too much nor too little. The rash man may be presumptuous, may set himself outside the order of things, but in doing so he weakens the great chain which links the cosmos together; and for his temerity he suffers that we may be persuaded to recognize the justness of the divine law. This thought runs straight through Greek literature, from the advice of Theognis:

Be not over-eager in any matter; best is due measure in all human affairs; oft is a man eager in pursuit of gain, only to be misled into great loss by an eager spirit which easily maketh what is evil seem to him good, and what is good seem evil.

to the considered belief of Plato:

God, as was said of old, holding that the beginning and end and middle of all things that have being in the natural course of his revolution moves directly to his end. Justice ever attends him as the punisher of those who forsake the divine law; closely following Justice, in humility and perfect orderliness, is he for whom a blessed lot is in store; whereas if any man be puffed up with boastful pride, whether of wealth or rank, or with foolish vanity of youthful beauty, and is inflamed with insolence, as one needing neither guide nor ruler, but setting up to guide others, such an one is left without God, and taking him to himself others no less abandoned makes general confusion with his antics. Many will take him for a great man; but

after no long time Justice exacts a full retribution, and he over-
turns not only himself but his household and city.

No clearer diagram of the pattern of Aeschylean and Sophoclean tragedy could be drawn; the ethos which informed their
plays and lifted them to their high level is here given its defini-
tive statement. Those who hold to the romantic interpretation
of the legend of Prometheus ought to study this passage from
the *Laws* as a useful corrective.

Somewhere in this region is to be discovered, I suspect, the
secret of the word *catharsis*. Pity, terror, awe: these are the
emotional responses, the aesthetic bridge as it were, which
make possible the passage from the action on the stage to the
heightened ethical consciousness in the mind of the spectator.
Pity for the tragic hero who, a man like us, must suffer that we
may learn to live rightly; terror that he has dared to question
the justice of the order of nature; awe because that order has
been reaffirmed more triumphantly than ever: such is the effect
of tragedy. Perhaps no critic has realized this more keenly than
Aristotle, nor has put this conception in more stimulating
language. Unfortunately, Aristotle has been more than once
altogether misinterpreted because it has not been seen that he
has translated the ethical norm of tragedy in terms applicable
to art, and more specifically, in terms of the conditions created
by a particular medium, in this case, tragedy. Thus, in dis-
cussing tragedy, he insists on the necessity for action over and
above ideas and characters because it is primarily through the
action on the stage that tragedy expresses itself. In a word,
what he has done is to center attention on the aesthetic implications of Greek cosmology in an attempt, and it is a successful
attempt I think, to discover what effect will be produced on a
work of art by the expression of the informing element in that
cosmology through the particular medium employed. As a
result of the romantic confusion of the arts, those paintings in
poetry, symphonic poems, and musical verses of the late nineteenth century, we have forgotten the salutary lesson of classi-

cism, namely, that each medium has its own specific laws which must be complied with, and, whenever this is not done, whenever the conditions created by the medium are disregarded and the philosophy is forced into the forefront, bad art, or more simply, propaganda, is the result. Marxists are so often accused of advocating propaganda in art and of judging the worth of a work of art by its opinions alone that it is worth calling attention to Engels' opinion of the subject:

I am not at all opposed to propaganda poetry as such. The father of tragedy, Eschylus, and the father of comedy, Aristophanes, were both clearly poets with a thesis, as were Cervantes and Dante. . . . But I believe that the thesis must inhere in the situation and the action, without being explicitly formulated; and it is not the poet's duty to supply the reader in advance with the future historical solution of the conflict he describes.

To Aristotle, then, the affirmation of the idea of a world order was of paramount importance, but he recognized, as indeed any critic must, that the demands of the medium must be harmonized with the ethos involved.

One or two important considerations are evident as a result of this slight excursus into the nature of tragedy. We have seen that a man of strong character but possessed of some overbearing passion jeopardizes by the exercise of that passion the order of nature and must suffer so that the equilibrium may be maintained at the proper poise. But the conception of the order of nature changes: for the Hebrew prophets it was the remorseless working out of the historic process to fulfill the exacting demands of justice; for the Greeks it was a rational world order apprehended by the exercise of reason; for the Christians it was an immediate identification with God, the source and symbol of order; for the scientific rationalists of the seventeenth and eighteenth centuries, it was a mathematically proportioned universe guided by a few simple laws discoverable by all men by the application of science.

Each age gives order and coherence to experience in its own way.

Where in the welter of conflicting modern ideologies can we find the conception of an order of nature capable of inspiring men on the mythological plane by making nature intelligible to him, by explaining his past, by setting his goals, by making bearable the present world of strife and sorrow? It is at this point that I should like to suggest that Marxism is most capable of providing the ethos upon which a satisfactory theory of modern tragedy can be based. Marxism offers as an adequate explanation of the unintelligibility of the working of natural forces the idea of the conflict of classes, for it sees in the notion of the disorder of nature merely the reflection of the chaos of the present social structure. Insofar as men recognize the existence of the class struggle, they attain to an understanding of the blind movement of social forces and this understanding raises them from the ranks of ignorant, groping men to men of vision and purpose. As Engels puts it:

With the seizing of the means of production by society, production of commodities is done away with, and, simultaneously, the mastery of the product over the producer. Anarchy in social production is replaced by systematic, definite organization. The struggle for individual existence disappears. Then for the first time, man, in a certain sense, is finally marked off from the rest of the animal kingdom, and emerges from mere animal conditions of existence into really human ones. The whole sphere of the conditions of life which environ man, and which have hitherto ruled man, now comes under the dominion and control of man, who for the first time becomes the real, conscious lord of Nature, because he has now become master of his own social organization. The laws of his own social action, hitherto standing face to face with man as laws of Nature foreign to, and dominating him, will be then used with full understanding, and so mastered by him. Man's own social organization, hitherto confronting him as a necessity imposed by Nature and history, pass under the control of man himself. Only from that time will man himself, more and more consciously, make his own history—only from that time will the causes set in movement by him have, in the main and in a constantly growing measure, the results intended by him. It is the ascent of man from the kingdom of necessity to the kingdom of freedom.

Just as the bourgeoisie was able to assert its superiority over the medieval way of life by appealing to science, to the operation of natural law above and outside of men, as the justification for its actions, so now the proletariat identifies its needs with the movement of history as bringing about the destruction of capitalism and the advent of socialism. Thus Newton's dictum:

To tell us that every species of Things is endow'd with an occult specifick Quality by which it acts and produces manifest Effects is to tell us nothing: But to derive two or three general Principles of Motion from Phaenomena, and afterwards to tell us how the Properties and Actions of all corporeal Things follow from those manifest Principles would be a very great step in Philosophy, though the Causes of those Principles were not yet discovered.

which struck the final blow against the scholastic method and made the methodology of the examination of natural laws applicable not only to the field of science but to economics, religion, criticism, and other disciplines as well is paralleled by Engels' insistence that:

The appeal to morality and justice does not bring us forward a finger's breadth scientifically; economic science can see no proof in moral indignation, be it never so justified, but only a symptom. The task of this science is rather to explain the newly rising social evils as necessary consequences of the existing modes of production, but also at the same time as signs of its approaching dissolution, and to discover within the economic movement-form which is dissolving, the elements of the future new organization of production and exchange which will abolish those evils.

It is the Marxist view that the science of Bacon and Newton was essentially optimistic, for it followed Bacon's injunction to bear fruit, that is to say, to produce socially useful results. Unfortunately, if we contrast the social potentialities of science with its present limitations, we can see why so many scientists are decrying the future of science itself and why so many philosophers sound the note of hopelessness. The depth of despair has been voiced most poignantly by Bertrand Russell:

That man is the product of causes which had no prevision of the end they were achieving; that his origin, his growth, his hopes and fears, his loves and beliefs, are but the outcome of accidental collocations of atoms; that no fire, no heroism, no intensity of thought and feeling, can preserve an individual life beyond the grave; that all the labours of the ages, all the devotion, all the inspiration, all the noonday brightness of human genius, are destined to extinction in the vast death of the solar system, and that the whole temple of man's achievement must inevitably be buried beneath the debris of a universe in ruins—all these things, if not quite beyond dispute, are yet so nearly certain that no philosophy which rejects them can hope to stand.

But Marxism does reject them and still stands, for, if it does not assure the immortality of the individual man, it makes certain the immortality of the race. For it belongs to the great tradition of cosmic optimism which goes back to the very beginnings of man's attempts to depict a better picture of the world in which to live. "Every world-view," says Reinhold Niebuhr, "which finds the mechanisms of the cosmos either neutrally amenable or profoundly sympathetic to human ideals, is mythological and religious," and it is in this sense that Marxism is mythological and religious, the traditional fructifying forces of tragedy.

Nevertheless, Marxism is not at all willing to relinquish the element of moral judgment. Capitalism, it asserts, falls not only because it is structurally unsound but because it is morally bad, that is to say, it cannot any longer take care of its own. What part do men play in this double doom of capital-ism? Are they determined by the inevitable movement of the social process or are they free agents, able to choose or reject or disregard their part in this movement? Marxism, like all the religions which have had to face this question, seeks to strike a balance between absolute determinism and absolute free-dom. While it is true that men make their own history, they make it within the conditions created by the existing social organization. Under capitalism, those conditions are anarchic and therefore determine men's actions, but they are able to free themselves insofar as they recognize the ruthless sweep of the historic process, to see in it the pattern of the class struggle in which is woven the ultimate abolition of anarchy and the establishment of social order. Greatness in men consists in the degree of their recognition of the design in the pattern and to the extent to which they help work out the design. To Engels:

. . . freedom is the appreciation of necessity. 'Necessity is blind only in so far as it is not understood.' Freedom does not consist in the dream of independence of natural laws, but in the knowledge of these laws and in the possibility this gives of systematically making them work towards definite ends. This holds good in relation both to the laws of external nature and to those which govern the bodily and mental life of men themselves—two classes of laws which we can separate from each other at most only in thought, but not in reality. Freedom of the will, therefore, means nothing but the capacity to make judgments with real knowledge of the subject. Therefore the freer a man's judgment is in relation to a definite question, with so much the greater *necessity* is the content of the judgment deter-mined; while the uncertainty, founded on ignorance, which seems to make an arbitrary choice among many different and conflicting possible decisions shows by this precisely that it is not free, that it is controlled by the very object that it should itself control. Freedom, therefore, consists in the control over ourselves and over external nature which is founded on knowledge of natural necessity; it is therefore necessarily a product of historical development.

Again, the picture of the universe as painted by the Marxist brush is seen to be amenable to men's wills and desires.

At bottom, however, Marxism is profoundly deterministic as indeed every great religion has been. But it is by no means fatalistic or content to permit its adherents to sit idly by while the historic process works itself out to the preordained end. On the contrary, salvation, that is to say, the establishment of harmony between the individual and the historic process, is possible only when the individual consciously and actively works for the creation of the classless society. As Niebuhr puts it, the most redemptive action in communism is the avowal of the class struggle which, though the end is predetermined, the individual must by himself affirm through his own actions. The Marxist understands, and perhaps sympathizes with, St. Paul's dilemma that action often destroys the intention: "The good which I would I do not; but the evil which I would not, that I do," but he would insist that only in the complete identification of the individual with the historic process can the good which one would do actually come to pass. The apocalyptic faith of the early Christians did not hinder them from zealous proselytizing; indeed, Engels was keenly aware of the similarity between the early church and the socialist cause when he wrote:

The history of primitive Christianity presents remarkable coincidences with the modern workers' movement. Like the latter, Christianity was originally a movement of the oppressed; it first appeared as a religion of slaves and freedmen, of the poor, the outcasts, of the peoples subjected or dispersed by Rome. Both Christianity and and Socialism preach an approaching redemption from servitude and misery; Christianity assigns this redemption to a future life in Heaven after death; Socialism would attain it in this world by a transformation of society. Both are hunted and persecuted; their adherents outlawed, subjected to special legislation, represented, in the one case, as enemies of the human race, in the other as enemies of the nation, religion, the family, of the social order. And in spite of all such persecutions, both advance irresistibly. Three centuries after its beginning, Christianity is the recognized state religion of the Roman Empire, and in barely sixty years Socialism has conquered a place that renders its victory absolutely certain.

There is this striking difference, however: that Marxism is deeply humanistic, for it places man in the center of things, and attempts to discover what influences are brought to bear on him and how he is best able to work them in order to shape them to his own ends. It does not for one moment forget that the ultimate object of all its endeavor is the enthronement of man. It is this factor which distinguishes Marxism from fascism and other forms of totalitarianism and makes all attempts to equate the two specious and malicious, as Hans Kohn has so sharply pointed out. Nor is Marxism ever doubtful of the energy, creative power, and initiative of human beings even now under the most adverse circumstances. "I think," said Lenin in a conversation with Max Beer, "with Marx, that man makes history, but with the conditions and with the materials given by the corresponding period of civilization." "And," he went on to add (we must remember that he was speaking at a time when the Russian revolutionary movement was at its lowest ebb), "man can be a tremendous social force."

Nor was Trotsky any less deluded into mooning over the chimera of a communism which would automatically and painlessly eliminate human suffering in one, simple stroke for he writes: "As socialists we want a socialist world not because we have the conceit that men would thereby be more happy—those claims are best left to dictators—but because we feel the moral imperative in life itself to raise the human condition even if this should ultimately mean no more than that man's suffering has been lifted to a higher level, and human history has only progressed from melodrama, farce, and monstrosity, to tragedy itself." Thus for the first time in human history choice would not be determined by the accident of circumstances but would be free, dependent only on the moral bias of the individual. Trotsky's point of view takes us directly back to Aristotle's insistence on height or stature as an indispensable element in the tragic protagonist not because tragedy can happen only to gods, heroes, kings, princes, and aristocrats but because only such men are free from the trammels which enshackle ordinary men in the ordinary course of their lives: they alone possess the freedom to choose and the height from which to fall. Arthur Miller perversely reads the Aristotelian injunction in a literal sense as showing anti-democratic prejudice and as leading to the conclusion that the lives of ordinary men cannot be tragic. Yet I think Aristotle seems to be saying that the great mass of men are not free, that their lives are determined by the limitations imposed on them by their class, position, occupation, money—and especially the lack of money. Men who are enslaved by poverty, ignorance, disease, injustice, and discrimination are certainly not free, but men who think themselves free because they are in good health, have decent housing, and are secure financially and socially but who must grab and grub for a living, whose lives are ruled by cupidity, fear, and hatred are no more free than those they contemn, are in fact more enslaved because they are blind to their very chains. For most men, then, height and stature are denied them by their own circumstances; not having risen morally, they have no ethical distance in which to fall, and they cannot choose because they have no choice. Trotsky does not deny suffering; he knows it is the ultimate human condition; but he would free men so that they would no longer suffer in ignorance, sordidly, because they can do or know no better, but freely, and therefore nobly, because undegraded by circumstance or passion, they can freely choose—and therefore bear the responsibility for their choice.

Now the essential conservatism of Marxism stands revealed, for it derives its emotional and moral appeal from its link with a deep-rooted human experience, the desire to achieve a state of society in which men can be free from oppression, greed, and war, in which each is respected as an individual, and in which each works with and lives harmoniously with his fellow men, "from each according to his ability, to each according to his needs." It seems to me that this urge is basic to the Western mind, for it is the core of at least four of the fundamental philosophies which have molded it. In Greek thought, this urge takes the form of the golden age motif, the notion that at one time in the history of the race men either were or will be in a state of harmony with nature and with each other. For the most part, the Greeks tended to put this state in the past, and much of the nostalgic tone of Greek literature may be attributed to the belief that this state was irrevocably gone, and that as a consequence man's history is a record of steady and progressive degeneration. On the other hand, the Hebrew mind placed the condition of complete happiness at some future time, when a Messiah would come who would lead the peoples of the world into an era of universal brotherhood and good will. Instead of looking to the past, the Jews kept their attention fixed on the future, for they saw in history not a sorrowful tale of decay but rather the remorselessly moral working out of God's way toward a state of perfection. The Jews saw this state as coming here on earth; the Christians transferred it to the world beyond this one. Salvation was to be found in heaven, in the city of God; hence, the emphasis was on otherworldliness, on the rejection of the things of this world. But with the development of a kind of society which could produce more of the good things of life for more of the people, the appeal to otherworldliness lost its flavor and there was substituted for it the idea of progress which held forth the promise that though the present was good, the future would be better, and this is liberalism at its finest.

Now, what holds these ideas together is the fact that each rejects the world as it is, each refuses to trade the world as it ought to be for what it is now. Each, though in varying degrees, is critical of the present; each, again in varying degrees, attacks the present for its failure to realize the best potentialities in human nature. In short, each is basically an ethical attitude which dares condemn the existing order in all its manifestations; in this sense, then, the desire for the more perfect state is as eternally revolutionary as it is eternally conservative. Thus, Marxism is in the pattern of the most artistically inspiring traditions which have gone to make up the Western mind. It is at one and the same time a drama in itself and the source of drama. It sees mankind engaged in a great struggle in which the issue is no less than the future of the race itself. Though the victory of the world-to-be is assured by the ruthless march of history, salvation for the individual comes by his identification with and submergence into the forces which are bringing about the triumph. For from lowliness comes exaltation, from the struggle comes peace, from death comes life.

I have been encouraged to follow this line of analysis of Marxism by a number of recent studies which have taken it seriously as philosophy and as myth, and I need not add that to consider Marxism in this way does not mean that those who do so must by that very fact expose their covert membership in the Communist Party nor that in their heart of hearts they secretly and stealthily follow the twists and turns of Communist policy; indeed, the train of history of the Communist Party is now, by a lovely irony, in the same predicament as its once-proud arch enemy, the railroads of classic capitalism: both are regularly behind the times. After all, we do not accuse Harry A. Wolfson of Arianism; Barbelo-Gnosticism; Creationism; Docetism, and its other forms neo-Docetism and Docetic Monophysitism; Dyenergism; Dyophysitism; Ebionism, and its other forms Ebiotic Monophysitism and neo-Ebionism; Eutychianism; Gnosticism, and its variants in Apelles, Basilides, Carpocrates, Cerdo, Epiphanes, Justinius, Lucian, Marcion, Menander, the Nassenes, the Ophites, Perates, Ptolemy, Saturninus, the Settians, and Valentinus; Modalism; Monenergism; Monophysitism and its other forms Apollinarian, Eutychean, Severian, Ebionitic, Docetic, and

Sidereal; Monotheletism; Nestorianism; Polyphysitism; and Sabellianism just because he has written about them and has not publicly declared that he is not forty-three different kinds of heretic. The drama of Marx's thought and the dramatistics of dialectics have been perceived by Norman O. Brown in *Life against Death* (1959); in many passages in Kenneth Burke's work; by Mircea Eliade in *Cosmos and History* (1949), and in *The Sacred and the Profane* (1957); by Erich Fromm in *Marx's Concept of Man* (1961); by Wylie Sypher in an article, "Aesthetic of Revolution," in the Summer, 1948 issue of *The Kenyon Review;* and by Robert C. Tucker in *Philosophy and Myth in Karl Marx* (1961). The most recent, and by far the most perceptive study of Marx's work as imaginative literature is in Stanley Edgar Hyman's exciting *The Tangled Bank* (1962).

But if Marxism is capable of producing authentic tragedy, why is it that so far no tragedies in the Marxist pattern have been written? The answer to that question lies in the intellectual climate out of which tragedy appears. If we examine the ideological atmosphere from which both Athenian and Shakespearean tragedy emerge, we shall discover a number of arresting and significant similarities. Conversely, if we then contrast these conditions with other periods in which tragedy seemed ideologically possible yet did not appear, we shall have a double check on the reliability of my analysis of the intellectual conditions which govern the creation of tragedy.

Fifth-century Greece and Elizabethan England were both ages of faith: faith in the justice of the gods in the one case, faith in the justice of God in the other. Both were profoundly religious periods; the establishment of the nature of man's relation to God was for each a real and moving need. Yet at the same time both ages were equally sceptical. The winds of new doctrine swept through the streets of Athens and of London and left the old and conventional modes of religious thought bare to the probing of doubt. It was the function of the Greek dramatists to reconcile the old religion with its unpredictable and arbitrary gods, to the new philosophy with its belief in a rational world order. This they did by effecting a new synthesis which now included the concept of inevitable retribution; they thus provided a simultaneously religious and humanistic solution to the union of faith and reason. Similarly, Shakespeare took the medieval concept of an ordered and static society with its corresponding hierarchy of stratified values and infused it with the vitality of Renaissance humanism, the insistence on all men's goodness and freedom. He combined the need for order with the need for life. He thrust aside ritual but retained faith; at the same time, he avoided the extremes of Renaissance politics and science which enabled him to see through the shams of convention to the reality beneath; finally, there emerged the picture of free men responsible to a just order of things. In both the Athenian and Elizabethan climates of ideas, therefore, tragedy emerges when what is viable in the new is kept and what is extreme rejected, and when the fusion of the best in each is effected in a new synthesis on a plane ethically more satisfying than either.

Tragedy, therefore, cannot exist where there is no faith; at the same time, it cannot exist where there is no doubt; it can exist only in an atmosphere of sceptical faith. The genuineness of the faith of the Middle Ages cannot be questioned yet its greatest expression is appropriately called the *Divine Comedy*, not only for critical reasons, but for more fundamental aesthetic and ethical reasons as well. The Middle Ages could produce no tragedy because it had no doubt; it could not question to reaffirm, but was capable only of affirmation by reiteration. There can be no suspense over the outcome of man's fate if the issue is never in doubt and this is the weakness of the art of the Middle Ages and of the Hebrews as well. On the other hand, there can be no tragedy where there is no faith because doubt alone can only inquire but cannot affirm. From the eighteenth century to the present, no genuine tragedies have been written because no faith has been strong enough to permit the artist and his audience to base themselves on it. The eighteenth century concern with exact poetic justice vitiated the element of doubt; the romantic preoccupation with the rebellious hero endlessly and hopelessly at odds with society undermined the possibility of belief in either; and the nineteenth century's attempt to account for man's behavior, history, and future on the basis of forces over which he had no control and of which at best he had but an imperfect understanding left him without a fate at all, for in the Western tradition the concept of man's fate has always insisted on man's participation in and responsibility for the settling of that fate. It is no wonder that in our time recourse is so often had to the escapist fatalism of the East or to the fatalistic ritualism of the church. Tragedy, as I have said, can exist only in an age of sceptical faith.

Though Marxism has had the courage to advocate a faith for our times, its followers have not had the corresponding courage to question that faith. That, baldly, is the reason for the failure to produce tragedy in the Marxist pattern. What was once live and flexible is being systematically ossified by considerations which, though extraneous to the artistic way, have increasingly come to dominate it. The result has been the production of propaganda, effective enough for its purposes, to be sure, but not art. The genuine artist must be left free to understand his faith by questioning it, and no great artist has been unable to return to his faith, strengthened by his victory over his doubt. But he must be free to walk his path alone.

(1953, 1962)

Some Meanings of Myth

WORDS, NO LESS than clothes, are subject to the whims of fashion, and the fashionable word today is myth. The superior design of mythic originals is first displayed in the *recherché* quarterlies, good copies are soon after shown in the middlebrow monthlies and weeklies, and before long, mass-produced imitations flood the daily press. The mythic mode has succeeded in dislodging from their eminence in the vocabulary of criticism such high-style favorites as objective correlative, organic, and perceptive. But it has done so mainly at the expense of traditional religious conviction; one more example of the dying-reborn god motif can hardly be expected to claim the uniqueness which exclusive devotion demands. But if mythography has managed to shoulder aside religious sentiment, the impulse to religion has in its turn succeeded in filtering back into myth. The critic who would be condemned for his *naiveté* if he expressed himself in religious terms has only to substitute the vocabulary of myth to be praised for his sophistication. Once but an innocent and innocuous synonym for classical legend, the meaning of myth has been expanded to sweep the entire range of belief, from *Weltanschauung* down to outright lie. On opposite pages of the same issue of a recent *New York Times Book Review* I found these virtually antonymous uses of myth: "The man and the artist have become a living myth that is still growing," and a review of Wolfe's *Khrushchev and Stalin's Ghost* headed, "Destroyer of the Myth." Myth has even become a strong-point for conservatives and liberals to fight over: because some conservative writers have taken advantage of the aura of mystery which myth suggests, political liberals have promptly condemned it as mystical nonsense, and the two *Nations* bristle with examples of the word used in every pejorative sense, from the merely mistaken to the viciously perverse, a heritage of those far-off days of the thirties when Rosenberg could boast that the Nazi myth of the twentieth century had effected "a new standard of value by which all things are to be judged," forcing Mann to castigate this fascist fabrication as "cheap, filthy backstairs mythology."

Since mythography today is essentially a coalition of several independent disciplines—anthropology, archaeology, classics, criticism, folklore, the history of religion, philology, philosophy, and psychoanalysis—we confidently turn to them for professional guidance through the twists and turnings of the labyrinth of myth. But so many are our guides, so divergent their techniques, and so disparate their directions, that not only are we uncertain which alleys to follow, but we are no longer sure where the maze of myth is, if indeed there is one at all, and, as we stand perplexed and frustrated, our guides, Clotho-like, spin out their threads, implacably immobilizing us in a cocoon of tangled lines. How artless, after all, was Ariadne's way out of the Minotaur's den: a simple ball of string unwound, retraced,—and—freedom! Well, it is quite beyond my powers to separate each single string from the knotted skein, but I thought it would a little lighten our way through the dark wood if I managed to clear at least a narrow path by considering four approaches to myth which between them sum up and illustrate the many views of myth which now clamor for our adherence.

The first of these approaches to myth I call the poetic view of myth, and it seems to me to have been most cogently expressed in a recent book by George Whalley called *Poetic Process.* "A myth," he writes:

is a direct metaphysical statement beyond science. It embodies in an articulated structure of symbol or narrative a vision of reality. It is a condensed account of man's Being and attempts to represent reality with structural fidelity, to indicate at a single stroke the salient and fundamental relations which for a man constitute reality. A myth in this sense is primitive, communal, and religious in origin; and its only possible mode of expression is Poetic. Myth is not an obscure, oblique, or elaborate way of expressing reality—it is the *only* way. Myth has as its purpose, its source and end, revelation; myth is not make-believe but the most direct and positive assertion of belief that man can discover. Myth is an indispensable principle of unity in individual lives and in the life of society.

The poetic view of myth appears to derive from a number of assumptions: first, that there is a real and valid difference between the mythopoeic and scientific modes of thought; second, that the mythopoeic mode is anterior and superior to the scientific mode of thought; third, that myth is a link to and expression of archetypal experience; fourth, that it is a permanent manifestation of human consciousness independent of historical circumstances; fifth, that it is socially functional, but only in a spiritual or religious way; and finally, that the indelible and moving images of myth, and therefore of art, are built into the very constitution of the mind. In the poetic view of myth, then, it is a belief beyond belief, a vision of reality beyond reality, and speaks in an utterance beyond language.

These assumptions stem directly from the Jungian concept of the archetype, from Cassirer's exposition of the categories of thought of the mythopoeic mind, and from Malinowski's functional view of myth, taken, however, in a Pickwickian sense; ultimately, they originate in the myth speculation of German romanticism and in Christian mysticism. But even

Jung has had increasing difficulties with his concept of the archetype; in his attempt to explain the puzzling Trickster figure which Radin has recently portrayed from the mythology of the Winnebago, he is forced to speak of successive stages of the development of consciousness and to admit that the therapeutic savior element in Trickster is a late accretion. But then, can archetypes undergo historical development and differentiation, and, if they can change so radically in meaning, why are they archetypes to begin with? Indeed, one may very well ask, how many archetypes does, or should, the Jungian pantheon contain? All this accomplishes is to add the difficulties of psychoanalytical euhemerism to the difficulties of historical euhemerism without clarifying either. Finally, cannot Trickster be accounted for equally as well as a later and debased, rather than an earlier and pristine, version of the dying-reborn god of primitive ritual? Given the date of transmission and the intellectual level of the Winnebago, is Trickster actually as archaic as Radin insists? Comparison of Trickster with the Bearson-Beowulf hypothesis of Panzer and with the Salmoxis-Sisyphus-Odysseus line projected by Carpenter suggests to me a ritual rather than an archetypal origin of the comic spirit in terms of the Impostor-Antagonist double first developed by Cornford. This is not to say that the psychoanalytic and the ritual mythogonies are necessarily incompatible with each other, but only that at the present moment at least their connections are not yet tightly fitted together. Indeed, I regret the missed opportunity afforded by the Trickster myth for relating conclusively the observed double personality of psychopathology, the historical Impostor-Antagonist double of Greek drama, and the shadow figure of Jungian theory.

Again the poetic view of myth usually ends up by asserting that Christianity alone is the only permanently valid myth. Whalley goes to some length to dispose of Greek myth in order to give primacy to Christianity in which he finds a ". . . luminous constellation of primordial symbols combined

with a fresh myth of inexhaustible vitality." While all exponents of the poetic view of myth agree that it is revelation,
they disagree, unfortunately, as to what it is a revelation of: to
Arthur Machen it was orthodox Roman Catholicism; to G.
Wilson Knight, orthodox Anglicanism; to Alan Watts, the
philosophia perennis, with a larger admixture of Christianity
than of Hinduism; to Coomaraswamy, the *philosophia perennis* again, but this time with more Hinduism than Christianity;
to Philip Wheelwright, in the proper liberal spirit, all together equally; he says: "Each embodies an archetypal idea—
a set of depth-meanings of perduring significance within a
widely shared perspective, and transcending the limits of what
can be said via ordinary literal speech." The Christianizers of
myth do no more than repeat in new form the old errors of
the allegorization of myth, and while they are certainly
entitled to listen for the "message from heaven," as Watts
calls myth, they do mythography no service by confusing it
with theology.

In the Introduction to *The Greek Myths,* Robert Graves
soberly informs us that his method has been ". . . to assemble
in harmonious narrative all the scattered elements of each
myth, supported by little-known variants which may help
determine the meaning, and to answer all the questions that
arise in anthropological terms." But this admirable caution
is rudely thrown to the winds by his pugnacious practice
which, with uncritical gusto, combines several antithetical
methods of myth interpretation. To begin with, he defines
myth as ". . . the reduction to narrative shorthand of ritual
mime performed on public festivals, and in many cases
recorded on temple walls, vases, seals, bowls, mirrors, chests,
shields, and the like." At first glance, this appears to be in
the Harrison-Murray-Cornford ritual view, but Graves im-
petuously converts it into a monomyth of his own devising:
"The antique story," as he calls it in *The White Goddess,*
"which falls into thirteen chapters and an epilogue, of the
birth, death, and resurrection of the God of the Waxing Year;

the central chapters concern the God's losing battle with the God of the Waning Year for love of the capricious and all-powerful Goddess, their mother, bride, and layer-out." We have already gone no little distance from the records on temple walls and the like, not to mention anthropology.

But Graves presses on: he rewrites the history of poetry in terms of the opposition between the mythopoeic and the scientific modes of thought: "My thesis," he declares in *The White Goddess*, "is that the language of poetic myth anciently current in the Mediterranean and Northern Europe was a magical language bound up with popular religious ceremonies in honour of the Moon-Goddess, or Muse, some of them dating from the Old Stone Age, and that this remains the language of true poetry. The language was tampered with in late Minoan times when invaders from Central Asia began to substitute patrilinear for matrilinear institutions and remodel or falsify the myths to justify social changes. Then came the early Greek philosophers who were strongly opposed to magical poetry as threatening their new religion of logic, and under their influence a rational poetic language (now called the Classical) was elaborated in honor of their patron Apollo and imposed on the world as the last word in spiritual illumination." But even as we look on in wonder, Graves' wildly-beating pinions are suddenly transformed into plodding *weldschoen:* "A large part of Greek myth," he declares in *The Greek Myths,* "is politico-religious history," and a large part of *The Greek Myths* is devoted to out-and-out euhemerism. Yet, as Hyman has argued in defense of the ritual view, ". . . myths are never the record of historical events or people; they never originate as scientific or aetiological explanations of nature, but freed from their ritual origins they may be so used." Thus, everything which Hyman said against Thompson and everything which Thompson said against Hyman and everything which I said against both in recent pages of *The Journal of American Folklore* may be said against Graves.

Frazer seems to have been thinking as much of himself as of

Apollodorus when he wrote of the author of the *Library:* "He was neither a philosopher nor a rhetorician, and therefore lay under no temptation either to recast his materials under the influence of theory or to embellish them for the sake of literary effect." Fortified by Apollodorus' sturdy common sense, Frazer staunchly resisted the vice he professed to find in Euhemerus, ". . . the vice inherent in all systems which would explain the infinite multiplicity and diversity of phenomena by a single simple principle, as if a single clue, like Ariadne's thread, could guide us to the heart of this labyrinthine universe" of myth. Nor was Frazer's suspicion of generalization the expression of years of gradual and painful disillusionment, for more than thirty years before the edition of the *Library,* virtually on the threshold of *The Golden Bough,* he had written: "In no branch of learning, perhaps, has this proneness to an attractive and fallacious simplicity wrought more havoc than in the investigation of the early history of mankind; in particular, the excesses to which it has been carried have done much to discredit the study of mythology and primitive religion. Students of these subjects have been far too ready to pounce on any theory which adequately explains some of the facts, and forthwith to stretch it so as to cover them all; and when the theory, thus unduly strained, has broken, as was to be expected, in their unskillful hands, they have pettishly thrown it aside in disgust instead of restricting it, as they should have done from the outset, to the particular class of facts to which it is really applicable." And to the "peaceful limbo of forgotten absurdities," he cheerfully consigned the solar myth theory, the theories of totemism, magic, and taboo, the rosy Dawn, Noah's ark, Max Müller, Jacob Bryant, and all.

Yet, despite his disclaimers, Frazer did allow himself the luxury of an occasional generalization, and, in the introduction to the *Library,* he actually defined myth; it is a characteristic definition, astringent, sceptical, and, from the poetic view of myth, perverse. "By myths," he writes, "I understand

mistaken explanations of phenomena, whether of human life
or of external nature. Such explanations originate in that
instinctive curiosity concerning the causes of things which at
a more advanced stage of knowledge seeks satisfaction in
philosophy and science, but being founded on ignorance and
misapprehension they are always false, for were they true, they
would cease to be myths." The subjects of myths are as
numerous as the questions which men can raise: the origin
of the world and of man, the motions of the heavenly bodies,
the recurrence of the seasons, the invention of the useful arts,
the beginnings of society—"in short," as he says, "the range
of myths is as wide as the world, being coextensive with the
curiosity and ignorance of man." And in a footnote to this
definition, he casually blows up the school which both its sup-
porters and opponents have honored by regarding him as
founder and first head: "By a curious limitation of view," he
observes "some modern writers would restrict the scope of
myths to ritual, as if nothing but ritual were fitted to set men
wondering and meditating on the causes of things. No doubt
some myths have been devised to explain rites of which the
true origin was forgotten; but the number of such myths is
small, probably almost infinitesimally small, by comparison
with myths which deal with other subjects and have had
another origin." And as though this were not enough, he
actually accuses the Cambridge school of ignorance of the
primary materials of myth study: "It might have been thought
that merely to open such familiar collections of myths as the
Theogony of Hesiod, the *Library* of Apollodorus, or the
Metamorphoses of Ovid, would have sufficed to dissipate so
erroneous a conception; for how small is the attention paid
to ritual in these works!" He fires his parting shot more in sorrow than in anger: "The zealous student of myth and ritual,
more intent on explaining them than on enjoying the lore of
the people, is too apt to invade the garden of romance and
with a sweep of his scythe to lay the flowers of fancy in the
dust. He needs to be reminded occasionally that we must not

look for a myth or a rite behind every tale, like a bull behind every hedge or a canker in every rose." Having thus shaken Harrison, Murray, and Cornford from his coat-tails, he then repays Freud's generous praise of his work with this: "The utilitarian creed is good and true only on condition that we interpret utility in a large and liberal sense, and do not restrict it to the bare satisfaction of bodily instincts on which ultimately depends the continuance both of the individual and of the species." One cannot help wondering why, if *The Golden Bough* is the "melancholy record of human error and folly," as he himself described it, he kept at it so doggedly, decade after decade, pen in one hand, nose in the other, the very Gibbon of anthropology.

Finally, there is the view of myth which transfers to the age of mythopoeic thought (at once the world of pre-historic, primitive, folk, and contemporary, non-Western speculation) the values and virtues of the golden age and of the noble savage. To put it crudely in this way is of course to do a disservice to its most sophisticated and eloquent exponent, Mircea Eliade, who does indeed devote a chapter in *Myths, Dreams and Mysteries* to an analysis of the idea of the noble savage in modern, Western thought but who, in his characteristic way, manages to reverse and convert the implied unfavorable verdict into a criterion for his own "moral, political and social disquisitions." Instead of the invention of the "good savage," he says, we ". . . really ought to speak of the mythicised memory of his exemplary Image," for, as he argues, ". . . the savage took pains not to forget what had come to pass *in illo tempore.*" And it is this very "return to the past," this *regressus ad originem,* which is precisely what the work-object obsessed Western world has forgotten and has thereby been betrayed into falling victim to history, time, and death, and their attendant anxieties. Thus there arises in Eliade's work the ever-present contrast between the sturdy, solid virtues of the men of the traditional civilizations, and in our own time especially those of the non-Western world, and India in particular, men who, though, or rather because, they were and are primitive (in its meliorative sense) believed without doubt and without the corrosion of the intellect in a simultaneously consoling and consistent, a well-consolidated system, as Eliade calls it, into which both man and the cosmos fitted easily and naturally. In contrast to this picture of simple, natural man at ease in his cosmic surroundings is modern man, caught up in the terror of history, uncreative and unfree. Indeed, Eliade goes so far as to put in the mouth of primitive man an attack on modern man and a defense of his own way of belief in *Cosmos and History;* I should add that he uses the same tactic of attacking modern, Western man by using his own invented Indian advocate of Yoga, Buddhism, and Vedanta in *Myths, Dreams and Mysteries;* this graceful eighteenth-century gambit is, however, in deadly earnest here. Eliade writes in *Cosmos and History:*

It is becoming more and more doubtful, he might say, if modern man can make history. On the contrary, the more modern he becomes—that is, without defenses against the terrors of history—the less chance he has of himself making history. . . . Modern man's boasted freedom to make history is illusory for nearly the whole of the human race. At most, man is left free to choose between two positions: (1) to oppose the history that is being made by the very small minority (and, in this case, he is free to choose between suicide and deportation); (2) to take refuge in subhuman existence or in flight. . . . On the contrary, the man of the archaic civilizations can be proud of his mode of existence, which allows him to be free and create. He is free to be no longer what he was, free to annul his own history through periodic abolition of time and collective regeneration. . . . Furthermore, archaic man certainly has the right to consider himself more creative than modern man, who sees himself as creative only in respect to history. . . . Oriental techniques attempt above all to annul or transcend the human condition.

What, then, does Eliade leave us? The cat out of the bag: "Basically, the horizon of archetypes and repetition cannot be transcended with impunity unless we accept a philosophy of freedom that does not exclude God." But note the negative way in which the formulation is put, very much like Othello's "I do not think but Desdemona's honest," which deserves Iago's sanctimonious "Long live she so! and long live you to think so!" Eliade continues: "In fact, it is only by presupposing the existence of God that modern man conquers, on the one hand, freedom (which grants him autonomy in a universe governed by laws or, in other words, the 'inauguration' of a mode of being that is new and unique in the universe) and, on the other hand, the certainty that historical tragedies have a transhistorical meaning, even if that meaning is not always visible for humanity in its present condition." And he shakily concludes: "Any other situation of modern man leads, in the end, to despair," just as Othello replies doubtfully to Iago: "And yet, how nature erring from itself . . ." Iago: "Ay, there's the point. . . ." And there indeed is the point: the horrible alternative, if not Christianity, what else? and the burden of proof is suddenly thrust upon our unsuspecting shoulders.

For myself, I see no reason for believing that the primitive mentality was and is superior to the modern mentality, either in the mode of operation or in the efficacy of its beliefs; in this respect, at least, I remain a simple follower of Frazer, an old-fashioned son who feels no need to kill his father. I believe that primitive man was and is (the confusing tense sequence is the consequence of Eliade's insistence that the primitive both was once in the pre-historic past and is now in the non-Western world) confronted with the same problem of attempting to create a tolerable existence in an essentially indifferent universe as we are and he succeeded to some degree through the invention of the myth and ritual pattern. I say to some degree only, because there is evidence enough that his techniques did not always work nor did he pay a small price in human suffering for their enactment; indeed, I am not so sure but that the price of Indian philosophy is

Indian poverty. But now that it is no longer possible to admire the picture of the happy medieval peasant content with the devoted protection of his lord and of his priest, Eliade seems to me to be overlaying it with the bright colors of the happy primitive man well adjusted to his cosmic environment. But the history of myth has been the history of the demythologizing of myth, and any attempts to revive myth as a viable organ of belief, in the same sense in which primitive man believed it, from even the best of motives, seem to me doomed to failure. For we must remember that belief in myth is not a personal attainment alone; it is more, much more so, a social phenomenon and depends for its efficacy on group acceptance and adherence; a private myth, however admirably expressed in whatever form, is therefore an ultimate, irreconcilable contradiction. All of us, believers in gods, myths, and formulae alike, must, in the long run, face up to the fact that despite our blandishments, bribes, and blusters, the indifferent universe, whatever we may read into it for whatever compelling reasons of our own, remains indifferent.

Well, in the present state of myth study, Frazer's scepticism is a useful antiseptic to have at hand, but if, as he warns us, ". . . it is a mistake to search for a mythical or magical significance in every story which our rude forefathers have bequeathed us by word of mouth" and ". . . an error to interpret in the same sad and serious way every carving with which they decorated the walls of their caverns," what, then, is left of mythography? Still, we must face the unpleasant fact that no one theory of myth is as yet capable of unifying the multiplicity and diversity of phenomena which mythography must take into account. Stubborn problems of method and approach insistently confront us. If the mythographer accepts from psychoanalysis the concept of the archetype, he must reconcile the primordial paradigm with the almost endless variations of form which folklore has accumulated. If the structure of early religion and art, and indeed of all early thought and expression, is derived from the same ritual pattern, as the Cambridge school holds, how can the mythographer square this explanation of myth-inception with the diversity of historical, real origins postulated by euhemerism? Can the ritual practices of peoples as different in time, place, and custom as those of Africa, Oceania, America, and the ancient Near East be traced back to an *ur*-ritual; does the available archaeological evidence substantiate the transmission of a single ritual form, or does it rather suggest a series of indigenous inceptions growing out of similar but separate social circumstances? Is myth but a definable, historical step in the intellectual ascent of man, or is it rather a universal expression of human consciousness; is it, in other words, the transient vocabulary of the savage, as Frazer rather surprisingly insisted, or is it the eternal language of the dreamer and the poet, as Freud and Jung, each in his own way, believed? Are the images of myth inseparable from the nature of the mind itself, ever changing in mode of expression yet ineradicable in structure and significance, or are the similarities of motif in myth after myth merely accidental, essentially unrelated, as the folklorists would appear to argue?

These, then, are the primary questions which have to be answered. Yet, even if satisfactory answers can be given them, there remain the equally obstinate problems posed by the application of the myth and ritual approach to literature itself. Basically, this approach consists in taking the myth and ritual pattern as fundamental and anterior to the form or work of art being considered, irrespective of its chronological, national, or social origins, and passing the form or work over the pattern, as tracings over the original drawing, in order to reveal the changes, modifications, and alterations made in the pattern by the subsequent form or work. The pattern itself being first and fixed, departures from it in the form or work immediately appear on inspection and thereby reveal variation, and it is these variations from the original pattern which enable the critic to define with a nice precision the uniqueness of the form or work with which he is concerned. We have, in short, a critical technique for dealing with literature very much like the iconological method of the art historian which has in recent years yielded up such remarkable results both in art history and in art criticism.

But when we begin to apply the method in detail, to specific forms or works, we come face to face with very disturbing methodological problems. These, derived from a study I have recently made of current applications of the method to Shakespeare's plays, may be listed as follows. One, there is no agreement as to what the myth and ritual pattern actually is. As a matter of fact, no myth and ritual pattern as such exists or ever existed in any real sense; it is a modern, scholarly reconstruction of diverse materials drawn from divergent sources, and no two experts agree as to its exact constitution. Two, there is no agreement as to the aesthetic and ethical effects of the pattern on works of literature; using the same pattern, different critics come up with antithetical conclusions as to its effect on the same work. Thus, as I have been confused to note, to one group of critics the Shakespeare of the last plays is a kind of Christian Olympian, a kind of Sophocles and Goethe in one; to another group, he is a tired, disillusioned old man, playing technical tricks for his own cynical amusement; yet both groups profess to follow the same method. Three, there is no satisfactory way of explaining how the pattern enters into the work of art. Are there demonstrable historical or psychological steps involved; is the use of the pattern a conscious, deliberate aesthetic decision of the artist himself? Or is myth inherent in the work of art, and, if so, how is one to be distinguished from the other? If the artist reshapes the pattern for his own purposes, and I know of no instance where a sophisticated work of art follows the myth and ritual pattern point by point, what is the need of the pattern to start with? Finally, four, what is the critical validity of a method which in effect sets up a pattern derived from sources outside the texts and then judges their success or failure in terms of their approach to or distance from conformity to that pattern?

So many and so difficult, then, are the problems which the myth and ritual approach faces, yet it continues to fascinate the critic. And no wonder: for, as Gilbert Murray long ago pointed out, it puts the work of art in that "strange, unanalyzed vibration below the surface," in that ". . . undercurrent of desires and fears and passions, long slumbering yet eternally familiar, which have for thousands of years lain near the root of our most intimate emotions and been wrought into the fabric of our most magical dramas." This, I submit, is no small accomplishment but to speak of it as a method is, I think, to assume what has still to be determined: we do not yet have a fully articulated and integrated theoretical structure. If I may venture a homely image: myth study at present has not so much the purity and integrity of an homogeneous regional cooking as it has the syncretistic flavor of international *cuisine:* a dash of Cassirer, a dollop of Freud, a grain of Frazer, a minim of Graves, a pinch of Harrison, a smidgeon of Jung, a taste of Thompson, all intriguing flavors in themselves, excellently cooked, but, still and all, not really a style.

(1959)

Myth, Method, and Shakespeare

Read at the English Institute, New York, September, 1958.

I WANT IT SPREAD on the record that when the subject of Shakespeare's sources was first proposed to me I fell into a sadness, then into a fast, thence to a watch, thence into a weakness, thence to a lightness, and, by this declension, into the madness whereon now I rave, for who else but a man bereft of his reason would undertake such an assignment? That my aversion to Bedlam is not shared by others, however, the annual bibliographies amply attest to, and now, with the simultaneous publication of Bullough's and Muir's multi-volumed anthologies of Shakespeare's analogues and sources, I feel as though I were in the cabinet of Dr. Caligari where every book printed before and up to the very last moment when Shakespeare put the last period to the last line of the last manuscript he ever wrote has been brought forward as a possible source, and, if we go on to define source somewhat loosely as intellectual milieu, we can find mentioned as his sources books published even after his death. My last hope of sanity was the

typescript of an article which my good friend Fred Johnson
said he was sending me expressly to aid me in my labors; you
may well imagine with what eagerness I read it; you may well
imagine, too, my despair when I realized that the paper was a
classic demonstration of the futility of source hunting. As the
most eminent practicing authority on the proverb today, Comrade Khrushchev, would say: a friendly Tartar is worse than
an angry bear.

In the course of preparing these remarks, I sincerely tried
to make as fair a sampling—for no man could read them all—
of books and articles on Shakespeare's sources as I could, and
now generalizing from my admittedly unscientific procedure,
I would say that they can be pretty much reduced to two
kinds, though both follow the same methodological techniques, and that they are by and large directed toward three
different ends, whose literary value is almost in inverse proportion to the numbers of studies devoted to them. I should like
to say a few words about each of these procedures and purposes
as I have found them in current practice and then go on to
propose what, in my presumption, I think source study might
well be and what this can accomplish.

As I read through my list of source studies, I was soon struck
by how methodologically unaware so many appeared to be.
That is, it was assumed at the outset that the juxtaposition of
an analogue or source to a passage in Shakespeare was inherently meaningful, and that, further, the more sources and
analogues which could be adduced, the more Shakespeare was
thereby somehow understood. The analogy by which the
source hunters seemed to operate was to the procedure for
solving a jig-saw puzzle: you have a number of separate pieces
laid out before you; you know that once they are fitted together they will constitute the picture; *ergo,* you fit them
together, and you have your picture. The flaw in the analogy
is, of course, that when you have fitted together all the pieces
of the puzzle, the jig-saw puzzle picture remains a jig-saw
puzzle picture, and not a work of art. The method makes

additional assumptions: first, that the writer draws his ideas and images from books alone. Lowes rather revealed the source hunter's frame of mind when he declared of Chaucer: "I have trailed him, as I have trailed Coleridge, into almost every section of eight floors of a great library," as though Chaucer, too, had spent his days and nights in the Widener and had, as a kind of sly challenge to the future, cunningly concealed throughout those same eight floors of books the clues for others to track down, nor is this attitude limited to literary historians, for Gombrich has said: "All pictures owe much more to other pictures than they do to nature." Another assumption is that all writers read as much or as intensively as we are supposed to do, as though Shakespeare was, in fact, the library cormorant that Coleridge said he was. But how much time for source hunting did Shakespeare himself have during the years 1600-02, for example, besides writing *Twelfth Night, Hamlet, Troilus and Cressida,* and *All's Well 'That Ends Well;* taking an active part in the management of his company, and, I suspect, in the production of his plays, perhaps even acting in them; enjoying the Elizabethan equivalent of TV, engaging in lawsuits; going home to Stratford; brooding over dark ladies; and listening to the university wits show off *their* small Latin and less Greek. To avoid the charge of hitting below the belt, I refrain from adding that he has been supposed to be at this very same time a sailor, a lawyer, a soldier, a physician, an astrologer, an herbalist, a falconer, and the front or rear man of a literary cabal. Finally, and much more serious, a source study proceeds by a kind of simple bookkeeping in which the debit column of poetry, so to speak, is made to total up to and equal the credit column of sources, the balance of literary creation being struck by means of a naive, additive associationism.

I do not mean by this to derogate all source study; rather, I hope only to make a little clearing, a methodological oasis, in the thicket—jungle or desert would be too ungracious a word—of scholarship. I call the two kinds of source study I referred to before the immediate and the proximate. The first, much more limited in its ambitions than the other, seeks the direct, verifiable echo of the source in the lines of the poet; it pins down the text to a text; but, because it keeps its eyes so closely glued to the heels of the writer, it does not actually see where he is going or what is ahead of him, so that when he nimbly jumps over a stone in his path, it clumsily stubs its toe, or, less fancifully, the single, immediate source turns out to be a commonplace. Moreover, it reduces the writer's role to that of an operator of an adding machine: he punches the keys of his sources, pulls down the lever of his imagination, tears off the tape, and hands you the poem. Though this technique may to some extent elucidate the work of academic authors who may deliberately strew their lines with learned allusions, images, and symbols which are meant to be picked up by the alert and equally academic reader, it has not been as rewarding in the case of popular authors such as Shakespeare whose reading, while small in scope and conventional in choice, was nevertheless consciously and boldly manipulated. Moreover, when an author has truly digested his sources, his own restatement of them is usually so full and so clear that recalling them is redundant, if not downright impolite. Thus, to take a simple example, when Horatio adjures the Ghost, he cites three explicit reasons why Ghosts become revenants: to ease their pain, to warn the state, and—rather anticlimactically I have always thought—to reveal where their ill-gotten gains have been buried. I must confess that I do not see why it is necessary to annotate this passage with learned references to medieval and Renaissance ghost-lore for the text explains itself, and, as a matter of fact, explains itself much more clearly and succinctly than a number of notes on the passage I have seen which not only managed to obscure its sense but confused it by misreading. Or take this comment on lines 1077-78 of Book IX of *Paradise Lost:* "And in our faces evident the signs of foul concupiscence; whence evil store;": *"concupiscence:* Wholly selfish sexual desire. To understand the exact effects of the fall on the sexual relations of Adam and Eve, the reader needs a knowledge of medieval scholastic ideas of sin and virtue. In some systems (Bonaventura), love and its nature is all-important; in Aquinas, intellect and control by reason is necessary. In still others (Scotus), the will is made dominant. Milton implies that the fall caused Adam and Eve to lose their sense of balance." And, I suppose, scholars their sense of proportion. For if it needs a course in scholasticism to make these lines come alive, then Milton has failed as a poet, but one has only to read them to experience the revulsion to the change in Adam and Eve which Milton is conveying, to acknowledge that Milton succeeds here, not as a scholastic, which is, after all, not his business, but as a poet, which is his business and which is what does count. I am not arguing that we must read the poem *qua* poem, whatever that may mean, but that identification of the source will not by that act make a poor poem good, nor a good poem better. Moreover, while source study may be applied at will, and has, it is inherently incapable of discrimination; that is, it can tell us only that two poems may be derived from the same source but it cannot tell us on the basis of that information alone, and that is the only information it may legitimately deal with methodologically, why one poem is better than the other; Milton, even more than Shakespeare, has been a victim of this fallacy. I might also add that source study cannot make a deaf ear hear.

Dissatisfaction with the single source technique has led to multiple source study in which a writer is now placed in his milieu, or intellectual environment, or tradition, or convention, or any other suitable synonym. Where before he was stretched out on the dissecting table and his bones one by one stripped and laid bare, now, like the Icarus of Breughel's painting, he is indifferently shunted into a corner of the vast canvas of his tradition; he is, in fact, lost in his own picture. By the time one has read all the comic plays, revenge plays, morality plays, history plays, political plays, satire plays, romance plays, and other miscellaneous forms and types, which preceded Shakespeare and which established the conventions within which he had presumably to write, one can only wonder that he had anything left to write at all; if one adds to this list of genres his reading sources in history, psychology, scholasticism, political science, sermons, theology, neo-Platonism, the literature of the occult, travel books, popular science, novel, essay, and the like, it is obvious that if he did any writing at all, he wrote not with a pen but with a scissors. And all this in the case of an author who is presumed not to have read very much to start with; in the case of a poet as learned as Milton, the sky, not surprisingly, is the limit. Allowing both for my amateur Milton scholarship and for the inadequacies of my arithmetic, I have counted from my far from complete notes on recent scholarship devoted to *Paradise Lost* some 2,000 authors from whom Milton is supposed to have derived in one way or another, or 167 authors per book, or one new author for each 5 lines, or .19 authors per line. Of course, this is an absurd *reductio,* but it does point up the lack both of proportion and of direction of source studies which in numbers and panoply are deployed and conducted like armies—or academic administrations. It seems to me closer to the truth of things to say that while a man shares in the environment of his contemporaries, he lives in the milieu of his own choosing or making, so that it may be laid down almost as a rule that by the time an author goes to a source he no longer needs it; he is rather confirming what he has already thought and felt, else he would not recognize the significance of the source to him. Let me put the problem of defining milieu in another way. Here we are a group united, it would appear, by many common bonds: we are intellectuals in a world indifferent to us, academics in a creative world which scorns us, teachers of English in an academic world suspicious of us, and indeed, the special kind of teachers of English who attend the English Institute; we share a common language and may even miraculously share common critical concepts, though by your smiling you seem to say no. Yet, to narrow down the difference even more exactly and to speak only of our colleagues who live in this one city, must we not ask, are the intellectual environments of Columbia, Fordham, New York University, and City College, to mention no others, all the same? I will go further: I share with a colleague the same office, we both teach English literature, in fact, we both specialize in the Renaissance, we both oppose the administration as a matter of principle, we even get pretty much the same salaries and have identical opinions about them, but we do not read the same books and magazines, we approach our subject in quite different ways, we do not teach alike, we are not moved by the same causes, the issues of the day which upset me do not bother him, he lives in a paid up colonial and I in a heavily mortgaged contemporary house (I have never heard of any other kind). To set us, so close to each other and yet so far apart, in the same general intellectual milieu would be undiscriminating, imprecise, and even misleading. How much more callous is it, then, to toss an author pell-mell into the broad ocean of western culture—for that, after all, is what Milton's 2,000 authors amount to—and announce triumphantly that we have placed him in his milieu. Rather limbo, I would say, than milieu.

Examined from this point of view, source studies may be diagnosed as suffering from the same methodological malady as do imagery studies, an ailment which, aping my betters, I presume to name the tautological fallacy. In English this means making the assumption that if you walk around in a circle and come out at your starting point, you think you have arrived somewhere else. So, for example, a recent article declares with an air of discovery and surprise that after the author had compiled a list of the images used in *Macbeth* he found them to be centered around night, hate, murder, death, and bloody knives. To which one can only say that had they been centered around light, love, marriage, life, and cakes and ale, they would have been *Twelfth Night*. For how else can a poet recreate an experience except by the manifestation of the imagery derived from and/or associated with it, imagery which is either traditionally appropriate to it or freshly extracted from it, but in either case, exquisitely and nicely apposite to it? The addition of all the images in a poem, plus the addition of all the sources of all the images, plus even the addition of the symbols, difficult and praiseworthy a feat as this may be, is not yet the poem itself. What remains to be asked, and it is this portion which seems to me by far the larger and more significant part left, is, to what ends are the sources, images, and symbols being put, and in what ways? Thus, Miss Raine's brilliant demonstration of the traditional content of Blake's seemingly esoteric symbols in "The Sea of Time and Space" fails of entire conviction because it does not raise the more searching question of Blake's particular use of them; that is, while Blake may very well want us to associate the symbol with its traditional meaning, is he not at the same time even more concerned that we should be aware that he is using it unconventionally, and so deliberately startling us into a fuller and fresher consciousness of the unique, that is, the Blakeian, vision he is offering? In her last paragraph, Miss Raine does come up against this very problem, for she recalls that when she first saw the tempera painting from Arlington Court, it reminded her of "Joyce's *Finnegan's Wake,* through the common theme of a cycle of descent and return, from sea to cloud, and river to sea." "Yeats' use of river and sea symbolism"—she goes on to add —"might equally have come to mind, though the cycle is peculiarly Joyce's theme. The similarities are not accidental; for these three great artists in myth are all scrupulously exact in their use of traditional symbols, though each has a different statement to make, within these terms." The qualification is, of course, the heart of the problem, else how are we to distinguish among them, or, for that matter, among the many other writers who have used the same symbols and the same sources, and indeed the sources themselves from the works which drew upon them? Nor does Miss Raine's discovery of Blake's source in Porphyry altogether allay the feeling, which it is the purpose of her paper to dispel, that ". . . some critics have thought this painting too personal to be an illustration of any allegory but Blake's own." The employment of myth, even with the greatest faith and sincerity on the part of the poet who is using it, does remain personal if the circumstances of belief in myth have changed; it takes at least two to make myth viable. Coleridge, who certainly should have known, said:

Imagery (even taken from nature, much more when transplanted from books, as travels, voyages, and works of natural history); affecting incidents; just thoughts; interesting personal or domestic feelings; and with these the art of their combination or intertexture in the form of a poem; may all (like the color on the marble peach) by incessant effort be acquired as a trade, by a man of talents and much reading, who as I once before observed, has mistaken an intense desire of poetic reputation for a natural poetic genius; the love of the arbitrary end for the possession of the peculiar means. But the sense of musical delight, with the power of producing it, is a gift of the imagination; and this together with the power of reducing multitude into unity of effect, and modifying a series of thoughts by some one predominant thought or feeling, may be cultivated and improved, but can never be learned.

In effect, this has been the procedure followed by the best source studies; reading Coleridge's warning recalled to my mind Miss Tuve's most sensible opening remarks in her *Images and Themes in Five Poems by Milton* or Whittaker's *Shakespeare's Use of Learning;* above all, I heard again Panofsky's lecturing on Durer's "Melancolia" in the course of which the seemingly arbitrary conglomeration of apparently pointless and random symbols was elucidated and their connections established; and as I understood, so was I moved; those dead bones do live.

Up to now I have been suggesting that if source studies have a methodological justification, this resides not so much in their being an end in themselves but in the uses to which they can be put. It is worth knowing that Shakespeare read North's translation of Plutarch; it is more valuable to know why he was interested in Plutarch; but it is most revealing to know what he did with his reading, and this same scale of values may be applied equally as well from Spenser's dependence on the medieval and Renaissance encyclopedists, to Milton's use of the hexameral tradition, to Coleridge's reading for *The Ancient Mariner,* to the romantics' wandering along the shores of darkness, to Yeats' dalliance with myth, to Auden's flirtation with Marxism, and to Eliot's courtship of Christianity. The things an author passes over in his sources, the things he takes from them, the things he changes, and to what extent and in what directions—all these together constitute a series of road signs pointing us toward his creative purposes. And, at the same time, they provide a kind of stake or mark against which his skill and originality may to some fair degree be measured. The source being fixed, variations from it can be plotted, described, and even evaluated; the more source studies establish that Shakespeare used conventional sources, the more the study of the use of the sources establishes his unconventional manipulation of them: the specifically Shakespearean emerges from the generally conventional. It is the awareness of this crucial distinction which distinguishes Whittaker from, say, Baldwin; Tuve from McColley; Bush from Starnes and Talbert; it is the sign of the Warburg school from Warburg himself through Saxl, Panofsky, Yates, Gombrich, and Wittkower.

But the recognition of this difference answers only one of my questions, to what end are the sources being put; the other, in what ways, has been much neglected, though it appears to me even more fruitful in that it can put us on the road leading directly into the operations of the poet's mind. And even when the question has been raised, as in Lowes' *The*

Road to Xanadu, the answers have been disappointing because we do not have a technique sophisticated enough to deal with the complexities of the process involved, that is, of course, the creative process itself. Lowes contents himself either with a naive associationism or, when that fails him, with appeals to the mystery of the creative mind, and, to a large degree, these two explanations, if explanations they can be called, are resorted to by students of Shakespeare's adaptation of his sources and of his imagery; even Armstrong, whose analysis of Shakespeare's imagery seems to me of greater insight than either Spurgeon's or Clemens', suffers from the inability to demarcate description from etiology. To have recourse to the hidden springs, to the mystery of creation, is to take refuge in the great analogy, to use Nahm's phrase, of aesthetics: just as God is the creator in his greater sphere, so is the artist in his lesser, but the mode of operation is in each case the same; indeed, it is the spirit of the greater creator dwelling in the lesser which actually guides the pen which the artist merely holds. The poet of the *Ion,* of the *Phaedrus,* and of the *Symposium,* exalted though he may be, is in the very moment of his highest inspiration reduced to serving as the mouthpiece of the demiurge of the *Timaeus* and his function is to confirm by his hymns of praise, composed and conducted by the greater creator in the first place, the cosmological order which the greater creator has himself ordained:

> That we on Earth with undiscording voice
> May rightly answer that melodious noise,
> As once we did, . . . till disproporn'd sin
> Jarr'd against nature's chime, and with harsh din
> Broke the fair music that all creatures made
> To their great Lord, whose love their motion sway'd
> In perfect Diapason, . . .
> O may we soon renew that Song,
> And keep in tune with Heaven, till God ere long
> To his celestial consort us unite, . . .

Both John Hollander and Mrs. Finney have demonstrated the extent and significance of this musical analogy in Renaissance thought in their recent books. It is an unbeatable system, I must confess, and I cannot help noting that the spiritual god-artist relationship has been in the *Republic* and the *Statesman* rather crassly politicized into the guardian as sponsor—in its contemporary or pejorative sense—of the poet, though I suppose there may be a difference between Urania visiting the poet nightly or efficiently presenting herself by day with forms to be signed in triplicate. On those occasions when Lowes frees himself from the mysteries of creation, he promptly makes himself the prisoner of Coleridge's own incomplete psychology; time and again, he brings up Coleridge's catch-phrases: "the hooks-and-eyes of memory" (like the hooks of Lucretius' atoms, and as misleading), "the tenacious and systematizing memory," "the streamy nature of association," "the twilight realms of consciousness," and then, in a sharp shift quite unperceived on his part, connects them with James' "the deep well of unconscious cerebration." But James' phrase comes from quite another psychological context than do Coleridge's phrases which rather point back to and recapitulate neo-Platonic and Christian mysticism plus a strong admixture of German philosophical romanticism culminating in the Hegelian dialectic. I am not enough of a Jamesian to know how much Freud he knew, if at all, but his phrase directs us not back to Coleridge but forward to Freud. I am now not speaking of the application of Freud's psychopathology to character or author analysis; if Freud himself failed at these misdirected attempts, I do not expect his followers to be able to do better. Rather, I have in mind, as a means of getting closer to the actual mechanisms of source adaptation and of image and symbol formation, whose complexity and multi-faceted character neither the theory of demiurgical inspiration nor that of simple associationism is equipped to handle, the techniques used by Freud in his analysis of wit. Stanley Hyman has acutely observed that this technique, potentially of such usefulness to the critic, has been, ironically, the least appreciated, and he has been able to cite but few honorable exceptions to this rule. In *Wit and Its Relation to the Unconscious,* Freud pointed out that: "The interesting processes of condensation with substitutive formation, which we recognized as the nucleus of word-wit, directed our attention to the dream-formation in whose mechanism the identical processes were discovered. Thither also were we directed by the technique of the thought-wit, namely, displacement, faulty thinking, absurdity, indirect expression, and representation through the opposite—each and all are also found in the technique of dreams." I would suggest that the processes of source adaptation and of image and symbol formation can be subsumed under these same categories; that is, when an author recasts his sources or revises his lines, his mind is operating by means of condensation, displacement, dramatization, and secondary elaboration. I would suggest, too, that at least part of the pleasure in art may be defined in nearly the same way that Freud defined the effect of tendency-wit; that is, it produces new pleasure by removing suppressions and repressions through the mechanism of the economy of psychic expenditure. And finally, I would suggest that the difference between art and dreams is the same as the difference between wit and dreams as Freud himself characterized it:

The most important difference lies in their social behavior. The dream is a perfectly asocial psychic product. It has nothing to tell anyone else; having originated in an individual as a compromise between conflicting psychic forces it remains incomprehensible to the person itself and has therefore altogether no interest for anybody else. Not only does the dream find it unnecessary to place any value on intelligibleness, but it must even guard against being understood, as it would then be destroyed; it can only exist in disguised form. For this reason the dream may make use freely of the mechanism that controls unconscious thought processes to the extent of producing undecipherable distortions. Wit, on the other hand, is the most social of all those psychic functions whose aim is to gain pleasure. It often requires three persons, and the psychic process which it incites always requires the participation of at least one other person. It must therefore bind itself to the condition of intelligibleness; it may employ distortion made practicable in the unconscious through condensation and displacement, to no greater extent than can be deciphered by the intelligence of the third person. . . . No matter how concealed, the dream is still a wish, while wit is a developed play. Despite its apparent unreality, the dream retains its relation to the great interests of life; it seeks to supply what is lacking through a regressive detour of hallucinations; and it owes its existence solely to the strong need for sleep during the night. Wit, on the other hand, seeks to draw a small amount of pleasure from the free and unencumbered activities of our psychic-apparatus, and later to seize this pleasure as an incidental gain. It thus *secondarily* reaches to important functions relative to the outer world. The dream serves preponderantly to guard against pain, while wit serves to acquire pleasure; in these two aims all our psychic activities meet.

That this objective language is still capable of arousing an almost primordial antipathy needs no demonstration, though I do not see why the same antipathy does not arise when, for instance, we see Steinman's mathematical formulae upon which his beautiful bridges are dependent. In either case, the language of Freud and the language of Steinman are merely the means by which phenomena in motion may be described with the utmost simplicity and economy and suggest neither approval nor disapproval—as though these expressions would, in any event, make any difference—for just as Steinman is saying that this is the way physical phenomena operate, so Freud is saying this is the way psychical phenomena operate. But this antipathy has kept the critics from taking advantage of the scalpel which Freud has so carefully sharpened for the anatomy of the creative process. And certainly it is a tool far more adept to the critic's hand than the Jungian approach which, like the magician's cloak, misdirects

and confuses the eye in its swirls, which is why I suppose
it has gained more adherents than Freud's insistence on the
rationality of the irrational.

I have so far commented briefly and altogether too inade-
quately on some of the methods of source study and have
indicated some of the uses to which they can be put. But
there is yet another meaning of source which deserves our
most serious consideration, source in a sense more profound
and fructifying than the others we have examined up to now.
For source may also mean the springs of belief and faith,
the deepest bed-rock of conviction, the soil in which our
very being is rooted and from which it draws its nourishment
and growth, source, in short, as Othello conceives it when he
pledges his life on Desdemona's faith. I feel that I need not
persuade you that the concept which has in our time best
succeeded in encompassing our own beliefs and the faiths
of our fathers and the superstitions of their fathers before
them and in compressing them into the ultimate archetype
of conviction is myth. I feel, too, I need not persuade you of
the centrality of myth to literature; one by one the varieties
of literature have been brought within the purvey of myth;
Wheelwright's *The Burning Fountain* and Frye's *Anatomy
of Criticism* signalize the final acceptance of the myth and
ritual approach to literature into the pantheon of contemporary criticism. And if these propositions are applicable to
the study of literature as a whole, they have become virtually
axiomatic for the study of Shakespeare in particular. I will
not bore you with a long list of names to prove how widespread is the application of the myth and ritual approach
to Shakespeare; I simply call to your attention the reversal
in attitude toward G. Wilson Knight in the thirty years since
Myth and Miracles was first published. The map of Shakespeare's spiritual progress ". . . from spiritual pain and de-
spairing thought through stoic acceptance to a serene and
mystic joy" which Knight first sketched in and which was
greeted with derision and hostility has now been accepted as

the most illuminating guide of all; and indeed, one can almost plot the widening acceptance of Knight merely by graphing the increasing amount of space given Knight and his followers in each succeeding issue of *Shakespeare Survey;* in Edward's review, for example, "Shakespeare's Romances: 1900-57," published in 1958, Knight has risen.

An advocate of the myth and ritual approach to literature myself, I should be the last person to object to this gratifying trend; I should not, as Sam Goldwyn might say, look a gifted horse in the mouth. It was unexpectedly flattering to the myth school to find at the end of Wimsatt and Brooks' *Literary Criticism* the declaration that in the myth and ritual approach to literature ". . . we have the most imposing of the several recent critical trends. Surely the hugest cloudy symbol, the most threatening, of our last ten or fifteen years in criticism, is the principle of criticism by myth and ritual origins." Here, unmistakably, is the Enemy: "War, then, war open or understood must be resolved." Well, I am not on the side of the angels, at least not those angels, but if I am to be of the devil's party, I want him to be in fact the subtle serpent he is supposed to be; that is, I want the myth and ritual approach as fit an instrument of criticism as it can be made, and that means ruthless self-criticism. I am not going to repeat certain criticisms of myth and ritual study in general and of their application to Shakespeare in particular which I have made elsewhere. My concern here is only this: just as I have been protesting against the indiscriminate use of source studies, so now I want to warn against the indiscriminate use of myth. While I freely grant the premise that myth does underlie literature, I must at the same time deny the implied corollary that it underlies each single work of literature equally, uniformly, and in the same way. Having first excavated the *ur*-pattern of myth, so to speak, and having established its relevance to literature—and even Bush's irony cannot halt the wave—the myth critics are pressing on to show that in every work of literature the pattern is ultimately the same, that is, both the architecture and the ideology of myth provide the architecture and ideology of literature, so that every work of literature can in the long run be shown to exhibit the same pattern of death, conflict, and rebirth. Not only would I object to this on the grounds of boredom alone, but it seems to me grossly to oversimplify the method which is certainly capable of more subtlety than that, but, much more important, it bleaches out the colors of literature into a gray sameness; again, the singular is not differentiated from the general. I must note at this point the force of a very powerful motive at work here: to bring back, in the guise of myth, the allegorical interpretation of literature, and by that means, as through a double back-door, to reintroduce the Christian interpretation of literature, so that myth, which ought to be universal, has been baptized and thereby rendered parochial, while Christianity, which ought to be unique, has been mythologized, and thereby rendered common. To use a figure appropriate to the fall athletic season, this double-reversal play has so confused the players that the opposing backfields have wound up playing behind their opponents' lines.

It is my contention that while all writers may very well use myth, they do not use it in the same way nor for the same ends; that while myth may be accepted by one writer, it may be rejected by another; and that it is the business of the myth critic to mark these crucial differences between means and ends; but it is emphatically not his business to force every work of literature into the same mold, nor does his happening to be a Christian confer upon him the privilege of playing a religio-critical shell game, as do, I believe, the contributors to Nathan Scott's symposium, *The Tragic Vision and the Christian Faith*. But let us see what a disinterested application of the myth and ritual approach to Shakespeare does tell us. I begin with endings. You no doubt remember Antony's final benediction on Brutus: "This was the noblest Roman of them all," a speech which, according to the myth critics, rounds off the play in a spirit of reconciliation. But they forget it is Antony speaking, the Antony who always says what is appropriate to the occasion; who, if he does not welcome Caesar's death, is ready to take advantage of the turmoil it erupts: "Mischief, thou art afoot,/ Take thou what course thou wilt!"; who plays on Brutus' vanity to save his neck; who has seen more days than Octavius and brutally dismisses Lepidus: "Do not talk of him/ But as a property"; who marries for his peace but in the East his pleasure lies; who loses the world for one more gaudy night; and whose magnanimity is ticked off by Enobarbus who, in reply to Agrippa's:

> Why, Enobarbus,
> When Antony found Julius Caesar dead,
> He cried almost to roaring; and he wept
> When at Philippi he found Brutus slain.

says:

> That year, indeed, he was troubled with a rheum;
> What willingly he did confound he wail'd,
> Believe't, till I wept too.

Reconciliation, with the whole world in confusion, and power up for grabs? Consider next Hamlet's penultimate speech to Horatio:

> O good Horatio, what a wounded name,
> Things standing thus unknown, shall live behind me!
> If thou didst ever hold me in thy heart,
> Absent thee from felicity a while
> And in this harsh world draw thy breath in pain
> To tell my story.

Horatio does not answer but we may assume that Hamlet is satisfied that Horatio will tell his story as soon as opportunity presents itself, and we may also assume that Hamlet is satisfied that Horatio will tell his story aright. And the opportunity does present itself only a few lines later when Fortinbras and the English Ambassador, standing aghast at the havoc before them, demand to know its meaning; Horatio speaks:

> And let me speak to th'yet unknowing world
> How these things came about. So shall you hear
> Of carnal, bloody, and unnatural acts,
> Of accidental judgments, casual slaughters,
> Of deaths put on by cunning and forc'd cause,
> And, in this upshot, purposes mistook
> Fall'n on the inventors' heads: All this can I
> Truly deliver.

"Let us haste to hear it," Fortinbras replies, and, lest we did not altogether understand what he has just said, Horatio repeats: "But let this same be presently perform'd/ Even while men's minds are wild, lest more mischance,/ On plots and errors, happen." Is this lurid billboard poster advertising a melodrama by Seneca the meaning of Hamlet's story? Is this Hamlet's cause: "Report me and my cause aright/ To the unsatisfied." Is this what Shakespeare wanted us to get out of the play and take away with us as its final impression? Is this the moment of illumination and reconciliation? Next let us visualize the staging of the final scene of *Othello*. It begins with the smothering of Desdemona by Othello: "It is the cause, it is the cause, my soul,—/ Let me not name it to you, you chaste stars!—/ It is the cause."; Othello, too, has a cause. Less than 400 lines later, Desdemona is dead, Emilia is dead, Othello is dead; of the principals of the play, only Iago is alive: "Demand me nothing; what you know, you know./ From this time forth I never will speak word." Can Lodovico's threats harm him; can physical torture reach him; why is he still alive, still unexplained, still evil? Is this reconciliation? Again, in the myth and ritual pattern, the moment of rebirth is the moment of trumph of good over evil; in tragedy, this

moment has been secularized into the moment of self-awareness: "Speak of me as I am." If this is the case, then that moment comes for Lear when, stripped of all the trappings of
power and reduced to his quintessential humanity, that is, a
man like all other men, he says:

> Pray, do not mock me.
> I am a very foolish fond old man,
> Fourscore and upward, not an hour more nor less;
> And, to deal plainly,
> I fear I am not in my perfect mind.

Lear has suffered and has learned from his suffering but now
he is reborn, and this point is repeated for emphasis: the
Doctor says to Cordelia: "Be comforted, good madam; the
great rage,/ You see, is kill'd in him"; Lear turns to her and
once more says: "You must bear with me. Pray you now, forget and forgive; I am old and foolish." What more is there
to add and should not, therefore, the play end at this moment
of illumination and reconciliation? But these lines are spoken
at the end of Act IV; what, then, is the purpose of Act V with
the unexpected and unnecessary defeat of the French forces,
the seizure of Lear and Cordelia, Edmund's swift secret dis-
patching of them, Regan's poisoning, Edgar's appearance as
the unknown champion whose challenge and joust succeed in
making everyone forget that Cordelia is at that very moment
being hanged, the suicide of Goneril, the death of Cordelia,
the defeat of Edmund, the return of Lear's madness followed
hard upon by his own death? No wonder Kent asks: "Is this
the promis'd end?" And answers himself: "All's cheerless,
dark, and deadly." The world has indeed been turned topsy-
turvy; Edgar has the last word: "The oldest hath borne most;
we that are young/ Shall never see so much, nor live so long."
Edgar is too optimistic: there are to come yet Macbeth who,
starting from: "Things bad begun make strong themselves by
ill . . ." goes on to:

Myth, Method, and Shakespeare

> I am bent to know
> By the worst means, the worst. For mine own good
> All causes shall give way. I am in blood
> Steep'd in so far that, should I wade no more,
> Returning were as tedious as go o'er.

to:

> I have liv'd long enough. My way of life
> Is fallen into the sear, the yellow leaf;
> And that which should accompany old age,
> As honour, love, obedience, troops of friends,
> I must not look to have; but, in their stead,
> Curses, not loud but deep, mouth-honor, breath
> Which the poor heart would fain deny, and dare not.

and on to:

> I have supp'd full of horrors;
> Direness, familiar to my slanderous thoughts,
> Cannot once start me.

and finally to his moment of dark illumination:

> I gin to be aweary of the sun,
> And wish th'estate o'th' world were now undone.;

Timon of Athens ". . . who, alive, all living men did hate"; Antony, betrayed how many times by his cold morsel and more by his own passion, fooled into committing suicide and bungling that, too: "How! not dead? not dead?," refused a decent death by his own guards, his almost lifeless body lugged, tugged, and hauled about the stage, his epitaph Octavius' grudging: "The breaking of so great a thing should make/ A greater crack"; and last, the irony of Aufidius' pronouncement on Coriolanus:

> Though in this city he
> Hath widow'd and unchilded many a one,
> Which to this hour bewail the injury,
> Yet he shall have a noble memory.

But why should he; what has he learned?

> O mother, mother!
> What have you done? Behold, the heavens do ope,
> The gods look down, and this unnatural scene
> They laugh at. O my mother, mother! O!

The gods send ghosts to terrify us; then look down and laugh.
Let us go back to the comedies, starting with *Troilus and Cressida*. Who, in this play, escapes from having his true nature exposed, either by the contradiction between his thoughts and his deeds or by the savage observation of others, themselves exposed too? Ajax and Achilles, "two curs who shall tame each other"; Troilus, so lovesick he will not fight for family and home: "Is this the generation of love—hot blood, hot thoughts, and hot deeds? Why, they are vipers. Is love a generation of vipers?"; Patroclus, "an effeminate man/ In time of action"; Paris and Menelaus alike in their dotage on Helen:

> He merits well to have her that doth seek her,
> Not making any scruple of her soilure,
> With such a hell of pain and world of charge;
> And you as well to keep her, that defend her,
> Not palating the taste of his dishonour,
> With such a costly loss of wealth and friends.
> He, like a puling cuckold, would drink up
> The lees of a flat tamed piece;
> You, like a lecher, out of whorish loins
> Are pleased to breed out your inheritors.
> Both merits poised, each weighs no less no more;
> But he as he, which heavier for a whore.;

Helen herself:

> For every false drop in her bawdy veins
> A Grecian's life hath sunk; for every scruple
> Of her contaminated carrion weight,
> A Troyan hath been slain. Since she could speak,
> She hath not given so many good words breath
> As for her Greeks and Troyans suff'red death.

Cressida no less:

> Fie, fie upon her!
> There's language in her eye, her lip,
> Nay, her foot speaks; her wanton spirits look out
> At every joint and motive of her body.
> O, these encounters, so glib of tongue,
> That give accosting welcome ere it comes,
> And wide unclasp the tables of their thoughts
> To every tickling reader! Set them down
> For sluttish spoils of opportunity
> And daughters of the game.;

Agamemnon brainless; Diomedes a false-hearted rogue; Nestor a stale old mouse-eaten dry cheese; Ulysses a dog-fox; even Hector, whose momentary flash of reason is quenched by Troilus' romantic rhetoric and obstinately goes to his bitter death, ambushed while unarmed and resting, by the brave Achilles and his bullies. So the great matter of Troy is reduced to clapper-clawing and: "Lechery, lechery; still wars and lechery; nothing else holds fashion." There is, I fear, no room for reconciliation here, but perhaps the next two comedies, *All's Well that Ends Well* and *Measure for Measure,* will prove more amenable, and indeed no other play in the canon, with the possible exceptions of *The Winter's Tale* and *The Tempest,* has been more Christianized than *Measure for Measure.* But how well does, in fact, *All's Well* end? Whatever one may think of Bertram, and in spite of all the medieval conventions behind the play, one cannot help sympathizing with his account of Helena:

> Certain it is I lik'd her,
> And boarded her i' the wanton way of youth.
> She knew her distance and did angle for me,
> Madding my eagerness with her restraint,
> As impediments in fancy's course
> Are motives of more fancy; and, in fine,
> Her infinite cunning with her modern grace,
> Subdu'd me to her rate. She got the ring;
> And I had that which any inferior might
> At market-price have bought.

Nor can one help wondering how well this marriage is going to turn out when, only a few lines later, under the threatening eye of the King, Bertram is forced to declare: "I'll love her dearly, ever, ever dearly." Similarly, one cannot help wondering whether Vienna is going to be any better off when, at the end of *Measure for Measure*, the Duke, congratulating himself on his performance as a meddling friar and casting a calculating look on Isabella, resumes his seat after the "mad fantastical trick of him to steal from the state, and usurp the beggary he was never born to" than it was before, when, for fourteen years, he failed to uphold the "strict statutes and most biting laws,/ The needful bits and curbs to headstrong steeds" which he had expected Angelo to enforce overnight. When even the Duke himself has to admit that under his rule "quite athwart/ Goes all decorum," Friar Thomas rightly chides him: "It rested in your Grace/ To unloose this tied-up justice when you pleas'd," yet the Duke persists in making excuses:

> Sith 'twas my fault to give the people scope,
> 'Twould be my tyranny to strike and gall them
> For what I bid them do; for we bid this be done,
> When evil deeds have their permissive pass
> And not the punishment.

Whose evaluation, then, of the Duke's character is correct: his own: "Wise! Why, no question but he was. . . . Let him be but testimonied in his own bringings-forth, and he shall appear to the envious a scholar, a statesman, and a soldier," or Lucio's: "Ere he would have hang'd a man for the getting a hundred bastards, he would have paid for the nursing a thousand. He had some feeling of the sport; he knew the service, and that instructed him to mercy." And who shows more tolerance when, speaking of Angelo, Lucio says:

> A little more lenity to lechery would do no harm in him.
> Something too crabbed that way, friar.
> Duke: It is too general a vice, and severity must cure it.
> Lucio: Yes, in good sooth, the vice of a great kindred, it is well allied; but it is impossible to extirp it quite, friar, till eating and drinking be put down.

And to think what convolutions Coghill had to go through in order to turn poor blabbermouth Lucio into a very big and very bad devil so that the Duke could be converted into a rather ineffectual Christ. As for Isabella, is she ever, like the Lady in *Comus*, in any real danger of being tempted, for, unlike the same Lady, she has no need of attendant Spirits, Brothers, Sabrina, conscience, hope, chastity, and a glistering guardian to keep her life and honor unassailed; she has her hard mind:

>   I'll to my brother.
> Though he hath fall'n by prompture of the blood,
> Yet hath he in him such a mind of honour,
> That, had he twenty heads to tender down
> On twenty bloody blocks, he'd yield them up,
> Before his sister should her body stoop
> To such abhorr'd pollution.
> Then, Isabel, live chaste, and, brother, die;
> More than our brother is our chastity.

And, like the Duke, she too is capable of the highest Christian charity; she is replying to her brother's plea, "Sweet sister, let me live":

> O you beast!
> O faithless coward! O dishonest wretch!
> Wilt thou be made a man out of my vice?
> Is't not a kind of incest, to take life
> From thine own sister's shame?

She then calls him a bastard, and continues:

> Take my defiance!
> Die, perish! Might but my bending down
> Reprieve thee from thy fate, it should proceed.
> I'll pray a thousand prayers for thy death,
> No word to save thee.

And why, if it was so loathesome for Isabella to sleep with Angelo, was it quite all right for Mariana to do so, and if Angelo was the heel the Duke knew him to be, as he demonstrates when he tells Isabella that Angelo dropped Mariana when he discovered her brother's drowning had deprived her of her dowry, why then did the Duke appoint him deputy in the first place and test him with a test he must have known Angelo was bound to fail? La Fontaine says in one of his fables that it is a double pleasure to deceive a deceiver, and indeed it is, but somehow that doesn't quite strike the right Christian note. If Shakespeare had wanted to write a Christian allegory, I am sure he was artist enough and Christian enough to have been less ambiguous. As a matter of fact, if it were not for the intractableness of the dates, I would be ready to argue that *Measure for Measure* was written as a parody on *Comus;* perhaps it is Shakespeare's revenge for having had to read Spenser.

As for the four final romances, I am more than willing to concede the presence in them of all the ritual devices; indeed, there are more deaths, rebirths, magical musics, spirits, visions, sorcerers, doctors, storms, caskets, rescues, reconciliations, illuminations, and the like in them than in all the plays before them, and that precisely is the trouble. These plays are all ritual and no myth; the spirit is gone from them, and only the letter remains. The last plays are the mere machinery of ritual, functioning beautifully no doubt, but to no end. But it must not be thought that Shakespeare failed to delineate the ideal God-king-hero-protagonist; in fact, there are three versions of him: Henry V, Fortinbras, and Octavius, the first so coolly calculating that he had to be warmed by a French romance, the second callous and grasping, and the third concerned only with power and prestige: "the wild disguise hath almost/ Antick'd us all," and besides he does not reprove Dolabella for speaking ill of the teaching profession:

> Caesar, 'tis his schoolmaster.
> An argument that he is pluck'd, when hither
> He sends so poor a pinion of his wing.

This is unforgivable, but then what else could be expected from such as Henry V, Fortinbras, and Octavius, their cold eyes staring down their long noses at us? Grace?

I have been trying to show that the myth and ritual approach is a critical tool which cuts both ways, that it can differentiate between acceptance and rejection of the myth pattern itself, and that it need not impose itself on the materials with which it deals and force them to conform to a predetermined ideological pattern which by its very nature must be less than the variety and intensity of literature itself. I am afraid there is very little consolation in this and I regret having to destroy the image of Shakespeare as seer or Olympian or even Christian. That some artists merit this designation is, of course, incontrovertible, but not as many as we would like to believe, nor are these few necessarily the greatest. The vision of order, justice, and mercy is a tenacious one and not easily eradicated; the alternative is too fearsome to contemplate. Yet order, regularity, law, and the like are not inherent in nature; they are imposed upon it by the frantic fears of man. They are read, not out of nature, but into it, and not by mathematics and physics and chemistry, but by mathematicians, physicists, and chemists, who have their illusions, too. Science is the pathetic fallacy writ large on government subsidy. If it takes faith to believe, it takes courage not to, and who is to say which is the deeper and more truthful. One can answer that question only for himself; and, speaking for myself, when I look about me and see things as they are and not as I would like them to be, which is how I think Shakespeare looked at them, too, I can say only this: one can stand bolt upright in the waters of existence and sink immediately, as Milton did; one can yield oneself to them and ultimately sink, as Shakespeare did; in any case, they cannot be walked. When, as a result of writing *Tragedy and the Paradox of the Fortunate Fall,* I arrived at the formula of tragedy as the passage from ignorance through suffering to understanding, I thought then that understanding meant the vision of what men could be. I now know it means the sight of what they are.

(1958)

The Mythic Origins of the
Creative Process

ONE OF THE MINOR, though still annoying, effects of the Madison Avenue influence is the commercial debasement of respectable critical terms. The latest such word to be given the ad-mass treatment is "creative." Apparently, Madison Avenue has discovered that there is a certain cachet attached to the word and, with its usual all or nothing energy, has promptly prefixed it to every product and activity it can exploit, so much so, in fact, that the adding of "creative" to selling has become in its own right "creative" advertising. It is therefore almost embarrassing to undertake to deal with the creative process because of the unfortunate associations which have been foisted upon it. Nevertheless, the phenomenon of artistic creativity is of such aesthetic significance and is yet so little understood that, Madison Avenue to the contrary, it deserves our most serious consideration. Indeed, if I may be permitted a wild generalization, I would say that from Aristotle to Coleridge the concern of the critic has been with the work of art existing outside of and apart from both artist and reader, while from Coleridge on, the concern of the critic has been with the work of art as a continuous process of becoming, ranging uninterruptedly from its psychological origins in the mind of its maker to its psychological effects on the mind of its reader, all forming one inter-acting continuum.

I should, therefore, like to examine the nature of the creative process as I understand it, and to suggest something of the way in which it works, and I begin with one of those casual remarks of Aristotle: "But the greatest thing by far," he says in the *Poetics* (Bywater translation, XXII, 7-10), "is to be a master of metaphor. It is the one thing that cannot be learnt from others; and it is also a sign of genius since a good metaphor implies an intuitive perception of the similarity in dissimilars." As usual, Aristotle's note-taker was unable to keep up with the lecture so we do not have the professor's development of his idea, but I suspect it would have gone something like this: "Imagery (even taken from nature, much more when transplanted from books, as travels, voyages, and works of natural history); affecting incidents; just thoughts; interesting personal or domestic feelings; and with these the art of their combination or intertexture in the form of a poem; may all . . . by incessant effort be acquired as a trade, by a man of talents and much reading, who as I once before observed, has mistaken an intense desire of poetic reputation for a natural poetic genius; the love of the arbitrary end for the possession of the peculiar means. But the sense of musical delight, with the power of producing it, is a gift of the imagination; and this together with the power of reducing multitude into unity of effect, and modifying a series of thoughts by some one predominant thought or feeling, may be cultivated and improved, but can never be learned." Coleridge may have been a born Platonist, but he studied Aristotle; in any event, both classical and romantic aesthetics are agreed on the centrality of metaphor.

I am concerned, then, with the perception of the similarity in dissimilars which is the mode of operation of metaphor which in turn is the mode of operation of imagery which, together with metaphor, is the mode of operation of the creative process. For metaphor is essentially a process of arrangement and re-arrangement, of combination and re-combination, of connection and inter-connection, above all, of selection. In this sense, metaphor does not originate, but rather places the unfamiliar side by side with the familiar and makes it customary; it puts the unexpected next to the expected and makes it awaited; it draws the unknown into the known; and, at the same time as it domesticates the strange, the terrible, and the unusual, it emboldens the conventional, the habitual, and the obvious: the shut eye sees, the closed ear hears. Metaphor pries open the closed lips of the deadened consciousness and breathes in new life; it relates. This I take to be the meaning of Coleridge's description of the imagination: "It dissolves, diffuses, dissipates, in order to recreate."

I take as my evidence the introspection of artists, their own statements of how they created as they did, and I do this in full awareness of the dangers inherent in the method. The artist is as capable of deceiving himself and others as we are, but if we can draw upon the observations of enough artists in enough different arts over a large enough range of time and area of distribution, then idiosyncrasy yields to probability and generalization becomes possible. The difficulty which confronts us here is not to find the evidence but rather how to convey to you the significance of the enormous mass of evidence which can be found. I do not have the voice to repeat nor you the patience to hear statement after statement from writers describing in detail how they work. I am therefore afraid that I will have to ask you to assume that I have done my homework and that there are and that I have read and analyzed a not inconsiderable number of introspections of creative people, artists and scientists alike. For once one begins to look for evidence of this kind, the wonder is that there is so much of it to be found and, even more astounding, that the multiplicity and variety of introspections can be assimilated within a comprehensive theoretical framework. For the sake of my reputation as a scholar, let me mention but a few of the more outstanding statements on the nature of the creative process drawn from the introspections of artists. From among the poets, Valéry's "Poetry and Abstract Thought," Amy Lowell's "The Process of Making Poetry," C. Day Lewis' "The Poet's Way of Knowing," Karl Shapiro's "The Meaning of the Discarded Poem," Spender's "The Making of a Poem," Tate's "Narcissus as Narcissus," Auden's "The Dyer's Hand," and Herbert Read's "Myth, Dream, and Poem"; I take for granted the gold to be found in the criticism, letters and notebooks of Wordsworth, Coleridge, Shelley, Keats, and Yeats. From among the painters, Ben Shahn's *The Shape of Content,* Michelangelo's poems 84 and 101, and Van Gogh's letters. From among the composers, Brahms' conversations with the violinist Arthur Abell, Tschaikowsky's letters to Madame von Meck, Roger Sessions' "The Composer and His Message," and Michael Tippet's "The Birth of an Opera." From among the novelists, Conrad's notes on the making of *Nostromo;* Henry James' *Notebooks,* particularly the entry dated January 4, 1910; Joyce Cary's *Art and Reality;* and Thomas Mann's account of the genesis of *Dr. Faustus, The Story of a Novel.* But my most telling example is simply the whole of Wordsworth's *Prelude,* to my mind the most revolutionary poem of modern times. I call it that because its theme, the autobiography of a poet's mind, is in effect the first new theme of poetry since Homer. For just as Homer opened up to the artist the exploitation of the world outside of man, Wordsworth opened up to him the world inside of himself and began those explorations of the inner life beside which the journeys into the interior of Africa to discover the sources of the Nile seem pallid, for the source of the Nile was found and Africa lost its mystery but that other voyage of discovery which Wordsworth began has not ended, nor is it likely to end:

> Visionary power
> Attends the motions of the viewless winds,
> Embodied in the mystery of the words:
> There, darkness makes abode, and all the host
> Of shadowy things work endless changes,—there,

As in a mansion like their proper home,
Even forms and substances are circumfused
By that transparent veil with light divine,
And, through the turnings intricate of verse,
Present themselves as objects recognised,
In flashes, and with glory not their own.

I believe that we have now had enough illustrations of the creative process from musicians, novelists, painters, and poets to venture some generalizations. I realize, of course, that the creative process is a continuous one with both simultaneous and overlapping stages, yet I think it will help our understanding of it if we describe it in terms of successive stages as follows: first, the stimulus, the need to react to a force naggingly pushing from within or without; second, the struggle to overcome the irritation, to reduce it to form, to make it cohere, to make it make sense in terms of what has already made sense up to then; third, the frustration, the bitterness of defeat as the irritant appears stronger than the ability to overcome it; fourth, the agony of despair, the blackness and bile as the creative impulse seems destroyed by the very weight and mass of the indigestible lump of the not-becoming and the not-being; fifth, the flash of insight, the vision which takes one unawares, the solution which suddenly stares one in the face, the right and the inevitable word and phrase and form; sixth, the feeling of exhilaration, of triumph, the sheer satisfaction of rightness; seventh, the labor of composition, with its false starts and wrong turns yet coming out in the right place at the end, the effort of labor this time lightened by the inevitability of conquest; and eighth, the sense of achievement, the lifting to a higher plane of understanding, the effect of illumination and insight, the attainment of order and shape and integration. I am not suggesting that in each and every instance each and every step is taken in precisely the same order in which I have arranged them, but I think our evidence justifies my conviction that this scheme does constitute the architecture of the creative process in an idealized form.

Nor am I suggesting that this kind of scheme is original with me. In his *Art of Thought,* Graham Wallas distinguishes four stages of thought, as preparation, incubation, illumination including intimation, and verification, and the psychologist, Catherine Patrick, uses these same terms in her effort to answer the question, *What Is Creative Thinking?,* as does the poet Richard Wilbur in a paper, "The Problem of Creative Thinking in Poetry." Rosamond E. M. Harding concentrates on inspiration in her book, *An Anatomy of Inspiration;* and the psychiatrist Eliot Dole Hutchinson examines in detail "The Period of Frustration in Creative Endeavor" and "The Nature of Insight," two stages from his own division of the creative process into periods of preparation, renunciation, insight, and verification, in a series of papers published in *The Journal of Psychiatry.* Robert N. Wilson names the stages of the creative process somewhat differently in *Man Made Plain:* ". . . selective perception of the environment; acquisition of technique; envisioning of combinations and distillations, elucidation of the vision; and the end of the poem and its meaning to the poet," and of these he singles out the moment of vision as of "pre-potent significance." The psychologist Julius Portnoy proposes three stages: sensory perception, then ". . . impressions and memories received through the senses undergo a period of incubation or unconscious elaboration," and the rising of this latent material to a conscious level during which the artist shapes his material. Exposure, incubation, illumination, and execution are the terms suggested by the industrial psychologist Irving A. Taylor. Though both Brewster Ghiselin and Robin Skelton collect many valuable introspections, particularly Skelton's previously unpublished letters from contemporary poets, neither attempts a schematic treatment of their material, nor do, for that matter, either Freud or Jung, despite their absorption in the problems of the creative process, though in *An Autobiographical Study* Freud comes close to a formulation:

The Mythic Origins of the Creative Process

The realm of imagination was evidently a "sanctuary" made during the painful transition from the pleasure principle to the reality principle in order to provide a substitute for the gratification of instincts which had to be given up in real life. The artist, like the neurotic, had withdrawn from an unsatisfying reality into this world of imagination; but, unlike the neurotic, he knew how to find a way back from it and once more to get a firm foothold in reality. His creations, works of art, were the imaginary gratifications of unconscious wishes, just as dreams are; and like them, they were in the nature of compromises, since they too were forced to avoid any open conflict with the forces of repression. But they differed from the asocial, narcissistic products of dreaming in that they were calculated to arouse interest in other people and were able to evoke and to gratify the same unconscious wishes in them too.

A little later on, I shall consider some neglected aspects of the Freudian theory of creativity, but I want to mention in connection with other examples the stage analysis of the creative process of F. C. Prescott who, in *The Poetic Mind,* converts the Freudian formulation into virtually a mathematical formula, and Kenneth Burke's more liberal translation of the Freudian insights into purpose, passion, and perception. Finally, mathematicians have been no less interested in the creative process than have critics and psychologists. Henry Poincaré's lecture, "Mathematical Creation" is well known, but Jacques Hadamard's *The Psychology of Invention in the Mathematical Field* is a more extensive and well developed treatment of the creative process in mathematics and uses the Wallas arrangement of stages as its framework, but he adds one more surprising element—surprising in view of the reluctance of artists to use the word: "But with Poincaré, we see something else, the intervention of the sense of beauty, playing its part as an *indispensable* means of finding." The mathematician Marston Morse is even more emphatic about this: "The first essential bond between mathematics and the arts is found in the fact that discovery in mathematics is not a matter of logic. It is rather the result of mysterious powers which no one understands, and in which the unconscious recognition of beauty must play an important part. Out of an infinity of designs a mathematician chooses one pattern for beauty's sake, and pulls it down to earth, no one knows how. Afterwards the logic of words and of forms sets the pattern right. Only then can one tell someone else. The first pattern remains in the shadows of the mind."

The creative process, then, conforms to a more or less definable pattern which is more or less similar for the many and varied fields of creative endeavor and which functions more or less alike in the many and varied actors in the drama of creation. Indeed, one could go on to other areas of mental experience and demonstrate the presence and persistence of the pattern I have described. Thus it would be possible, I think, to show that the varieties of religious experience can be subsumed within this pattern, all the way from the kind of religious experience which may be called that of rational conservatism as described in Gerhart Ladner's *The Idea of Reform* to that middle of the road religion about which Ronald Knox has written so engagingly in *Enthusiasm* to the extreme left-wing millenarianism and chiliasm of apocalyptic religion as it has been comprehensively treated in Norman Cohn's *The Pursuit of the Millennium*. In one way or another, the religious experience would appear to follow the program which Miss Underhill has described: awakening or conversion; self-knowledge or purgation; illumination; surrender, or the dark night; and union. Indeed, the very process of conversion, of which the religious variety is merely the first which comes to mind, but which is characteristic of any dramatic change of belief, as much from faith to unbelief as from unbelief to belief, follows the same pattern: first, irritation and frustration caused by the feeling that all is irrational, combined with an almost overpowering sense of chaos and meaninglessness leading to despair and instability of mind; then this state gives way when the pieces of the puzzle seem all at once to fit together under the impetus of conversion, and there is an almost overwhelming feeling of exhilaration which comes from the effect of strong conviction, and above all, the feeling of knowledge and power which comes from having ascended from ignorance to light, the recognition of order and design in the world which had hitherto seemed empty of them. St. Augustine's: "No further would I read; nor needed I. For instantly even with the end of this sentence, by a light as it were of confidence now darted into my heart, all the darkness of doubting vanished away," might well have served as the theme of Tolstoi's last novel, fittingly called *Resurrection*.

You will have noticed, I am sure, that I have had to describe the creative process dramatistically, in the form of an action whose plot is that of birth, death, and rebirth. But this is the very same plot of the action called myth, a drama in which the divine king in his own person engages in combat with an opposing force, suffers, is defeated, dies, is reborn triumphantly, celebrates his victory by the act of creation in the divine marriage and by the sacred procession, and grants the fruits of that victory in the settling of destinies in which the people, for whom and with whom he undergoes his suffering, death, and rebirth, are raised to a new and higher stage of understanding and justice. To be sure, the order of acts in the drama is not everywhere the same, nor are all the scenes necessarily enacted; with the passage of time, some scenes are subordinated to others, some given increased prominence, while others are eliminated altogether, but whatever changes have been made, the shape and intent of the pattern remain the same: the depiction of the triumph of light, life, and good through suffering over dark, death, and evil. Thus it would appear that on the conscious level the creative process is a parallel re-enactment of the myth and ritual pattern and draws its force and vitality from it.

But this is to think of the myth and ritual pattern as fundamental and anterior to the creative process, at which point we would have to call a halt to our excavations, as it were, since no further penetration below would be possible. If, however, we reverse the positions of myth and creation, we are able to continue our digging so as to open up even deeper layers than we have so far managed to probe. As far as creativity is concerned, its mode of operation is common to all its manifestations, varied only by their predisposition as to purpose and form. We may liken the creative process to a long tunnel through which all cars must pass in a single lane, turning only as they emerge into different exists taking them to different destinations. Seen from this point of view, the myth and ritual pattern now becomes the symbolic representation of the creative process, that is to say, the mind's figuring forth of itself. So that what I have been calling the creative process appears to be nothing less than the mode of operation of the mind itself.

The concept of the mode of operation of the mind as essentially dramatic and dialectical, of proceeding by what amounts to a series of leaps, falls, and higher leaps is, I know, offensive to us since we have managed to persuade ourselves that while we may perhaps think this way in our emotional, irrational, and therefore poetic moments, we think in a straight, clear line in our logical and rational moments, that is, when we think we think scientifically. But our evidence will not allow us this well-intentioned delusion: the mind thinks in the same way in any case, and only the form of presentation, depending on difference of intention, is different. Or, to put the matter less starkly, the mind leaps out into an intuition of apprehension along which it has painfully to crawl back and then forward again for its justification. I myself have hitherto thought that a genuine distinction could be made between mythopoeic and scientific thought, but I must admit that I am no longer able to maintain that distinction. The essence of mythopoeic thought is analogy, the perception which relates seemingly individual and specific likenesses to each other; it says that things are like each other because they, or parts of themselves, look enough like each other so as to constitute a contiguous relationship of hitherto unperceived significance. On the other hand, I held that the scientific mode of thought says that things equal each other, not because they have any necessarily observable physical characteristics in common, but because they are capable of being encompassed within the same abstraction. The one appeared to me concrete, emotive, and anthropomorphic; the other abstract, rational, and disengaged. In this, I had been following the lead of Cassirer, and especially of the Frankforts in their brilliant introduction and conclusion to their collection of papers on the ancient Near East, *Before Philosophy*. I no longer find their sharp distinctions between myth and science (and/or reason) tenable; their notion of the emancipation of thought from myth is too suggestive of an actually observable, linear historical development when it would appear to me that we must use a much more sophisticated image, something like Darwin's tangled bank or Marx's entangled net or Frazer's woven web of varicolored threads. Both the mythopoeic and the scientific modes of thought address themselves to the same fundamental problem: that of seeking to create a world of order, justice, and reason in a universe constitutionally indifferent to those values, values which man has read into it but which he cannot ever prove are inherent in it. Both, then, propose the same ends and use the same means, that is, the creative process, but differ as to the language of their formulations, and it is a moot point indeed whether one has been in the long run more successful than the other. I will, of course, admit that the tactical successes of science are certainly more lustrous but the scientists themselves will not, I am sure, make the same claim for its strategic ends. I am even quite prepared to backtrack on my concession concerning the tactical successes of science whose intrusion into culture has amended the law of civilization to read: the more sordidly man lives, the fewer men, and with more difficulty, he can kill; the more splendidly he lives, the more men, and with greater ease, he can kill.

I must apologize for taking so tortuous a journey to reach so obvious a destination, that when we think, we think in metaphors, that is, in leaps and jumps from correspondence to correspondence as in a long corridor of mirrors. Thus it would appear that the primal law of the inner life of man is that ontogeny recapitulates phylogeny, just as it would appear that it is the law of history and of nature itself. As I try to visualize the movement of the mind during the creative process, I see an unfolding from within, a reaching beyond, another unfolding, and another stretch; an ever shifting center radiating out to ever widening circumferences, not circular, but irregular, with deep bays of regression, flat beaches of futility, and sudden promontories of achievement. In any event, I do not see the movement as a circle, of a beginning returning in on itself, but rather as an uneven, ascending spiral. I suppose that from the point of view of God as he looks down on the process it is a circle (as I suppose it is too from the point of view of Satan as he looks up at it) but from the point of view of man standing midway and looking head-on, the circle is a spiral, and what hope he has comes from the difference in location and angle of vision. You will have noticed, of course, that I am doing my best to avoid the idea of progress, but I am forced to take recourse to the symbol of the spiral in order to account for change, variety, and, above all else, originality.

The inclusion of innovation in the process of phylogeny recapitulating ontogeny, or, in mythical terms, the dialectical transformation of the highest stage of the settling of destinies into the lowest stage of the next sequence of the myth drama, seems to me to solve a major stumbling block which any theory of the creative process must overcome, and I owe this idea to one of Freud's most illuminating insights. In one sentence in *Moses and Monotheism,* he summed up his contribution to psychoanalysis: "Early trauma-defence-latency-outbreak of the neurosis—partial return of the repressed material: this was the formula we drew up for the development of a neurosis." And then, in a magnificent leap, he went on to relate the inner life of man to history itself: "Now I will invite the reader to take a step forward and assume that in the history of the human species something happened similar to the events in the life of the individual. That is to say, mankind as a whole also passed through conflicts of a sexual-aggressive nature, which left permanent traces, but which were for the most part warded off and forgotten; later, after a long period of latency, they came to life again and created phenomena similar in structure and tendency to neurotic symptoms." Do not be put off by the word neurosis: after all, the capacity to be irritated, to react to the aggravation of not knowing, to be dissatisfied is the measure of difference between the bovine and the intelligent. The creative process is therefore by its nature profoundly revolutionary, a built-in device which immediately upsets any state of equilibrium or stasis it encounters. By its interposition, it transforms rest into motion, altering and recasting, until the friction of resistance and effort slows it down into form or formula, a new state of rest, whose balance it again upsets, so that now each mirror in the long corridor reflects one subtly altered image after another. As I was groping for a figure to concretize this idea, Toynbee's image of the pollarded willow and Yeats' question about the dancer and the dance and Beethoven's Great Fugue came to my mind, but, most vivid of all was that recurring theme of Picasso's of the artist at his easel with his model calmly looking over his shoulder at his painting of her. No wonder that the central preoccupation of artist and scientist alike is that of metamorphosis.

So far we have been following the creative process along the track of its vicissitudes, a journey symbolized in the rites of passage of the mythological god-king-hero himself. We have now to examine the mechanism of the mode of its operation, that is to say, the process of image and symbol formation. In *Wit and Its Relation to the Unconscious* Freud pointed out that: "The interesting processes of condensation with substitutive formation, which we recognized as the nucleus of word-wit, directed our attention to the dream-formation in whose mechanism the identical processes were discovered. Thither also were we directed by the technique of the thought-wit, namely, displacement, faulty thinking, absurdity, indirect expression, and representation through the opposite—each and all are also found in the technique of dreams." I would suggest that the processes of image and symbol formation can be subsumed under these same categories; that is, the creative process proceeds by means of condensation, displacement, dramatization, and secondary elaboration. These motions of the mind can be observed in virtual laboratory conditions in notebooks and manuscript and printing revisions but to reproduce for you a manuscript leaf of Milton's "Lycidas," or Blake's "The Tyger," or of Swinburne's "Rococo," or of Yeats' "Among the School Children" and "After Long Silence," would not be illuminating without burdensome detailed analysis. Luckily, however, we can cite the evidence of the reflections of poets themselves on their own revisions; my example of the techniques of the creative process at work in the making of a poem is W. D. Snodgrass' "Heart's Needle, vi," about which he himself has written so discerningly in his paper, "Finding a Poem":

I showed this poem, for criticism, to a number of my friends at the University of Iowa. Most of them liked it in a luke-warmish way; one said that it sounded a little like an imitation of my earlier poems about my daughter. And, when I came back to it, I had to admit that I still didn't know what it was about. I could see that the image of hacking the limbs off the trees was related to my separation from my daughter (I had previously described this as an animal gnawing off one of its limbs to get out of a trap); the pigeon fluttering out of my hands was related both to my letting her go in the separation and also to the way she sometimes ran away to make me chase her. The blackbird in the last stanza seemed to be my first wife "protesting" her nest; the killdeers crying over their flooded nests implied some sense of grief over the breaking up of the home. These things all made sense and were all memories which the child's return might cause to be reborn in me. But this did not seem enough. No adequate pattern had emerged. I wasn't sorry to have written the poem, but I couldn't say that I thought much had happened.

Besides, what was the Fourth of July (stanza 3) doing in my Easter poem? Of course there *had* been a terrible windstorm that night in Iowa City. Many wires and trees came down, the power failed, and all the people watching fireworks in the park barely escaped when the storm passed ten feet over their heads. I knew that my daughter had been in the park with her mother that night, though I was not. At that time I was separated from the family; that particular evening I was at a birthday party for the girl who later became my second wife. Thus, that night had held a good deal of significance for me. Yet none of it was *in* the poem, nor did it seem to me that it *should* be. While I was writing this stanza, most of these problems had already occurred to me, yet something had wanted to keep that phrase about the Fourth of July. I had a moment of wild panic at the thought that perhaps I was becoming patriotic in my old age. Happily, I was soon able to quell *that* chimera. Yet, I still had my dilemma: if the Fourth of July didn't mean patriotism, what *did* it mean?

At this point, I put the poem aside, hoping that something might happen if I looked the other way. One Sunday morning several weeks later, I was sitting in a Quaker meeting when one of the members said something that annoyed me. In rough paraphrase it went, 'The measure of man's freedom is that he alone is given the power to reject God.' I am always bothered by people, especially Quakers, who talk about God—I started going to meetings to escape people who talk about things they don't know about. My own habit is to paraphrase such statements, substituting for the term "God" either "Nature" or "Life," since those are at least terms about which I think a person might know something. When I tried paraphrasing the Quaker's statement, I found myself confronting one of my own central problems. Shortly, I heard myself saying that, in Nature, man alone has the choice to withdraw from the reality in which he lives, and so has the power to die, either metaphorically or literally. I was specially concerned about this then, because I had recently returned from my sister's funeral. It seemed to me that she, disapproving the life about her and unwilling to find any other, had withdrawn into a very destructive and self-deceiving relationship with her mother. This, of course, had satisfied none of her real needs, but she was unable to change her course; she developed a severe case of asthma. One's breath *is* one's life; it seemed to me that in refusing to breathe, she had taken the next step in rejecting her life. When her problem became progressively worse and she reached the age at which it must have been clear that she would never marry or have any independent career, she took the logical last step. On the morning of the Fourth of July (one year after the storm of which I spoke earlier), her heart simply quit beating. To die on Independence Day seemed an act of terrible and destructive blamefulness, yet this may have been, in its way, the easiest solution of her dilemma—she had died spiritually (that is, as an animal moved by aims and opinions) years before. But I was now once again disturbed about this, for my daughter had just had an asthma attack. I felt that this was *her* way of refusing *her* life. (It happens that I was wrong about this, but that has no essential bearing on the poem; what matters is that I *did* believe this and was profoundly disturbed by it.) I felt that I must find some way to tell her that she must choose what reality was possible—that she was, of course, full of rage and regret for what she could not have, but that she was hardly alone in that. She still must choose what was unavoidable. This was the particular rebirth I wanted that year.

It was not until after the meeting that I realized I had been talking about my poem. It must have been this whole complex of problems about freedom, breathing and asthma which had smuggled the Fourth of July into the poem. This, too, must link with the ironic rhyme-word 'free' in the passage about cutting limbs off the trees, and again with the lines about snarling the pigeon in a net, for I apparently felt that I had helped snarl my daughter in a tangle of smother-love. It seemed to me—and I have often found this to be so—that my poem could develop a structure adequate to my experience only if, like the old sonata form, it carried two separate thematic areas at the same time. Plainly, the whole problem of freedom and guilt, which had at first been so very subordinate, must now be developed into a major thematic area, perhaps into the dominant theme.

I went about this in two ways. First, I added new material. After my original first stanza, I added a new one about the time when the child took her first breath and, with it, accepted her life. At the end of the poem, I added two stanzas: first, one stanza about her present refusal of breath (presented, however, as a memory of an earlier attack); finally, a stanza to sum up what I wanted to say to her, and what could only be said more or less doctrinally, but which I hoped was new enough, or personal enough, to be worth an abstract statement.

Since this new material brought with it a progression from the time of the child's birth to her present illness, it seemed that the material already in the poem should be rearranged to fit this chronological order. This involved numerous small changes which will be obvious; the largest change involved taking the original last stanza (about the blackbird and the killdeers), which dealt with the breakup of the marriage, and moving this material back before the original third stanza (about hacking the wrenched limbs off the tree), which dealt with the divorce and separation.

I found also, that to make these additions and changes, I had to change my stanza pattern by adding one more syllable in each of the first three lines of every stanza, and two more syllables in the fourth line. Finally, I had to give up my lines about stone-skipping and the Sunday lovers on the river-bank. This nearly broke my heart, but I promised myself to work them into a later poem. Like almost every other promise I have ever made myself, this one remains unfulfilled.

And a passage from a recent talk by C. Day Lewis on his unpublished poem, "Travelling Light":

I was thinking in the repetitive way that poets think . . . when suddenly the words came into my head, 'streamlined whales and hulls.' And then the word 'dilate' came into my head. And that did have a meaning for me. . . . Somehow I connected it with the Cotswolds and the time when I was a schoolmaster and used to walk over them, when the whole world seemed to dilate into a kind of boundless possibility. It is a romantic feeling but it is perfectly genuine. One other line came into my head a little later than the hulls and whales—'the course in view, the wake in flower.' And I thought, 'My word, how beautiful this is.' If one did not occasionally feel that, one would really stop in despair attempting to write verse.

It is obvious that something far more complex and sophisticated than simple notions of memory or association is needed to describe the dialectical movement of the creative process and it seems to me that the Freudian terms I have been employing come closer to conveying the dimensions and the texture of the creative process than, say, the naive associationism upon which Lowes had to depend for his study of Coleridge.

Will knowing about the operations of the creative process enable one to discriminate between a good poem and a bad one? Despite Goethe's letter of recommendation on behalf of the study of the creative process, my first impulse is to hide behind a lab coat and to say, with the meteorologist, I don't like tornadoes and I don't make them; all I do is study them. One can study the making of Snodgrass' poem and one can study the makings of another Michigan poet who is no doubt a welcome guest in an eternal Greenfield Village, and I suppose with equal success. But the last paragraph of Snodgrass' paper will not let me get away with a cheap answer; he writes:

I am left, then, with a very old-fashioned measure of a poem's worth—the depth of its sincerity. And it seems to me that the poets of our generation—those of us who have gone so far in criticism and analysis that we cannot ever turn back and be innocent again, who have such extensive resources for disguising ourselves from ourselves—that our only hope as artists is to continually ask ourselves, 'Am I writing what I *really* think? Not what is acceptable; not what my favorite intellectual would think in this situation; not what I wish I felt. Only what I cannot help thinking.' For I believe that the only reality which a man can ever surely know is that self he cannot help being, though he will only know that self though its interactions with the world around it. If he pretties it up, if he changes its meaning, if he gives it the voice of any borrowed authority, if in short he rejects this reality, his mind will be less than alive. So will his words.

Let us recall the journey of the mythological hero who, as I have tried to show, may be taken as the symbolic representa-

tion of the creative process. You will remember that in his rites
of passage he encounters an opposing force, he suffers, he dies
but revives, he continues his struggle, and, in the end, conquers. But the struggle he engages in must be a real struggle
in which the outcome must be uncertain and dependent on his
genuine efforts to conquer; he must win on his own, at whatever the cost to himself; anything less than this is false for the
very efficacy of his sacrifice, that is, the well-being of the community for whom he undergoes his agony, is inextricably tied
up with the honesty of the conflict and of the combatants alike.
What I am trying to say, then, is that the intensity and the
genuineness of the struggle to bring the poem to birth and to
realize its meaning fully in all its aspects, to make it convey the
totality of the experience it expresses is, in the long run, the
measure of difference between a good poem and a bad one.
We need not accept the poet's vision but we must be changed
by it, and he can change us only after he has changed himself.
He must meet and face up to and finally conquer the double
antagonism of the creative crisis: to fulfill its form as he fulfills its meaning. I have recently received from Dr. John
Paterson of California a dramatic demonstration of this dual
demand in *The Making of "The Return of the Native."* My
friend and colleague, A.J.M. Smith, has, I think, expressed
the poet's twofold obligation with classical elegance in his
poem, "To a Young Poet":

> Tread the metallic nave
> Of this windless day with
> A pace designed and grave:
> Iphigenia in her myth
>
> Creating for stony eyes
> An elegant, fatal dance
> Was signed with no device
> More alien to romance

Than I would have you find
In the stern, autumnal face
Of Artemis, whose kind
Cruelty makes duty grace,

Whose votary alone
Seals the affrighted air
With the worth of a hard thing done
Perfectly, as though without care.

I suppose that by now it will be assumed that I am going to jump on the Jungian bandwagon. But this I am not going to do, first, because of the irrational reason that I have an almost pathological antipathy to the Jungian mystique, and second, because as much as I would like to say that the closer a work of art comes to the myth and ritual pattern the greater it is, the last vestige of scholarly honesty in me prevents me from doing so. As I have argued on another occasion, there are at least five questions which have to be answered before the myth and ritual approach can be accepted. First, there is no agreement as to what the myth and ritual pattern actually is. As a matter of fact, no myth and ritual pattern as such exists or ever existed in any real sense; it is a modern, scholarly reconstruction of diverse materials drawn from divergent sources, and no two experts agree as to its exact constitution. Second, there is no agreement as to the aesthetic and ethical effects of the pattern on works of literature; using the same pattern, different critics have come up with antithetical conclusions as to its effect on the same work. Thus, as I have been confused to note, to one group of critics, the Shakespeare of the last plays is a kind of Christian Olympian, a kind of Sophocles and Goethe in one; to another group, he is a tired, disillusioned old man, playing technical tricks for his own cynical amusement; yet both groups profess to follow the same method. Third, there is no satisfactory way of explaining how the pattern enters into the work of art. Are there demonstrable historical or psychological steps involved? Is the use of the pattern a conscious, deliberate aesthetic decision of the artist himself? Or is myth inherent in the work of art, and, if so, how is one to be distinguished from the other? If the artist reshapes the pattern for his own purposes, and I know of no instance where a sophisticated work of art follows the myth and ritual pattern point by point, what is the need of the pattern to start with? Fourth, what is the critical validity of a method which in effect sets up a pattern derived from sources outside the texts and then judges their success or failure in terms of their approach to or distance from conformity to that pattern? Finally, if the end of the myth and ritual pattern is accommodation to and acceptance of the order of nature, the imposition of the will to believe and the will to live in dignity with justice in accordance to reason in a universe quite devoid of those values, what are we to make of those artists who in the end have turned away from that vision and have told us, like the little boy in the fable, that the emperor is naked, that the universe is indifferent, and that man's efforts are vain and in vain; I have in mind the Shakespeare who could leave Othello dead and Iago alive.

It will be noticed, I trust, that I have been considering the creative process as the central span in the bridge of communication between the artist and his audience. As a consequence of this attitude, I have also been thinking of art as essentially a social phenomenon, not as a thing in itself, the poem on the printed page, but rather as a relationship set up between the writer and the reader, as the means by which the former enlarges the experience of the latter in a manner so heightened, so sharpened, and so exactly focused that both the totality and the essence of that experience are re-experienced by the reader. And not only is literature itself a social phenomenon, but the very device by which it fulfills itself is also a social phenomenon, I mean the symbol. We can describe the mode of operation of the symbol only in paradoxical terms. It must be individual, yet typical; it must be unique, yet universal; being unmistakably the thing itself, it must be just as unmistakably the thing for which it stands. Whatever their origins, there appear to be certain symbols which have the power of immediately quickening our interest and of deepening our understanding, for they seem to us as wells of significance in whose bottomless waters we discern endless depths of meaning. Nor does there appear to be any area of experience from which symbols cannot be derived. From the observation of nature have come the symbols of the tree of life, the sad cry of the nightingale, the lily of the field, the dove, the lamb, the deer, the wasteland, the cherry orchard, and the tiger burning bright. Again, the symbol may be an individual who sums up in himself in concentrated form all that our experience of human character has taught us: Ulysses the shrewd man, Achilles the man of wrath, Aeneas the dutiful man, Tristram the man of passion, Troilus the gull, Robinson Crusoe the self-sufficient man, and K. the man in the middle. Or experiences drawn from the passage of life itself may be of symbolic significance: an example is the symbol of the hero's journey combined with his quest. In its most generalized form, the hero goes forth, encounters obstacles and adversaries, engages in mortal combat, is defeated, dies, is reborn triumphantly, marries; at the height of his power seems to fade away into obscurity, and appears in the end in some form of apotheosis. In this connection, we remember the wanderings of Ulysses, Jason's quest of the golden fleece, the search for the Holy Grail, Dante's descent into the underworld, the adventures of Don Quixote, Pilgrim's progress, the search of the Ancient Mariner, Ahab's chase after Moby Dick, Hans Castorp's sojourn on, and descent from, the magic mountain, and—to complete the circle—the memorable day in the life of that other and later, yet the same, Ulysses. In other words, any object or any attribute may be invested with symbolic meaning: we know St. Sebastian by his arrows, justice by her scales, matrimony by its gold band; we know light by Apollo and Apollo by light; we know it is winter when Adonis is slain and we know it is spring when he is brought to life again; we know Eve by woman and woman by Eve; we know by signs and symbols. From this we learn that art abhors the abstract, the general, and the typical, yet by passionately concerning itself with the concrete, the unique, and the individual it gives our unlocalized feelings and generalized ideas viability, vivacity, and vision.

Art, then, takes up experience and boldly wrenches it into new shapes; it does not so much hold the mirror up to nature as it confronts nature with a new, fresh, and unique version of itself. And, in the space which lies between experience as it is and experience as it has been remade by art, arises the vision of experience as it ought to be. From this process of reshaping and re-forming experience, is derived that enlargement of experience which is the hallmark of art—an enlargement which is not one-dimensional but operates on all the levels of our being; for it is not merely aesthetic, or intellectual, or emotional, or moral alone, but all these together and more besides. Further, because it clarifies and crystallizes experiences, art cuts across those differences of temperament, time, place, and point of view which separate man from man; and this is especially true of literature, which is less burdened by the difficulties of technique as a medium of expression and communication than are the other arts. Despite the gulfs of time and custom which separate us from the Greeks of twenty-five hundred years ago, we can still feel in ourselves the agonies of Oedipus; from across the late Middle Ages we still hear the sound of the horns' warning and start up with Little Musgrave; the passage of a hundred and fifty years has not yet filled the aching void left by the death of Lucy.

Moreover, by virtue of the representative power of literature, we can participate in experiences which, were they to happen to us in the course of our everyday lives, would be too shattering to bear or understand. Surely, few of us would want —nor would we have the stamina—to pass through Othello's vicissitudes; yet, through the medium of tragedy, we can vicariously take part in his greatness, his suffering, his fall, and his rebirth. We have thus added dimensions of experience to ourselves safely, yet with the intensity needed to effect our growth in stature. It is far from certain that experience by itself is the best teacher, and life by itself can be cruel and pointless, quite devoid of humanity, meaning, and nobility. But once experiences have been put through the ordering and purging pressures of art, they yield up the qualities we need and seek. By vicarious participation, we can speak and act freely and greatly, we can safely release our pent-up feelings, we can cleanse ourselves of dross and of evil. We experience largeness of heart and mind, we are exhilarated by a sense of purpose, we see what man can be.

This process by which the artist reaches out into the mind and soul of his audience, the process by which in turn the audience reaches back into the mind and soul of the artist, this process, the creative process, is, then, by its very nature surely one of the most compelling means of human communion; it is a bond—I am tempted to say the bond—of the human community. But I should be putting a false gloss on the picture if I appeared to be giving the impression that it is a bond which invariably and permanently binds. Not all men, in fact very few men, respond to the bond of creation, and many of those who do, do so in ways crippling both to themselves and to the arts. The Greeks who were awed by Aeschylus could blithely betray each other in the halls of the Parthenon. The Romans whose ears were so attuned to the delicate ironies of Horace were deaf to the cries from Galilee. The Florentines who were safely led from hell to heaven by Dante repaid him by exile. The Germans who wept over the sorrows of Werther built Buchenwald. The French, of whom a Frenchman wrote: "For it is true that French intelligence has no equal; . . . it is the only intelligence that still exists in the world of today; we are the only people in the world, I repeat coolly, who know how to think," have demonstrated that intelligence at work in Algeria. The Russian, still thrilled by the performance of his favorite ballerina, does not notice the desecrated grave. And the American who sat in the halls where Emerson and Holmes and Brandeis once taught can order the resumption of nuclear testing.

For the bond of creation, like the bond of the human community, is man made, and what man can make, he can destroy. The choice is his, and no metaphysical imperative moves or stays his hand; he alone is the agent of his life and of his destruction. The arts more often than not lead him to the waters of love and life, but the furies of hate, avarice, ambition, stupidity, and pride harrow him into the desert of denial and death. In the never ending struggle between Eros and Thanatos, the arts, together with the fundamental mode of their expression, the creative process, stand beside Eros. It is a noble choice but it is not the decisive choice; that choice remains locked in the brain and breast of man. As of this moment, I do not know what that choice will be.

(1960)

The Agony and the Triumph

Pʀᴏᴍᴘᴛᴇᴅ ʙʏ ᴛʜᴇ publication of Francis Russell's *Tragedy in Dedham* to re-read the letters of Sacco and Vanzetti, I was once more struck by their power to move, and even to exalt, me. I cannot attribute this force to the recollection of personal involvement in the case; I was too young when it started and too uninformed when it ended; yet later cases of similar miscarriages of justice, particularly that of the Trenton Six, in which I took some part directly, have not affected me as much as the Sacco-Vanzetti case which has become for me the archetypal exemplar of the struggle for individual justice, just as the Spanish Civil War in its time became for me the archetypal exemplar of the struggle for international justice: both are the benchmarks for the test of conscience.

Nor am I alone in this conviction concerning the trial and execution of Sacco and Vanzetti. Though it is over thirty-five years ago since they were sent to their death, studies of the case still continue to appear regularly and to provoke argument. Russell's book came out in 1962; it concludes that Vanzetti was probably innocent and Sacco probably guilty; but even at this late date, this half-hearted verdict was strongly attacked in many of the reviews. Robert H. Montgomery's *Sacco-Vanzetti, The Murder and the Myth*, 1960, is one of the rare recent defenses of the Massachusetts courts: "Sacco and Vanzetti had a fair trial, and the case would never have become a *cause célèbrè* unless the Reds had made it one." One hears here the echoes of the era of McCarthy just as one hears loud and clear in the case itself the echoes of the era of the infamous Palmer Raids. The 1960 revision of Herbert B. Ehrmann's *The Untried Case,* first published in 1933, effectively disposes of Montgomery's arguments. Another example of the continuing grip of the case is Robert P. Weeks' *Commonwealth vs. Sacco and Vanzetti,* a collection of documents for classroom use, which was first published in 1958 and has undergone four printings since then. Nor has the American artistic imagination failed to be stirred by the case. Many writers and intellectuals of the time—Harry Elmer Barnes, Charles A. Beard, Robert Benchley, Heywood Broun, Malcolm Cowley, John Dewey, Bernard De Voto, Theodore Dreiser, John Dos Passos, Felix Frankfurter, Michael Gold, Granville Hicks, Rockwell Kent, James A. Landis, John Howard Lawson, William Ellery Leonard, Sinclair Lewis, Walter Lippman, Robert Morse Lovett, H. L. Mencken, Samuel E. Morrison, Lewis Mumford, William A. Neilson, Dorothy Parker, Bliss Perry, Katherine Anne Porter, William A. White, and Edmund Wilson, among them—voiced their protest in pamphlet, petition, and picket-line. For other writers, the case became the focal point of a number of their works, some still powerful, others admittedly disappointing, but together adding up to a sizeable list in which may be included Maxwell Anderson's and Harold Hickerson's plays, *Gods of the Lightning* and *Outside Looking In* (1928); Anderson's verse play, *Winterset* (1935); Nathan Asch's *Pay Day* (1930); Bernard De Voto's novel, *We Accept with Pleasure* (1934); Howard Fast, *The Passion of Sacco and Vanzetti* (1953); James T. Farrell, *Bernard Clare* (1946); Ruth McKenney, *Jake Home* (1943); Upton Sinclair, *Boston* (1928), as well as references to the case in *Between Two Worlds* (1941) and *World's End* (1940); and James Thurber's and Elliott Nugent's play, *The Male Animal* (1940). In 1932

Ben Shahn exhibited a group of twenty-three gouaches called "The Passion of Sacco and Vanzetti"; he later wrote of the aesthetic and ideological problem they posed in *The Shape of Content* (1957): "... there began for me the long artistic tug of war between idea and image. At first, the danger of such a separation did not appear." Absorbed by the Dreyfus affair, he did a series of portraits of the leading actors in the case and found within the Dreyfus pictures "... a new avenue of expression opening up before me, a means by which I could unfold a great deal of my most personal thinking and feeling without loss of simplicity." Still preoccupied with the problem of expressing idea in form, he turned naturally to the Sacco-Vanzetti case and did another group of portraits of the chief participants in the case in a style "... not unmindful of Giotto, and of the simplicity with which he had been able to treat of connected events—each complete in itself, yet all recreating the religious drama, so living a thing to him. ... I felt that my own work was now becoming identified with my person." Thus for one artist at least the Sacco-Vanzetti case had the effect of fusing eye, hand, and mind into the aesthetic-moral-social vision of "The Unifying Power of Art," as he calls it.

For Dos Passos, the fire in the crucible of the case burned even more fiercely. The beam which supports *The Big Money* (1936) is the metaphor of the two nations and, while the phrase itself is derived from Disraeli, the immediate motivating experience behind it is the experience of the Sacco-Vanzetti case; this, I should add, is the judgment of Louis Joughin and of Alfred Kazin as well. It is in "The Camera Eye" (50) where the image is given its most angry, bitter, and poignant expression:

America our nation has been beaten by strangers who have taken the clean words our fathers spoke and made them slimy and foul . . .

their hired men sit on the judge's bench . . . they have the dollars the guns the armed forces the power-plants . . .

all right we are two nations . . .

but do they know that the old words of the immigrants are being renewed in blood and agony tonight . . . the language of the beaten nation is not forgotten in our ears tonight . . .

the men in the death house made the old words new before they died.

It was in this same mood of angered betrayal of an ideal that Edna St. Vincent Millay wrote in "Fear" (1937):

These men were castaways upon our shore, and we, an ignorant and savage tribe, have put them to death because their speech and their manners were different from our own and because to the untutored mind that which is strange is in its infancy ludicrous, but in its prime evil, dangerous, and to be done away with. . . . For, although I was born in this country, and am possessed of that simple right of the citizen to hold any opinions he may hold, yet to avail myself of this right and to express opinions contrary to the opinions of the majority may become, as we have lately seen, a folly punishable by the extreme correction. . . . The world, the physical world, and that once was all in all to me, has at moments such as these no road through a wood, no stretch of shore, that can bring me comfort. The beauty of these things can no longer at such moments make up to me at all for the ugliness of man, his cruelty, his greed, his lying face.

But this is merely to enumerate effects, not to account for causes. I believe that as they underwent the harsh and bitter experiences of their arrest, the trial presided over by the implacable and insatiable Judge Thayer, and their conviction in Dedham; the appeals of their lawyers, the adverse rulings of the Judge, and of the Supreme Court of Massachusetts; the hopes and fears first for executive clemency, then the attempts to get a new trial on the grounds of judicial prejudice in the Superior Court of Massachusetts, the lower Federal Court, and finally before Mr. Justice Holmes and Mr. Justice Stone of the Supreme Court of the United States, all in the end denied; the arguments and bickerings over the tactics of legal appeal and public protest; the continuous imprisonment for seven years, first in Dedham Jail, afterwards in Charlestown State Prison, then in the death house on two separate occasions, and including for Vanzetti four months in the Bridgewater State Hospital for the Criminal Insane, and finally two last-minute stays of execution—under the blows of these battering experiences, Sacco, and even more, Vanzetti began to see them in the form of a drama in which they were cast in the role of the tragic proletarian protagonist engaged in a cosmic struggle against the overwhelming evil force of the cruelty of capitalism embodied in the state of Massachusetts and in Judge Thayer, the outcome of which would determine, not alone their fate, but the fate of all mankind for good or for ill. I believe too that this vision came to Sacco more as a result of his instinctive, perhaps naive, faith in the order and goodness of nature and less as a result of his philosophical and political convictions while to Vanzetti it was the product of his reading, his devotion to the principles of anarchism, and his own deliberate and powerful train of thought. And I am convinced that if the letters of Sacco and Vanzetti are read within the framework of this tragic vision, and furthermore, if the ultimate sources of this vision are at the same time recalled and continually borne in mind, then surely a commanding explanation of their strength to sway us is thereby revealed.

The theme of the beneficence of nature makes a very early appearance in Sacco's letters. Writing to Mrs. Cerise Jack, February 26, 1924, Sacco nostalgically recalls his father's vineyards, last seen by him sixteen years ago, a loss made all the more unsupportable by his imprisonment. In a letter to Mrs. Elizabeth Evans, June 18, 1926, he speaks of ". . . the harmony of nature . . . resting upon the soil of the mother nature." (All citations from the Sacco and Vanzetti letters are taken from *The Letters of Sacco and Vanzetti,* edited by Marion Denman Frankfurter and Gardner Jackson, the paperback edition, 1960, published by E. P. Dutton and Co., Inc.; first edition, 1928, by The Viking Press, Inc.). Again, to Mrs. Jack, he laments the "sad bars" which confine him and exclaims: "But there between all the harmonies of the mother nature, under the radiant rays of sun where everything grows so vividly in the human mind and in the heart, love, life and all the vegetation beautifully. Oh life!" To Vanzetti, February 4, 1927, he expresses hope for both of them: ". . . I were thinking that after all these long persecution years instead to open our prison door, the storm continues to pass upon our shoulder one more cruel than another. But there between these turbulent clouds, a luminous path run always toward the truth, . . ." —home, wife, children—"And not far off but near this dearest vision, at the cypress tree, where the sun light were shining, your loyal and faithful picture of yesterday. Today in my eyes appear as a martyrdom." In almost his very last letter, he writes to his youngest son Ines, July 19, 1927: "For the things of beauty and of good in this life, mother nature gave to us all, for the conquest and the joy of liberty. The men of this dying old society, they brutally have pulled me away from the embrace of your brother and your poor mother. But, in spite of all, the free spirit of your father's faith still survives, and I have lived for it and for the dream that some day I would have come back to life, to the embrace of your dear mother, among our friends and comrades again, but woe is me!" What made Sacco's disappointment in the promise of American life even more difficult to bear was his identification of the beneficence of nature with the goodness of America itself, "the country that was always in my dreams." He tells Mrs. Jack, February 12, 1924, that Americans should be proud of Lincoln, and, mentioning Washington, Jefferson, and Lincoln together, he says: "The history of these three great Presidents strike the feeling of the humble reclus. . . ."

Characteristically, the idea of the link between America and nature does not occur in Vanzetti's letters. To him, nature is a source of strength and independence, and several times in his letters he mentions the fact that his father ran a successful farm to which he could have returned at any time he wished were it not that his ". . . conscience do not permit me to be a business man. . . ." Rather, ". . . I am the son of Nature, and

I am so rich that I do not need any money. And for this they say I am a murderer and condemned me to death" (letter to Mrs. Evans, July 22, 1921). To Mrs. L. N. Russell he writes, September 18, 1925: "My father own a beautiful garden and a good deal of land among the better veins and position of the town-territory, which extends itself at the feet of beautiful hills." He goes on to list the number of crops of hay it brought, the quantity of cows, the many tenants, the large size of the farm buildings, the up-to-date use of the rotation system, the careful raising of silkworms, the growing of many varieties of fruit—all told with evident pride and with a sense of his belonging to a productive, modern, and respectable family, and intended to prove that his rejection of property is a matter of principle not of necessity. Even more lyrical a description of his farm home is the letter of October 7, 1926, addressed to Mrs. M. O'Sullivan: "My Father has plenty of good land and a beautiful garden. . . . As for our garden, it takes a poet of first magnitude to worthy speak of it, so beautiful, so unspeakably beautiful it is. . . . Yet, I think that the wonder of the garden's wonders is the banks of its paths." No wonder he is capable of a phrase such as this from a letter to Mary Donovan, December 19, 1926: "With the fierce music of the cold and strong wind blowing through this bright morning. . . ." And no wonder that he begins his speech to the court, April 9, 1927, with the proud boast: "My father in Italy is in a good condition."

But nature as such was not sufficient enough a concept for Vanzetti. In a letter to Mrs. Virginia MacMechan, April 26, 1923, he turns the images of simple nature into metaphor for his belief in anarchism: "Just imagine what it would be, for a man confined in a miasmatic, muddy swamp, to feel at once his chains loose and freely walk toward the summits, to dive in the first stream of living waters, and then proceed, surrounded and deluged by sun and winds, height and height, and drink at the alpine springs and reach the highest summit, and from there dominate the immense vista of lands, waters and sky. . . .

Oh, friend, the anarchism is as beauty as a woman for me, perhaps even more since it include all the rest and me and her. Calm, serene, honest, natural, viril, muddy and celestial at once, austere, heroic, fearless, fatal, generous and implacable— all these and more it is. . . ." To Mrs. Evans he declares in winter of 1923: "For me, the moral sense come from the strongest instincts of every living being. I mean the instincts of conservation and happiness, which as soon as the intelligence comes, generates a third instinct, the love of the race. . . . But we have instincts that lead us, and intelligence that serves them, and after all, a nature fundamentally equal. Those things would be enough if man would not be susceptible of degeneration, as soon as he left his natural way of life." A year later, to Mrs. Evans again, he writes: "For the water in liquid state, freedom is, to flow from a relative up to a relative down; or vice versa when the water is in vapor state. For the fire, freedom is, to expand and to arise. In short, freedom is, for each and all things of the universe, *to follows their natural tendencies*—and to fulfill their own virtues, qualities and capacities." And he bursts into a paean of praise for nature: "O the blessing green of the wilderness and of the open land. . . . O the supreme extasies and mystery of the starry night, heavenly creature of the eternity." Yet not for Sacco and Vanzetti, chained and unfree ". . . to use our natural faculty of locomotion to carry us from our cells to the open horizon— under the sun at daytime—under the visible stars at night." So man and nature are fused into one being, for, as he writes to Irene Benton, March 29, 1927: "The dearest manifestation of Nature to me is mankind with his miseries and proudness, his glories and his shames, his smallness and his grandeur."

This, then, is the cosmic order of nature whose destruction by evil in the form of an unjust social order symbolized by the Commonwealth of Massachusetts and its representative, Judge Thayer, Sacco and Vanzetti see themselves blocking even to the death. The metaphor of cosmic drama and the concept which lies behind it is as old as the history of mankind itself, and what Sacco and Vanzetti have succeeded in doing is to link themselves to it, naively and even crudely, but for all that strongly and with entire commitment, and they draw their strength and endurance to confront their vicissitudes from it. In a letter to Mrs. Jack, April 9, 1924, Sacco recalls meeting an old comrade while walking the streets of Boston looking for a job: ". . . but this spontaneous affection it shows at all times in the heart of one who has reciprocal love and sublime faith and such a remembrance it will never disappear in the heart of the proletarian." A month later, in another letter to Mrs. Jack, he recounts a "terrible and beautiful" dream: a strike is taking place in a mining camp in Pennsylvania when a protest meeting is surrounded by soldiers with fixed bayonets; Sacco jumps up on a little hill in the middle of the crowd to appeal to the soldiers: "Brothers you will not fire on your own brothers just because they tell you to fire," but as he speaks, a soldier fires and strikes him through the heart; he falls, his hand upon his heart, and he awakes, his hand still upon his heart. On December 28, 1924, he assures Vanzetti that they will yet win because they are faithful to their comrades; on October 24, 1926, grieving over the death of Eugene Debs, he praises Debs' noble faith in the workers which is his own inspiration on ". . . the bright road for the conquest, the joy of liberty and the happiness of all." Even as the end approaches, his faith in his cause remains firm; writing to Leonard Abbott, April 1, 1927, he says: "In regards to me, I have love for nothing else than faith, which has given me courage and strength in all these terrible long years of struggle, and today and yesterday, I feel to be proud to have loved this faith. . . ." To Mrs. Evans, May 8, 1927: ". . . the right part has remain always the pride of an sincere faith which one have love and for it suffered and know to fall as he have suffered and loved. . . ." Again, to Gardner Jackson, June 14, 1927: "It is true, indeed, they can execute the body but they cannot execute the idea which is bound to live." But even for him, the burden becomes too great; to Mrs. Evans, June 23, 1927: ". . . none other should suffering no pain but I only should suffering and crusifice from this iniquitous law. . . ." And finally, he writes in his farewell letter to his son, Dante, August 18, 1927:

I say that our ineffable affection reciprocal, is today more than any other time, of course. This is not only a great deal but it is grand because you can see the real brotherly love, not only in joy but also and more in the struggle. . . . Much have we suffered during this long Calvary. . . . help the weak ones that cry for help, help the prosecuted and the victim, because that are your better friends; they are the comrades that fight and fall as your father and Bartolo fought and fell yesterday for the conquest of joy of freedom for all and the poor workers. In this struggle of life you will find more love and be loved. . . . Yes, Dante, they can crucify our bodies today as they are doing, but they cannot destroy our ideas, that will remain for the youth of the future to come.

"He that humiliate himself, exalt himself." "To know, to suffer is the sole real, heroism." These lines, the first from a letter to Alice Blackwell, September 15, 1924, the other from a letter to Mary Donovan, December 5, 1925, reveal at once the sharpness and style of Vanzetti's mind. For him the struggle for justice is the noblest aspiration of man: "It need," he writes Mrs. Glendower Evans, June 22, 1921, "love, light, spirit of sacrifice, ideas, conscience, instincts. It need more conscience, more hope and more goodness." And he reverts to a theme constantly in his mind, that a man of principle needs no money and cannot therefore be tempted to steal or murder for it: "The clearness of mind, the peace of the conscience, the determination and force of will, the intelligence, all, all what make the man feeling to be a part of the life, force and intelligence of the universe, will be brake by a crime. I know that, I see that, I tell that to everybody: Do not violate the law of nature, if you do not want to be miserable. . . . I am the son of Nature, and I am so rich that I do not need any money. And for this they say I am a murderer and condemned me to death. Death? It is nothing. Abbominium is cruel thing."

Vanzetti is fully aware of the two sides of his character

which his hard role in life has so forcefully brought out in him: on the one hand, the lover of mankind: "When one has passed through such a trial as mine . . . he loves as himself those who stand with him for the good cause" (letter to Francis Bigelow, December, 1922); on the other hand, the lonely, dedicated, and suffering strategist of principle: "The price of perfection is high, sorrowful. I suffered more in making my conscience, than in facing my trial. I am a bitter polemist, a merciless theorist, and I know I cause to others much anguish" (letter to Mrs. Elsie Hillsmith, May 6, 1923). And again to Alice Blackwell, January 24, 1924: "And I do not fear the consequences of my utterances. I am in their hands, let them crucify me if it fitted them. It is in these conditions that I am now that I like to take my ground and assume my responsibilities—no matter how dreadful." A month later, in another letter to Alice Blackwell, February 27, 1924, he sets forth his creed in some detail: "I abhor useless violence. I would my blood to prevent the sheading of blood, . . . And if tragedy is compelled to us, who knows; who knows if to speak now is not my duty? The champion of life and of the liberty should not yield before the death. The struggle for the liberty, between the oppressor and the oppressed, shall continue beyond the life, beyond the graves." The champion of liberty is impaled on the dilemma of action; on the one hand, he hates: "The sorrow of their victims torture me in blood and spirit. As for me, I would forgive them but I could not, for I would be a traitor of the race. . . . The only vengeance which could placate me is the realization of freedom, the great deliverance which would beneficiate all my friends as well as all my enemies; All." On the other hand, he would love: "The more I live, the more I suffer, the more I am inclined to forgive, to be generous, and that the violence as such does not resolve the problem of life." In this dilemma, then, in which the good he would do is perverted by the evil he must do, he is sustained by the rightness of his cause: "It is supremely sweet to me— my consciousness of superiority, of righteousness, to know that I can judge and that the future shall bow to me, the doomed, and curse my judges." But a year later, writing again to Alice Blackwell, October 27, 1925, he finds the sweetness of his righteousness has turned to gall and vinegar: "I am yet man enough to look straight into the eyes, the black ghastly reality and the tragedy of my life. And I would have the deadly joke to end, no matter how, this very moment." Yet he can overcome his bitterness in the contemplation of the meaning of his life; writing to Virginia MacMechan, May 15, 1926, he says:

But I was prompted by my nature to an ideal of freedom and of justice to all—and this is the worst of the crime to my enemies. The fact that for it and for consciousness I have renounced to a life of ease and of comfort, to wealth, to worldly ambitions, goods and honors, even to the joys of love—make me a terrible criminal to the eyes of my judges—a criminal capable of every crime. In fact, I voluntarily submitted myself to hard labor, poverty, dangers and persecutions. Had I renegated my principles after my arrest, I would not find myself, now, on the threshold of a death-house. I neither boast nor exalt, nor pity myself. I followed my call, I have my conscience serene, I regret nothing except the unspeakable agony that my destiny causes to my most beloved ones. And strange indeed, I cannot even hate my murderers and my diffamers. I even pity them. But oh! how they hate; how they fear; how unhappy they are! . . .

So, a few hours before his execution, in his last talk with W. G. Thompson, August 22, 1927, when Thompson suggested that he forgive his enemies, he said that he would think of it; he did, and just before he stepped in the chair, he thanked the warden and his guards for their kindness to him and then turned to the spectators and asked them to remember that he forgave some of his enemies.

Independent as was Vanzetti's mode and quality of thought, it was at the same time the product of considerable reading and study. In the course of his letters, he mentions as having read or quotes from Marcus Aurelius, Bakunin, Charles Beard, Dante, Debs, Emerson, Anatole France, Galleani, Godwin, Gori, Gorki, William James, Hugo, Kropotkin, Lincoln, Jack London, Malatesta, Michelet, Marx, Mirabeau, Pellico, Proudhon, Reclus, Renan, James Harvey Robinson, Shelley, Herbert Spencer, Mark Twain, Tolstoi, and Thoreau. The tradition of philosophical anarchism is of course very strong in him and from it Vanzetti derived his philosophy of history and the location of his place in history. As with all philosophers who are seriously concerned with the role and effects of action in history, he believed that the historic process would by its very character inevitably bring about the justice he sought; at the same time, he was fully aware that without the deliberate, active efforts of men on its behalf the historic process on its own alone was powerless to fulfill its mission. Writing to Alice Blackwell, June 10, 1925, he tells this revealing anecdote: "One beautiful morning, a young bandit, a lifer, with a young wife and two children, looked through the window of our shop, and said to me, 'What a wonderful good world this will be 5,000 years from now, if it will exist.' 'Yes, then it may be, 5,000 times better, or as well, 5,000 times worse than it is now. It depends on the people's will, actions and capacities.' Thus I answered and explained to him—because I had seen at once that he believed that the world must get better by force—I mean by its fate." Again, to Alice Blackwell, April 24, 1926: "I would like, but I cannot believe, that the triumph of good in this world is predestined. Yet, there is but two possible suppositions: either that we will be doomed, or else, by ourselves and other things, redeemed. The latter is hope no matter how foolish it may be; the former is despair, and better, a hundred times better, a foolish hope than a crazy desperation, for, all desperations are insane. But to keep myself near home, within the fence of the relative, I believe that a little more of voluntarism, and a little less of fatalism, in all what concerns the human powers and possibilities, would be more salutary to all. . . ." To Mrs. Maude Pettyjohn, December 11, 1926, he writes that his experience as a prisoner increases his understanding but diminishes his power of expression; he can no longer express himself at the best of his power:

The Agony and the Triumph

The crux of this inner drama is not only about expression—it is that I doubt my own thoughts, my opinions, my feeling, my sentiments, beliefs and ideals. I am sure of nothing, I know nothing. When I think of a thing and try to understand it, I see that in the time, in the place, and in the matter that thing is, both before and after, related to so many other things that I, following its relations, both backward and forward, see it disappear in the ocean of the unknown, and myself lost in it. It is easy to create a universal system, to human minds; that is why we are blessed by so many universal systems, while no one knows what a bed buck is. The sense of relativity and of measure is a progress on the sense of the absolute and infinite, for the former is a capacity of discernment, the second a mental abstraction, a symbol of the 'abroad' of our senses and relative knowledge.

He believes that man is born with the capacity to acquire ideas and their expression and that these are imposed on the individual from without by church, school, and state so that, against his will and intentions, he himself was made ". . . stupid, ignorant, vile, coward, arrogant, self-conceited, brutal, greedy, ferocious and filthy and falsely proud, and humble, that the best of my essence was choked in myself, or, what is still worse, distorted and aberrated." But it was ". . . by a rinnovation of [my] own previous self, through a self reaction, an inner tragedy which costed me the bleeding of my heart's blood, that I re-began and became what I am now." Therefore he is not a determinist but believes in ". . . hope, faith, optimism, confidence" which ". . . are good to the individual"; they are "part of the race wisdom; an historical experience." He concludes that we must look reality straight in the face, not to allow ourselves to be overwhelmed by adversity, not to be "scared by black prospects," but to fight them with all our force. From the philosophy of free will stems, he believes, ". . . the merciless of the law, the dishonesty of the State, the ferocity monstruous of the churches, and the immorality of the pure moralists"; from the philosophy of determinism comes the weakening of the human will, idle fatalism, self-indulgence, and irresponsibility; but "As for me, I believe to a certain extent in both, as limited and changeable phenomenum, interdependent, and dependent from some higher phenomenism. So, I have no ultimate word on them and I remain a *Voluntarist.*"

Vanzetti is often able to condense his thought into tough, aphoristic expression. On war: "We have war because we are not sufficiently heroic for a life which does not need war" (letter to Alice Blackwell, December 28, 1926). On words which are intended to conceal: ". . . in such contingence words are not the echo of the action—first motion, then thought— but symptoms of want of will. Then words are but empty voices to cloak a consciousness of nothingness, echoes, pretentions of want and of nothingness—and worse of course, to an aim or an object, than silence, might fall eloquent silence" (letter to Leonard Abbott, March 24, 1927). On learning from one's own experience: "It is a quarter century that I am struggling to dis-learn and re-learn; to disbelieve and re-believe; to deny and re-confirm. By little of school and very much experience (well and rightly understood) I became a cosmopolite perambulating phylosopher of the main road,— crushing, burning a world within me and creating a new —better one. Meanwhile I am having the worst of the worst one" (letter to Mrs. Gertrude Winslow, April 3, 1927). On the psychology of his enemies: "We dead, they think they will have rest, peace, retributions, and honors. How transparently it appears that the gods deprive of wisdom those they want to lose. The insanity of our murderers—who kill us for worldly honors and conservations of justice—does not consist in lack of wit, suttleness, or what not, but in being invaded by a sort of obsession which lead them into an abyss—to innihilation" (letter to Mrs. Elizabeth Evans, May 24, 1927). On the inter-mingling of good and evil in this world: "To my ultimate analysis, it seems to me that the forces of good and evil are of a same nature and that all the forces are essentially good inasmuch they create life, preserves life, are life them-

selves. Their good or bad influence upon us are determine by
the quantities, conditions, circumstances and forms in which
they exercise themselves" (letter to Mrs. Sarah Adams, May 25,
1927). On the form of justice in the future: ". . . a new conception of justice is plowing its way in the soul of mankind; a
justice that centered on man as man" (letter to Alice Blackwell, May 31, 1927). And on breaking out of the endless cycle
of historic repetition: "Anarchy, the anarchists alone, we only
can break these deadly circles and set life in such a way that
by a natural synchronism, produced by the very nature of
the things which create the new order, history will be
streamed toward the infinite sea of freedom, instead to turn
in the above said dead, close circle, as, it seems it did 'til
now" (letter to Li Pei Kan, July 23, 1927).

No better analysis of the characters of Sacco and Vanzetti
can be made than Vanzetti's own statement in the notes for
his address to Judge Thayer but which he was prevented from
speaking in court by the pronouncement of sentence. Of
Sacco, he said: "Sacco is a heart, a faith, a character, a man;
a man lover of nature and of mankind." On himself, he was
most severe: "Oh yes, I may be more witful, as some have put
it, I am a better babbler than he is," but W. G. Thompson
redressed the balance in his record of his last conversation
with Vanzetti: "In this closing scene the impression of him
which had been gaining ground in my mind for three years
was deepened and confirmed—that he was a man of powerful
mind, and unselfish disposition, of seasoned character, and
of devotion to high ideals. There was no sign of breaking
down or of terror at approaching death. At parting he gave
me a firm clasp of the hand and a steady glance, which
revealed unmistakably the depth of his feeling and the
firmness of his self-control."

Earlier, I named the American intellectuals who strove to
bring Sacco and Vanzetti the justice which in the end was
denied them. By itself, it is an impressive list, but if we place
against it another list of American writers who lived and

worked during the seven years of Sacco's and Vanzetti's arrest, trial, public agitation, and execution, and yet who kept silent, it shrinks to a small list of an honorable eloquent and compassionate few against the silent many. For purposes of comparison, I have made a list of American writers who could have lent the prestige of their names to the cause of Sacco and Vanzetti and what it then stood for but who, so far as I have been able to find out, chose not to do so. Here is a list of the writers born in the previous century; some are still at work today: in the 60's: Masters and E. A. Robinson; in the 70's: Gertrude Stein, Frost, Sherwood Anderson, Sandburg, Vachel Lindsay, Wallace Stevens; in the 80's: Pound, Jeffers, Marianne Moore, Eliot, O'Neill, John Crowe Ransom, Conrad Aiken; and in the 90's: Sidney Howard, MacLeish, Marquand, Cummings, Fitzgerald, Faulkner, Robert Sherwood, Thornton Wilder, Benet, Hemingway, Henry Miller, Hart Crane, and Allen Tate. Why did they not respond to that part of Anatole France's appeal addressed especially to them: "You are a great people. You ought to be a just people. There are crowds of intelligent men among you, men who think. I prefer to appeal to them. I say to them beware of making martyrs. This is the unforgivable crime that nothing can wipe out and that weighs on generation after generation. Save Sacco and Vanzetti. Save them for your honor, for the honor of your children, and for the generations yet unborn."

Is this failure to respond a failure of the American imagination or of the American conscience? In *The Continuity of American Poetry*, Roy Harvey Pearce takes as his thesis the American poet's compulsion to justify his existence as a poet, his overriding theme and need, and concludes his survey with a poem by William Carlos Williams:

> It is difficult
> to get the news from poems
>   yet men die miserably every day
>   for lack
> of what is found there.

The Agony and the Triumph

Well, it is a little difficult, I think, to get the news from poems if there is no news in them, and I would have thought that in the case of Sacco and Vanzetti at least, there was news enough, yet they died miserably, among other reasons, for what was not found there. I do not pretend to a scholarly knowledge of the American imagination, but I have the sense that, when confronted with a crisis of conscience, it seems regularly to avoid it, by change of setting ("go west"), by expatriation ("go away"), by return to childhood ("go back"), or, when these fail, by voyages of the discovery of self ("go inside"). In short, we respond by fleeing, an almost automatic reflex made possible perhaps by the escape hatch hitherto always provided by an endless physical frontier. Now, however, that we are stopped by Los Angeles on the west and by the threat of nuclear incineration all around us, where can we go to escape? And what form will that pent-up fear and frustration in us take when we realize we have no place left to go? I know that once before, in the case of Sacco and Vanzetti, we had the chance to choose, and our answer was death. Will we, this time, when the question is not alone one of justice for two wronged men but of the very survival of the race itself, will we be able to answer as Vanzetti did: "If it had not been for these things, I might have live out my life talking at street corners to scorning men, I might have die, unmarked, unknown, a failure. Now we are not a failure. This is our career and our triumph. Never in our full life could we hope to do such work for tolerance, for joostice, for man's understanding of man as now we do by accident. Our words—our lives—our pains—nothing! The taking of our lives—lives of a good shoemaker and a fish-peddler—all! That last moment belongs to us—that agony is our triumph."

(1963)